CHRONICLES OF DHAMMA

Selected Articles from the Vipassana Newsletter

Vipassana Research Publications

Vipassana Research Publications
an imprint of
Pariyatti Publishing
www.pariyatti.org

ISBN: 978-1-681723-54-9 (Print)
ISBN: 978-1-928706-37-3 (PDF)
ISBN: 978-1-938754-06-7 (ePub)
ISBN: 978-1-938754-07-4 (Mobi)

Printed in USA

CONTENTS

Introduction

The *Vipassana Newsletter* plays a unique role in the spread of Dhamma around the world. For old students in this tradition, the *Newsletter* provides a valued meeting-point, a living connection to the Dhamma community with its special combination of inspiration and information. Words of the Buddha are quoted alongside feedback from course servers; local activities are reported alongside international developments; lead articles are presented by S.N. Goenka and others about aspects of the teaching and its practical application in our lives.

'Chronicles of Dhamma' presents a selection of articles taken from the *Vipassana Newsletter* over the years in English. The sources for the material are two-fold: the edition published in India and the International edition published in North America. The articles themselves have been selected to reflect different aspects of the spread of Vipassana meditation in recent times. They are organised in broad thematic groups: Vipassana Teachings; Messenger of Dhamma; In the Footsteps of the Buddha; Applied Dhamma; The Spread of Dhamma. The articles are reprinted here exactly as they appeared originally (or with some editing), it has not been possible to standardise every variation in spelling, punctuation or usage.

Massive changes in communications technology over the past 40 years since S.N. Goenka left Myanmar and began his worldwide teaching mission on behalf of Sayagyi U Ba Khin have transformed the publishing and sharing of information about Vipassana. Through translation the *Newsletter* and local variations of it are now available in many languages, supporting the growing numbers of Vipassana meditators globally in their practice and service.

This compilation spans a period from the earliest improvised small Vipassana courses in India to established meditation centres by the score, increasing numbers of courses across five continents and the incomparable achievement of the Global Pagoda. It samples the successes, struggles and set-backs along the way. Looking back through the archives of the *Vipassana Newsletter*, we see the remarkable story of the revival of Vipassana in the modern age unfolding and illuminated. May this collection of Dhamma articles give confidence and strength to present and future generations walking on this Noble Path.

The history and significance of the International and Dhamma Giri editions of the *Vipassana Newsletter* have been well described in the following article.

A Voice for the Dhamma: The Vipassana Newsletter

In the early 1970s, the clock of Vipassana struck for a small but growing number of young people from Western countries. Like others of their generation, they journeyed to India and had the good fortune to encounter S.N. Goenka, who was beginning his own journey as an envoy of the Dhamma. Many of them decided to accompany him along the path. They followed Goenkaji all over the Indian subcontinent, sitting and serving in course after course.

But for all of them, sooner or later the time came to return to their own country. And then they all faced the questions: How can I continue doing this in everyday life, in my own culture? How can I maintain daily practice of meditation, and how can I interest other people so that they too will want to learn Vipassana?

This is always a big challenge and it was particularly tough in the early 1970s. Goenkaji's activities were confined to India, and his passport did not allow him to travel to the West. Even communicating with him was a challenge. There were only three options, each problematic: letters took weeks to arrive and might be lost en route; telegrams were fast but equally uncertain; and phone calls were expensive and the connection was always poor.

But there were hundreds of Goenkaji's students in the West, many of them filled with inspiration and enthusiasm. Several of them in different places had the idea for a newsletter that would connect them, enable them to support each other, and help them plan and publicize opportunities for meditation. The result in 1974 was the first issue of the *Vipassana Newsletter.* It was soon followed by a second issue, then a third, and it finally became a regular publication.

There was a model for it in India, where a Hindi newsletter appeared every month. Regularly Goenkaji would sit down and dictate an article to his secretary, then provide a quotation from the Pali texts and several dohas—verses of his own composition. The monthly *Vipaśhyanā Patrikā* often had a very personal tone and became a unique journal in which Goenkaji communicated with his Hindi-speaking students. It still is.

Obviously the *International Newsletter* could not replicate that tone or format, and in the beginning it was clearly struggling to find its voice. Early issues carried recipes, want ads and advice on making a meditation cushion, among other items. But they also carried words of the Buddha and sometimes articles from Goenkaji. And equally important, they featured lists of group sitting contacts and schedules of activities. People who felt alone suddenly learned that they were not. They also learned that they could join organized activities for the practice of Vipassana as taught by Goenkaji. As one of the earliest Western students says, "When I got the first newsletter, I realized there was something I could do, a way to continue practicing."

For that meditator and many others, the *Vipassana Newsletter* was a lifeline, their only channel for hearing about Vipassana.

Within a short time the *Newsletter* found that it had a devoted readership because it provided something that was available nowhere else: inspiration and information for the practice of Vipassana meditation in this tradition. Quickly the mailing list expanded beyond North America, and very soon the *Newsletter* started appearing in other Western languages. In France, for example, students would translate the lead articles from the English Newsletter, and then add local items plus a list of French activities and contacts. The template and much of the content came from the North American editors, but rounding this out was the key information needed by local meditators.

The *Newsletter* grew in importance as Goenkaji started traveling to the West because once again it was the sole channel for providing information to most of his students. It announced his itinerary and the dates of courses, explained how to apply, and later reported on each year's tour. From the early 1980s it performed an equally important function for the winter course program at *Dhamma Giri*. Hundreds of Westerners came to the center for the two or three months that Goenkaji spent there in that season. Once again they turned to the *Newsletter* to find out what the program was and how to enroll for the courses they wanted to sit.

In winter of 1981–82, the *Newsletter* was the channel through which Goenkaji announced the appointment of the first assistant teachers. From then on, once or twice a year the *Newsletter* would carry a list of people who had been asked to take on this responsibility.

Another milestone came in 1982, with the starting of the first centers in the West—*Dhamma Dharā* in the Eastern USA and *Dhamma Bhūmi* in Australia. Like dedicated meditators throughout the United States, the *Newsletter* packed up and moved to Massachusetts. From now on it would be published from a Vipassana center and would have much closer supervision from the Teacher.

At the same time another trend started that would go on and become increasingly powerful: Once there were centers—and the number quickly increased—each wanted to have its own channel for communicating with students in its area. At first this might be a sheet inserted with the *International Newsletter*. But it then quickly became a separate publication, a regional newsletter edited and distributed by local students. So one voice of Dhamma became a chorus.

As the years went on and activities increased, it became impractical to list all courses or all contacts in the *International Newsletter*. Instead this information moved to the regional newsletters, which increased in importance. An English-language version of the *Patrikā* started to appear in India, and it eventually became a separate publication of great value, appearing monthly.

But the biggest change was the advent of the Internet and the creation of the ***www.dhamma.org*** website. Suddenly there were endless opportunities for communication, and many channels through which meditators could find information.

All these are voices for the Dhamma. And all these have taken their cue from the small mimeographed publication that first appeared three and a half decades ago.

The basic goals remain the same: to provide information and inspiration for people who have taken a Vipassana course and who are looking for opportunities to continue on the path of Dhamma.

Today the *Newsletter* is only one among these many voices. And that itself is a sign of its success.

These days it is easy to take for granted that the funds and organisation will be there to prepare the *Newsletter*. That its regular publication could be both simplified and improved to such an extent through word-processing, desk-top design and e-mail. It was not always so, as early editors at the International edition, Bill and Virginia Hamilton, explain:

"The first newsletters were quite challenging to put together. They were prepared on a tiny screen of a little Macintosh computer and then everything was literally cut and pasted and taken to the printer. Soon the cut and paste operation became computerized which made our work easier.

The main articles had to be prepared six weeks in advance so they could be sent out to all the countries for translation. They usually used our lead articles; then they added their own information and the course schedule for their area.

When we returned to the printer to get the 10 or so cases of printed newsletters, we would excitedly open up one to see how the *Newsletter* looked. Invariably, each time, we seemed to find a spelling mistake that jumped out like a sore thumb, even though there were about six proofers that reviewed the newsletter before it went to press. Once we found Goenkaji's name without the "j"...Goenkai!

Every three months about 20 students would get together at somebody's home for a pot luck lunch and a newsletter mailing "party". We stapled, stuck on mailing address stickers on some 12,000 newsletters. Then we had to organize them for the different states in the US and other countries in the world. Finally took them to the post office in large mail bags. It took about six hours."

In September 2001 the International edition celebrated 100 issues of the *Vipassana Newsletter*. The lead article concluded:

"The history of the *Newsletter* is longer than that of any of the Vipassana centers that now provide focal points for activities. Before centers, before Goenkaji ever taught courses outside India, the *Newsletter* was the vehicle that helped Western students keep in touch with each other, with the course schedules, and with the inspiration needed to keep their practice alive in a culture that was often indifferent to Dhamma. It has long served as the only truly international repository of both information and funds to help with the ever growing work of Dhamma. It arrives in our mail—or more recently in our e-mail inbox—with a regularity and an ease that often belies the struggle to keep it alive. May it continue for hundreds more issues in the decades to come."

Internet access to the *Vipassana Newsletter* archives is as follows:
For the *Dhamma Giri* edition (in Hindi, English etc) go to ***www.vri.dhamma.org***
To access the International edition (in English etc) go to ***www.news.dhamma.org***

Acknowledgements

We would like to thank all past and present editors and contributors to the Dhamma Giri and International editions of the Vipassana Newsletter for their work.

In assembling this book we have received valuable help from many people. Maung Maung and Bill Hamilton with accessing archive material, Klaus Nothnagel with Pāli content, Jason Howells with design and formatting. In particular we are grateful to Bill Hart, Brihas Sarathy and others for their assistance with the editing of this material for publication.

May the merits of this service be shared with all of them.

SECTION ONE

VIPASSANA TEACHINGS

Vipassana Teachings—Introduction

The focus of the articles in this section (and associated Words of Dhamma) is specifically on the teaching, both its practice *paṭipatti* and theory *pariyatti*.

The standard exposition of Vipassana meditation is given during a 10-day course and Goenkaji's evening talks are collected in The Discourse Summaries, available at ***www.dhamma.org/os*** (for password details, please contact your local centre).

"The Buddha's First Discourse" article reminds us how the newly enlightened Siddhartha Gotama spoke to his sceptical friends and explained the Middle Path he had discovered through his own experience of Vipassana meditation. "Work Out Your Own Salvation" is an inspiring talk taken from a short course for old students, where the emphasis is on re-energising one's daily practice. "*Sīla*: The Foundation of Dhamma" is an extract from a public TV broadcast. The article "*Kamma*—The Real Inheritance" includes excerpts from discourses for long course students on the subject of cause and effect and the practical consequences of our actions. "The Factors of Enlightenment" describes the seven *bojjhangas*, whose development will lead to full liberation. "The *Maṅgala* Sutta", one of the best-known teachings of the Buddha, lists the many welfares to be attained by a householder despite the hindrances in everyday life. In another extract from a long course discourse, "The Snare of Māra", Goenkaji returns to a familiar theme—the danger in meditation of relishing and becoming trapped by the experience of pleasant sensations, instead of understanding their changing nature and observing them objectively in wisdom. "*Mettā*" is an important part of the practice of Vipassana and this article and accompanying questions and answers clarify what it is and how it should be done. Another of the *pāramīs* is discussed in detail in "The Gift of *Dāna*". The following two articles: "Gain the Strength of Dhamma" and "Fulfilling the Teaching of the Buddha" remind students of their responsibilities, having benefited from practising Vipassana at a deeper level, to apply Dhamma in their lives for the benefit of many. In "The Purity of Dhamma" Goenkaji cautions meditators, despite good intentions, to avoid mixing other practices with Vipassana as taught by the Buddha and preserved in this tradition by generations of Teachers, thereby risking compromising its effectiveness. The final article "Discovering the Buddha in the Tipiṭaka" encourages us to explore the Buddha's words for ourselves to gain confidence, understanding and direction in our practice on the path to liberation.

The Buddha's First Discourse

The following article, condensed slightly for publication in the Newsletter, is by Patrick Given-Wilson, who is Regional Teacher for Australia and New Zealand and author of the summaries of Goenkaji's Satipaṭṭhāna Sutta discourses.

Words of Dhamma

Idaṃ kho pana, bhikkhave, dukkhaṃ ariyasaccaṃ
jātipi dukkhā, jarāpi dukkhā, byādhipi dukkho, maraṇampi dukkhaṃ,
appiyehi sampayogo dukkho, piyehi vippayogo dukkho, yampicchaṃ na labhati tampi dukkhaṃ:
saṅkhittena pañcupādānakkhandhā dukkhā.

—Dhammacakkappavattana Sutta

This, monks, is the noble truth of suffering:
birth is suffering, aging is suffering, disease is suffering, death is suffering,
association with the unloved is suffering,
separation from the loved is suffering,
not getting what one wants is suffering,
in brief the five aggregates of grasping are suffering.

After his enlightenment, the Buddha gave his first discourse to the five friends who had accompanied him during most of his years of searching. It is called the *Dhammacakkappavattana Sutta*, the discourse that set in motion the wheel of Dhamma. It summarizes the Buddha's entire teaching.

The sutta starts:

Ekaṃ samayaṃ bhagavā Bārānasīyam viharati Isipatane Migadāye.

The scene is set in Isipathana, a sacred place near Varanasi frequented by recluses, hermits and other saintly people. Within it, Migada was a deer park and sanctuary where no animal could be killed.

Tatra kho bhagavā pañcavaggiye bhikkhū āmantesi.

The discourse was given to his five former companions. They were a skeptical audience, believing that the Buddha had failed in his quest because he had given up fasting and physical austerities. As they saw him approach, they agreed to show him no special respect. Nevertheless they listened, impressed by his serenity and the glow on his face.

He declared to them that he had become a Buddha. And to overcome their doubts, he explained how he had achieved enlightenment.

Dveme, bhikkhave, antā pabbajitena na sevitabbā. Katame dve?

Two extremes, bhikkhus, should not be practiced by one striving for liberation. What two?

... yo cāyam kāmesu kāmasukhallikānuyogo hīno gammo pothujjaniko anariyo anatthasaṃhito ...

... attachment and clinging to sensual pleasures, which is low, coarse, vulgar, unworthy, and profitless ...

He decisively repudiates the path of sensual pleasures. No one can attain liberation from sensual pleasures by indulging in them. This would have been obvious to his audience. But his second statement would have seemed radical: a decisive repudiation of the ascetic path they had been practicing together.

... yo cāyam attakilamathānuyogo dukkho anariyo anatthasaṃhīto

... attachment to self-torture, which is painful, unworthy, and profitless.

He then describes the actual path he took, the Middle Path, and states the result:

Ete kho, bhikkhave, ubho ante anupagamma majjhimā paṭipadā tathāgatena abhisambuddhā cakkhukaraṇī ñāṇakaraṇī upasamāya abhiññāya sambodhāya nibbānāya saṃvattati

Between these extremes the Middle Path, realized by the Tathāgata, gives vision, gives knowledge, and leads to calm, to insight, to enlightenment and to *nibbāna*.

"Tathāgata" was the term the Buddha used to describe himself. It means literally "thus gone," or one who has walked the path of truth.

He describes this Middle Path as the Eightfold Noble Path:

Ariyo aṭṭhaṅgiko maggo, seyyathidaṃ—sammā diṭṭhi sammā saṅkappo sammā vācā sammā kammanto sammā ājīvo sammā vāyāmo sammā sati sammā samādhi.

This Noble Eightfold Path, namely—right understanding, right thought, right speech, right action, right livelihood, right effort, right mindfulness and right concentration.

At one level, this was nothing new. The practice of morality already existed in India. Deep *samādhis* were also practiced, and Gotama himself had practiced these in the past. *Paññā* was also understood and accepted at least at the intellectual level.

However, the path starts with *sammā diṭṭhi*, and the *diṭṭhi* (understanding) must be *sāmma* (right). That means not only must it be understood, it must also be experienced. Something can only be understood properly if it is actually experienced; otherwise it remains a mere philosophy or view. Similarly, every step on the Noble Eightfold Path is preceded by the word *sāmma:* to be right, it has to be experienced.

He then states the keystone of his teaching, the Four Noble Truths. He describes each in turn:

Idam kho pana, bhikkhave, dukkham ariyasaccaṃ: jātipi dukkhā, jarāpi dukkhā, byādhipi dukkho, maranampi dukkhaṃ, appiyehi sampayogo dukkho, piyehi vippayogo dukkho, yampicchaṃ na labhati tampi dukkhaṃ—saṅkhittena pañcupādānakkhandhā dukkhā.

This, bhikkhus, is the Noble Truth of Suffering: birth is suffering, aging is suffering, sickness is suffering, death is suffering, association with the unpleasant is suffering, dissociation from the pleasant is suffering, not to receive what one desires is suffering—in brief the five aggregates of clinging are suffering.

Again at a mundane level, much of this was familiar to his audience. But there was a widespread belief that beings of the highest celestial realms were immortal. And here he states that all birth is *dukkha* and ends with a comprehensive rejection of clinging to any kind of existence.

Working deep inside, he had realized that any clinging to anything in the field of mind and matter was *dukkha*, suffering. The truth of *dukkha* had to be accepted in every aspect of existence. Even the most pleasant, subtle, tranquil experience had to be accepted as *dukkha* because of its impermanence.

... dukkhasamudayaṃ ariyasaccaṃ: yayaṃ taṇhā ponobbhavikā nandirāgasahagatā tatratatrābhinandinī, seyyathidaṃ kāmataṇhā, bhavataṇhā, vibhavataṇhā.

The Noble Truth of the Arising of Suffering is this craving, leading to rebirth, bound up with pleasure and desire, finding delight now here, now there, namely, craving for sense pleasure, craving for existence, and craving for annihilation.

The second Noble Truth is that suffering arises with *taṇhā*, craving. Sometimes *samudayaṃ* is translated as "the cause" of *dukkha*, but more precisely it means "arising." *Dukkha*, the agitation, starts as soon as craving, *taṇhā*, starts: they are simultaneous. This is experienced by a meditator at a subtle level. This craving is the actual problem that leads to rebirth, *ponobbhavikā.*

He describes three types of craving, or *taṇhā*. The first is the craving for sensual pleasures, *kāmataṇhā*. This can be easily understood, but eradicating it alone is not enough. The second is the craving for any kind of existence, *bhavatanhā*. Even if someone is free of sensual pleasures, there is the craving for survival: "The 'I' must survive. No matter what happens to the world or to other beings, I must be there in whatever plane of existence, to witness it and see it continue. Even liberation is something that 'I' must experience, 'I' must enjoy." This craving gives rise to further rebirths, and so the round of suffering continues. The third and final craving is the desire for annihilation, *vibhavatanhā*. Even craving for the end of existence is still craving.

Idaṃ kho pana, bhikkhave, dukkhanirodhaṃ ariyasaccaṃ yo tassāyeva taṇhāya asesavirāganirodho cāgo paṭinissaggo mutti anālayo.

This, bhikkhus, is the Noble Truth of the Eradication of Suffering: it is the complete eradication of that very craving, giving it up, relinquishing it, the liberation and detachment from it.

This craving must be totally eradicated, so that no root is left. Elsewhere, in the *Satipaṭṭhāna Sutta*, the Buddha describes in more detail how the eradication must be complete at every step of the mental process: in every part of the mind, at every sense door.

The fourth Noble Truth is the way to reach that goal, the Eightfold Noble Path.

... dukkhanirodhagāminī paṭipadā ariyasaccaṃ: ayameva ariyo aṭṭhaṅgiko maggo, seyyathidaṃ—sammā diṭṭhi, sammā saṅkappo, sammā vācā, sammā kammanto, sammā ājīvo, sammā vāyāmo, sammā sati, sammā samādhi.

The Noble Truth of the Path leading to the eradication of suffering is this Eightfold Path, namely right understanding, right thought, right speech, right action, right livelihood, right effort, right mindfulness, and right concentration

In essence, the four Noble Truths are very simple: accept the fact of suffering, understand how it arises, totally eradicate it, and so realize the path to its eradication. But the Buddha's enlightenment was actually to experience it. He elaborated, saying that each Noble Truth has to be realized in three different ways. Each truth is not a reality unless it is witnessed, or experienced.

Idaṃ dukkhaṃ ariyasaccam pariññeyaṃ... pariññataṃ.

This Noble Truth of suffering is to be experienced fully is experienced fully.

The fact of suffering, *dukkha*, had to first be accepted. But that was mere intellectual knowledge, merely a starting position. The second part was to understand the need to experience directly the entire field of *dukkha—pariññeyaṃ*—because unless the entire field is experienced, there might be some aspect, some part of *dukkha*, still considered free from *dukkha*. However, this was still an intellectual decision. The third step was *pariññataṃ*—he had explored the entire field of *dukkha* only when he had gone beyond *dukkha*. So even in this first Noble Truth, all the Four Noble Truths are included.

Idaṃ dukkhaṃ samudayaṃ ariyasaccaṃ pahātabbaṃ pahīnaṃ.

This Noble Truth of the arising of suffering has to be eradicated has been eradicated.

The same applies to the second Noble Truth, *dukkha samudaya*. Mere acceptance that craving is the cause of *dukkha* does not help. The craving has to be eradicated: *pahātabbaṃ*. But even this is insufficient. The third part must be completed—*pahīnaṃ*—*taṇhā* must actually be eradicated at the root level, so that not a trace is left. So the second Noble Truth also completes all the Four Noble Truths. If it is *pahīnaṃ*, totally eradicated, one is free from misery.

Idaṃ dukkhanirodhaṃ ariyasaccaṃ sacchikātabbaṃ sacchikātaṃ.

This Noble Truth of the eradication of suffering has to be witnessed has been witnessed.

The third Noble Truth is the stage where there is no more misery at all—the stage of *nibbāna*. Mere acceptance that there is a stage beyond mind and matter is not enough. It has to be witnessed—*sacchikātabbaṃ*. Then the third part is *sacchikātaṃ*—it is witnessed. When that was witnessed, he became free of all misery. All the four Noble Truths are included.

Idaṃ dukkhanirodhagāminī paṭipadā ariyasaccaṃ bhāvetabbaṃ bhāvitaṃ.

This Noble Truth of the path leading to the eradication of suffering has to be developed has been developed.

The fourth Noble Truth is the path. Again it has to be experienced fully. Only then can it be said to have been completed. The first step is acceptance that this is the path. The second is the intellectual decision that it has to be developed, *bhāvetabbaṃ*. Both are necessary. But only actually covering the entire path—*bhāvitaṃ*—could liberate him, and by walking it he had accomplished the other three Noble Truths. So all four Noble Truths, when actually experienced, are each complete in themselves and contain all the others.

Therefore, unless each Noble Truth is worked out in three ways, and the four Noble Truths thus become a twelvefold Noble Truth, they cannot give the result of liberation from suffering. If someone merely accepted the truth that there is misery, that there is a cause of misery, that there is total eradication of misery and that there is a way to eradicate the misery, the acceptance would be no more than a philosophy—logical but otherwise no different from any other philosophy. It could not have liberated him.

... pubbe ananussutesu dhammesu cakkhuṃ udapādi, ñānam udapādi, paññā udapādi, vijjā udapādi, āloko udapādi.

... I had never heard such Dhammas before: vision arose, knowledge arose, wisdom arose, understanding arose, light arose.

This is repeated for each part of each Noble Truth. These were truths, Dhammas that he had never heard before: *pubbe ananusuttesu dhammesu*. When he actually experienced them: *cakkhuṃ udapādi, ñañaṃ udapādi, paññā udapādi, vijjā udapādi, āloko udapādi,* vision arose, knowledge arose, wisdom arose, understanding arose, light arose. Each was his own direct realization.

The Buddha describes this path as *dukkhanirodhagāminī paṭipadā*, the path to the cessation of all misery. Elsewhere he describes the same path as *vedanānirodhagāminī paṭipadā*, the path to the cessation of all sensations. This is because the path has to be experienced. The word used for experience in those days was *vedanā*, which also means sensation. So *pariññataṃ* means that the entire field of *vedanā*, sensation, has to be experienced. Elsewhere, he says, *Yam kiñci vedayitaṃ, taṃ dukkhasmiṃ*—every sensation is connected with *dukkha*, with misery. Even the most pleasant sensation has to be understood as *dukkha* because it is *anicca*. There is the danger of clinging to this impermanent experience and of generating *taṇhā*, craving, toward it. Unless all sensation is understood as misery, there might remain a delusion that some sensation really does give happiness.

Yāvakīvañca me, bhikkhave, imesu catūsu ariyasaccesu evaṃ tiparivaṭṭaṃ dvādasākāraṃ yathābhūtaṃ ñāṇadassanaṃ na suvisuddhaṃ ahosi, neva tāvāhaṃ, bhikkhave 'anuttaraṃ sammāsambodhiṃ abhisambuddho'ti paccaññāsiṃ.

As long as my knowledge and insight into reality "as it is" was not pure in these three aspects, in these 12 ways, concerning the four Noble Truths, I did not claim to have realized matchless, supreme Enlightenment.

The Buddha describes his commitment to truth, the acceptance of reality "as it is," *yathābūtha*, at every stage—a commitment that underpinned his exploration and his practice. This led to *ñāṇadassanaṃ*—knowledge with insight, and purification. This had been his method of investigation: he remained always with the reality "as it is," without getting carried away by any philosophical belief, desire, speculation or imagination. Every meditator who wishes for enlightenment has to do the same.

Yato ca kho me, bhikkhave, imesu catūsu ariyasaccesu evaṃ tiparivaṭṭaṃ dvādasākāraṃ yathābhūtaṃ ñānadassanaṃ suvisuddhaṃ ahosi, athāhaṃ, bhikkhave, ... 'anuttaraṃ sammāsambodhiṃ abhisambuddho'ti paccaññāsiṃ

But now that it was so purified, he declared that "the matchless supreme enlightenment," '*anuttaraṃ sammāsambodhiṃ abhisambuddho*', had been realized. It is an emphatic declaration of his enlightenment.

Then finally comes the statement of the result:

Ñāṇañca pana me dassanaṃ udapādi—'akuppā me vimutti, ayamantimā jāti, natthidāni punabbhavo"ti

Knowledge and insight arose in me: "Unshakable is my liberation. This is the last birth. There is no more birth for me now."

This concluded the discourse, and the five companions were delighted. All their skepticism was gone.

Imasmiñca pana veyyākaranasmiṃ bhaññamāne āyasmato koṇḍaññassa virajaṃ vītamalaṃ dhammacakkhuṃ udapādi: "yaṃ kiñci samudayadhammaṃ, sabbaṃ taṃ nirodhadhamma"nti.

While this discourse was being given, the pure, stainless Eye of Dhamma arose in the Venerable Kondañña, that: "Whatever has the nature of arising, has the nature of ceasing."

The Eye of Dhamma, *dhammacakkhu*, now arose in Koṇḍañña, one of the five companions; that is, he experienced *nibbāna*. He understood that whatever has the nature of arising also has the nature of passing away.

This was a turning point because the discourse set in motion the Wheel of Dhamma. After an unimaginably long period of preparing and developing his *pāramī*, after successfully overcoming all obstacles to achieve enlightenment, the Buddha now had the capacity to teach others.

It must be understood that Koṇḍañña did not become enlightened simply by listening to what the Buddha was teaching. Instead, as he heard the Buddha's words, Koṇḍañña would have started focusing inside. He would have followed the same path, observing the reality, *yathābhūtaṃ*, "as it is," arising and passing throughout the mind-matter structure. Continuing to observe, he could reach the stage of experiencing *dukkhanirodha*, total cessation.

Koṇḍañña now worked vigorously and within a short time became fully liberated. He became known as "Koṇḍañña the Wise."

Koṇḍañña was the first of many who became liberated at that time. The path is the same for all, and we are fortunate that the technique is still available today. It is therefore incumbent on all meditators to make best use of this path, for their own liberation. It is a rare opportunity.

(International edition—August 2009)

Work Out Your Own Salvation

S. N. Goenka

The following article has been condensed from a discourse given by Goenkaji on the second day of a three-day old student course.

Words of Dhamma

Atha kho bhagavā bhikkhū āmantesi—
"handa dāni, bhikkhave, āmantayāmi vo,
vayadhammā saṅkhārā,
appamādena sampādetha" ti.
Ayaṃ tathāgatassa pacchimā vācā.

Then the Exalted One spoke to the bhikkhus:
"Now, bhikkhus, this I say to you:
Transient are all created things;
strive on untiringly."
These were the last words of the Tathāgata.

—Mahāparinibbāna Sutta, Dīghanikāya 16–6–7

At the surface, the mind plays so many games—thinking, imagining, dreaming, giving suggestions. But deep inside, the mind remains a prisoner of its own habit pattern; and the habit pattern of the deepest level of the mind is to feel sensations and react. If the sensations are pleasant, the mind reacts with craving; if they are unpleasant, it reacts with aversion.

The enlightenment of the Buddha was to go to the root of the problem. Unless we work at the root level, we will only be dealing with the intellect and only this part of the mind will be purified. As long as the roots of a tree are unhealthy, the whole tree will be sick. If the roots are healthy, then they will provide healthy sap for the entire tree. So start working with the roots. This was the enlightenment of Buddha.

When he gave Dhamma, the path of *sīla* (morality), *samādhi* (mastery over the mind) and *paññā* (experiential wisdom)—the Noble Eightfold Path—it was not to establish a cult, a dogma, or a belief. Dhamma is a practical path. Those who walk on it can go to the deepest level and eradicate all their miseries.

Those who have really liberated themselves will understand that going to the depth of the mind—making a surgical operation of the mind—has to be done by oneself, by each individual. Someone can guide you with all the love and compassion; someone can help you in your journey on the path. But nobody can carry you on their shoulders and say: "I will take you to the final goal. Just surrender to me; I will do everything."

You are responsible for your own bondage. You are responsible for making your mind impure, no one else. You are responsible for purifying your mind, for breaking all the bondages. No one else can do that.

And continuity of practice is the secret of success. When it is said that you should be continuously aware, this means that you must be aware with wisdom of the sensations on the body, where you really experience things arising and passing away. The awareness of *anicca* is what purifies your mind—the awareness of the sensations arising, passing, arising, passing.

Intellectualizing this truth will not help. You may understand: "Everything that arises sooner or later passes away. Anyone who takes birth sooner or later dies. This is *anicca*." You may understand this correctly but you are not *experiencing* it. It is your own personal experience which will help you purify your mind and liberate you from your miseries. The word for "experience" used in India at the time of Buddha was *vedanā*, feeling by experiencing, not just intellectualization. And this is possible only when a sensation is felt on the body.

Anicca must be experienced. If you are not experiencing it, it is merely a theory. And the Buddha was not interested in theories. Even before Buddha, and at the time of Buddha, there were teachers who taught that the entire universe is *anicca*; this was not new. What *was* new from the Buddha was the experience of *anicca*; and when you experience it within the framework of your own body, you have started working at the deepest level of your mind.

Two things are very important for those who walk on the path. The first is breaking the barrier which divides the conscious and the unconscious mind. But even if your conscious mind can now feel those sensations which were previously felt only by the deep unconscious part of your mind, that alone will not help you. Buddha wanted you to take a second step: change the mind's habit of reacting at the deepest level.

Coming to the stage where you have started feeling sensations is a good first step, yet the habit pattern of reaction remains. When you feel an unpleasant sensation, if you keep reacting—"Oh, I must get rid of this"—that won't help. If you start feeling a pleasant flow of very subtle vibrations throughout the body, and you react—"Ah, wonderful! This is what I was looking for. Now I've got it!"—you have not understood Vipassana at all.

Vipassana is not a game of pleasure and pain, pleasure and pain. You have been reacting like this your entire life, for countless lifetimes. Now in the name of Vipassana you have started making this pattern stronger. Every time you feel an unpleasant sensation you react in the same way with aversion. Every time you a feel pleasant sensation you react in the same way with craving. Vipassana has not helped you, because you have not helped Vipassana.

Whenever you again make the mistake of reacting because of the old habit, see how quickly you can become aware of it: "Look—an unpleasant sensation and I am reacting with aversion; a pleasant sensation and I am reacting with craving. This is not Vipassana. This will not help me."

Understand that this is what you have to do. If you are not 100 percent successful, it doesn't matter. This won't harm you as long as you keep understanding and keep trying to change the old habit pattern. If for even a few moments you have started coming out of your prison, then you are progressing.

This is what Buddha wanted you to do: practice the Noble Eightfold Path. Practice *sīla* so that you can have the right type of *samādhi*. For those who keep breaking *sīla*, there is little hope that they will go to the deepest levels of reality. *Sīla* develops after you have some of control over your mind, after you start understanding with *paññā* that breaking *sīla* is very harmful. Your *paññā* at the experiential level will help your *samādhi*. Your *samādhi* at the experiential level will help your *sīla*. Your stronger *sīla* will help your *samādhi* become strong. Your stronger *samādhi* will help your *paññā* become strong. Each of the three will start helping the others and you will keep progressing, progressing.

There were many techniques in India in those days, and also later on, practicing which meditators started feeling subtle vibrations throughout the body when the solidity had dissolved. The truth is that even the subtlest vibration one can experience is still a phenomenon in the field of mind and matter. It is arising, passing, arising, passing; still in the field of *anicca*, a field of constant change.

Some meditators of old tried to impose a philosophy on this subtle experience. Having reached that stage where they experienced nothing but vibrations, they postulated: "Throughout the universe, there is this subtle energy. This is God Almighty. I am experiencing this; I am with God Almighty. The entire universe is one. Every being is God. Why should I have any kind of preference or prejudice?"—A very positive mental suggestion. But it only helps at a superficial level.

The reality is that even this very subtle experience is still in the field of mind and matter. It is not the ultimate truth which is beyond mind and matter. All these suggestions, however positive they may be, cannot liberate anyone. You must be with reality, with the truth as it is. Things keep changing. All vibrations are nothing but a flux, a flow. This realization removes the deep-rooted habit pattern of reacting to the sensations.

Whatever sensations you experience—pleasant, unpleasant or neutral—you should use them as tools. These sensations can become tools to liberate you from your misery, provided you understand the truth as it is. But these same sensations can also become tools that multiply your misery. Likes and dislikes should not cloud the issue. The reality is: sensations are arising and passing away; they are *anicca*. Pleasant, unpleasant or neutral—it makes no difference. When you start realizing the fact that even the most pleasant sensations you experience are *dukkha* (suffering), then you are coming nearer to liberation.

Understand why pleasant sensations are *dukkha*. Every time a pleasant sensation arises, you start relishing it. This habit of clinging to pleasant sensations has persisted for countless lifetimes. And it is because of this that you have aversion. Craving and aversion are two sides of the same coin. The stronger the craving, the stronger the aversion is bound to be. Sooner or later every pleasant sensation turns into an unpleasant one, and every unpleasant sensation will turn into a pleasant one; this is the law of nature. If you start craving pleasant sensations, you are inviting misery.

Buddha's teaching helps us to disintegrate the solidified intensity that keeps us from seeing the real truth. At the actual level there are mere vibrations, nothing else. At the same time, there is solidity. For example, this wall is solid. This is a truth, an apparent truth. The ultimate truth is that what you call a wall is nothing but a mass of vibrating subatomic particles. We have to integrate both truths through proper understanding.

Dhamma develops our understanding, so that we free ourselves from the habit of reacting and understand that craving is harming us, hating is harming us. And then we are more realistic: "See, there is ultimate truth, and there is also apparent truth, which is also a truth."

The process of going to the depth of the mind to liberate yourself, is done by you alone; but you must also be prepared to work with your family, with society as a whole. The yardstick to measure whether love, compassion and good will are truly developing is whether these qualities are being exhibited toward the people around you.

Buddha wanted us to be liberated at the deepest level of our minds. And that is possible only when three characteristics are realized: *anicca* (impermanence), *dukkha* (suffering), and *anattā* (egolessness). When the mind starts to get deconditioned, layer after layer becomes purified until the mind is totally unconditioned. Then purity becomes a way of life. You won't have to practice *mettā* (compassionate love) as you do now at the end of your one-hour sitting. Later, *mettā* just becomes your life. All the time you will remain suffused with love, compassion and good will. This is the aim, the goal.

The path of liberation is the path of working at the deepest level of the mind. There is nothing wrong with giving good mental suggestions, but unless you change the blind habit of reacting at the deepest level, you are not liberated. Nobody is liberated unless the deepest level of the mind is changed. And the deepest level of the mind is constantly in contact with bodily sensations.

We have to divide, dissect and disintegrate the entire structure to understand how mind and matter are so interrelated. If you work only with the mind and forget the body, you are not practicing Buddha's teaching. If you work only with the body and forget the mind, again you are not properly understanding Buddha.

Anything that arises in the mind turns into matter, into a sensation in the material field. This was Buddha's discovery. People forgot about this truth, which can only be understood through proper practice. The Buddha said, *"Sabbe dhammā vedanā samosaraṇā"*—anything that arises in the mind starts flowing as a sensation on the body.

The Buddha used the word *āsava*, which means flow or intoxication. Suppose you have generated anger. A biochemical flow starts, which generates very unpleasant sensations. Because of these unpleasant sensations, you start reacting with anger. As you generate anger, the flow becomes stronger. There are unpleasant sensations and, with them, a biochemical secretion. As you generate more anger, the flow becomes stronger.

In the same way, when passion or fear arises, a particular type of biochemical substance starts flowing in the blood. A vicious circle starts, which keeps repeating itself. There is a flow, an intoxication, at the depth of the mind. Out of ignorance, we get intoxicated by this particular biochemical flow. Although it makes us miserable, yet we are intoxicated; we want it again and again. So we keep on generating anger upon anger, passion upon passion, fear upon fear. We become intoxicated by whatever impurity we generate in our minds. When we say that someone is addicted to alcohol or drugs, this is actually untrue. No one is addicted to alcohol or drugs. The actual truth is that one is addicted to the sensations that are produced by the alcohol or drugs.

Buddha teaches us to observe reality. Every addiction will be undone if we observe the truth of the sensations on the body with this understanding: *"Anicca, anicca*. This is impermanent." Gradually we will learn to stop reacting.

Dhamma is so simple, so scientific, so true—a law of nature applicable to everyone. Buddhist, Hindu, Muslim, Christian; American, Indian, Burmese, Russian or Italian—it makes no difference; a human being is a human being. Dhamma is a pure science of mind, matter, and the interaction between the two. Don't allow it to become a sectarian or philosophical belief. This will be of no help.

The greatest scientist the world has produced worked to find the truth about the relationship between mind and matter. And discovering this truth, he found a way to go beyond mind and matter. He explored reality not just for the sake of curiosity but to find a way to be free of suffering. For every individual, there is so much misery; for every family, for every society, for every nation, for the entire world—so much misery. The Enlightened One found a way to come out of this misery.

There is no other solution: each individual has to come out of misery. Every member of a family must come out of misery. Then the family will become happy, peaceful and harmonious. If every member of society comes out of misery, if every member of a nation comes out of misery, if every citizen of the world comes out of misery—only then will there be world peace.

There can't be world peace just because we want world peace: "Because I am agitating for world peace, it should occur." This doesn't happen. We can't agitate for peace. When we are agitated, we lose our own peacefulness. No agitation! Purify your mind. Then every action you take will add peace to the universe.

Purify your mind, purify your mind: this is how you can help society. This is how you can stop harming others and start helping them.

When you work for your own liberation, you will find that you have also started helping others come out of their misery. One individual becomes several individuals—there is a slow widening of the circle. But there is no magic, no miracle. Work for your own peace, and you will find that you have started helping the atmosphere around you to become more peaceful, provided you work properly.

The biggest miracle is changing the habit pattern of the mind from rolling in misery to freedom from misery. There is no bigger miracle than this. Every step that is taken toward this kind of miracle is a healthy step, a helpful step. Every other apparent miracle is only bondage. May you all come out of your misery, come out of your bondage. Enjoy real peace, real harmony, real happiness.

(International edition—May 1997)

Sīla: The Foundation of Dhamma

S. N. Goenka

The following is a translation of an article originally published in the August 1998 issue of the Vipaśhyanā Patrikā. It is an adapted excerpt from the third in a series of 44 public talks broadcast on Zee TV.)

Words of Dhamma

Sīle patiṭṭhāya naro sapañño,
cittaṃ paññañca bhāvayaṃ;
ātāpī nipako bhikkhu,
so imaṃ vijaṭaye jaṭanti.

—Visuddhimagga 1–1

The wise, ardent, and discerning meditator, well established in morality, who develops *samādhi* (concentration) and wisdom, unties the knots (of defilements).

To learn Vipassana, the technique of purification of the mind, it is necessary to go to a Vipassana meditation centre. This technique can be learnt only in a conducive atmosphere. If one wants to learn to read and write, one has to enrol in a school. To keep the body healthy and strong, one has to go to a gymnasium. To learn yoga and prānāyāma, one has go to a yoga school. Similarly, to learn this Vipassana technique, the quintessence of the Buddha's teaching, one has to go to a Vipassana meditation centre. It is not necessary to stay in a school or gymnasium or yoga school day-and-night. It is sufficient to learn the technique and then to practise it at home. But to learn the technique of Vipassana, at least in the beginning, one has to stay in the meditation centre for 10 days.

If the purpose of meditation is merely to concentrate the mind, one may learn a meditation technique based on a mantra or an image as an object of concentration from some guru and practise it at home. Such a technique may calm the mind, concentrate the mind, and may even purify the surface level of the mind. But Vipassana does not merely purify the surface part of the mind. It is a deep surgical operation of the mind and purifies the mind at the deepest level, where defilements arise and multiply. These are defilements that one has accumulated in the depth of the mind over innumerable lifetimes. Those who do not believe in past lives have accumulated so many defilements even in this lifetime. The mind has become a prisoner of the habit-pattern of generating defilements in the depth of the mind. It is such a great bondage. One has to liberate the mind from this bondage and change its nature of continuously generating defilements. A deep surgical operation of the mind is needed to achieve this purpose.

When one becomes physically ill, one goes to a hospital that is clean and hygienic. If surgery is necessary, one has to go to an operation theatre that is completely sterile. Vipassana is a serious operation on the mind. Therefore, one can learn it properly only in an atmosphere that is free from any kind of pollution not only from atmospheric pollution but also from the pollution generated by the defilements of the mind.

These Vipassana meditation centres have existed since ancient times and also exist today. The environment in a centre is kept very pure. There is abundant greenery, and no physical pollution of any kind. There is peace, silence and an atmosphere conducive for meditation. And most importantly, there is no activity of any kind other than Vipassana in these meditation centres. As only Vipassana is practised, the entire centre vibrates with the vibrations of pure Dhamma. So it is an ideal place to go for the first surgical operation on the mind. In addition, there are experienced and authorised people in a Vipassana centre who assist in this operation, in teaching this technique. It is not proper to try to learn this technique on one's own.

Vipassana is not complicated; it is a very simple technique. One may get the impression that one can start practising it after merely listening to such discourses or reading a book. But I wish to caution you. Vipassana is an extremely serious task, an extremely delicate task. Once, at least for the first time, one should learn this technique in a conducive atmosphere for 10 days, under the guidance of some knowledgeable, experienced, authorised person. After that, everyone is one's own master.

At home, it is not possible to meditate continuously for long hours. Therefore, the operation is not as deep at home. After learning Vipassana at a centre, one can practise Vipassana in the morning and evening at home. Whenever the need arises for another deep operation on the mind, one can again go to a Vipassana centre.

There is one more reason why Vipassana should be learnt in a meditation centre. The aim of the technique is to develop a pure mind. So during the 10 days when Vipassana is being learnt in the centre, one practises *Sīla* (morality) without breaking it in any way: one does not kill, one does not commit sexual misconduct but maintains celibacy for 10 days, one does not lie, one does not steal, one does not take any kind of intoxicant.

One understands that in order to live a life of morality, one has to gain control over the mind. If one cannot control the mind, how can one become virtuous? But one can learn this technique only while living a life of morality. So a great difficulty arises. To live a life of morality one has to gain control over the mind. The mind has to be purified. To master the mind, to purify the mind, one's life has to be a life of morality. Should one keep the horse in front or the cart in front? Should morality come first or should concentration and purification of mind come first?

To solve this problem, the wise teachers of our country established this tradition of going to a meditation centre to learn Vipassana. One is able to practise all the five *Sīla*s there, meaning one does not do any vocal or physical action that disturbs the peace and harmony of others. One should not do any action that causes harm to others. How? The atmosphere of the meditation centre, the discipline and heavy daily programme of a 10-day course is such that it is easy to maintain *Sīla*. The student is so busy from four o'clock in the morning to nine o'clock at night that there is no opportunity to break *Sīla*. In order to avoid lying and wrong speech, the meditation centre has one more rule: for the duration of the course one must maintain silence. There should be no communication with fellow students. Of course, one may talk to the teacher or guide to seek clarification about the technique, or speak to the management about any material problems. However, even while talking to them, one should remain very attentive not to break one's *Sīla*. One should not exaggerate or hide anything. In this way, even the *Sīla* of not telling lies can be easily maintained during the course.

So *Sīla* is maintained perfectly. The work of learning the technique begins on this foundation of perfect *Sīla*. If the student works as instructed, progress is certain. But if the foundation of *Sīla* is missing, the student will not progress.

During the time of the Buddha, there were many teachers, like some teachers today, who told their students, "What is the need for morality? Do whatever you wish to do. Enjoy yourself without restraint, indulge in sensual pleasures. Even then, I shall teach you a meditation technique that will give bliss!" Such so-called spiritual teachers attracted big crowds. People are always looking for the easy way out. If they can get exemption from the need for morality and still get bliss, what more do they want?

Such harmful delusions have no place in Vipassana, the true path of the Dhamma. The foundation of morality is absolutely necessary. One should understand why it is so necessary. After all, one has to operate on the mind. To merely fill the surface part of the mind with bliss is not the goal of Vipassana. One has to reach and purify the depth, the deepest part of the mind, where the defilements arise, where they are accumulated. It is a very deep operation. If the surface part of the mind is very disturbed, very agitated, it results in gross impure vibrations. These vibrations act as a barrier and prevent one from going to the depth of the mind.

Suppose one has to search for oil fields

under the ocean-bed. During the monsoon, the search has to be stopped because it is not possible to do this work of searching in the depth of the ocean when there are high tidal waves. When the monsoon is over and the rain has stopped, the high tidal waves subside. Now it is possible to search for oil fields even though the tidal waves have not completely ceased. Similarly, there are waves of defilements in the mind. But when one breaks any *Sīla* whether one kills or steals or takes intoxicants or tells lies or commits sexual misconduct there are such high tidal waves of impurities created on the surface part of the mind that one cannot go to the depth. If one has to work at the depth of the mind, a situation has to be created where even though there are waves of defilements, they do not multiply and cause such high tidal waves of impurities in the mind.

The entire atmosphere of the meditation centre is helpful in achieving this. The rules, the discipline, the timetable must be followed strictly. If one works with discipline, one gets the benefits. People comc to a meditation centre not to enjoy a picnic or a 10-day holiday from the responsibilities of life, but to meditate, to remove the defilements in the mind by practising extremely serious meditation. One has to work very seriously and continuously. Therefore, after understanding, accepting and following the rules, one begins to work earnestly.

(Dhamma Giri edition—September 1999)

Kamma—The Real Inheritance

S. N. Goenka

The following is adapted from a discourse given by S. N. Goenka for long course students.

Words of Dhamma

Sārañca sārato ñatvā
asārañca asārato
te sāraṃ adhigacchanti
sammāsaṅkappagocarā.

They who regard the essential as essential,
the nonessential as nonessential;
such persons realize the essence,
for they contemplate right thoughts.

—Dhammapada 12

Kammassakā, bhikkhave, sattā kammadāyādā, kammayonī, kammabandhū, kammapaṭisaraṇā, yaṃ kammaṃ karonti—kalyānaṃ vā pāpakaṃ vā—tassa dāyādā bhavanti

Oh meditators, beings are the owners of their deeds, the heirs of their deeds, born of their deeds, kin to their deeds; their deeds are their refuge. Whatever actions they perform, whether good or evil, such will be their inheritance.

—A-X-206

Kammassakā: Oh meditators, beings are the owners of their deeds.

The law of *paṭicca samuppāda* (dependent origination) is the universal law of cause and effect: As the action is, so the result will be. Mental volition is the driving force for action at the vocal or physical level. If this driving force is unwholesome, the vocal and physical actions will be unwholesome. If the seeds are unwholesome, then the fruits are bound to be unwholesome. But if this driving force is wholesome, then the results of the actions are bound to be wholesome.

For a Vipassana student who develops the ability to observe this law at the level of direct experience, the answer to the question "Who am I?" becomes so clear. You are nothing but the sum total of your *kamma*, your *saṅkhāra*. All your accumulated actions together equal "I" at the conventional level.

Kammadāyādā: the heirs of their deeds.

In the wordly, conventional sense, one says, "I received this inheritance from my mother or my father or my elders," and yes, at the apparent level this is true—but what is one's real inheritance? *Kammadāyādā*. One inherits one's own *kamma*: the results, the fruits of one's own *kamma*.

Whatever you are now, the present reality of this mind-matter structure is nothing but the sum total of and the result of your own accumulated past *kamma*. The experience of the present moment is the sum total of all that is acquired, inherited—*kammadāyādā*.

Kammayonī: born of their deeds.

One says, "I am the product of a womb, I have come out of the womb of my mother," but this is only apparent truth. Actually, your birth is because of your own past *kamma*. You come from the womb of your own *kamma*. As you start understanding Dhamma at a deeper level, you realise this. This is *kammayonī*, the womb which every moment produces the fruit of the accumulated *kamma*.

Kammabandhū: kin of their deeds.

None other is your relative, not your father, your mother, your brother nor your sister. In the worldly way we say, "This is my brother, my relative, or my near or dear one; they are so close to me." Actually, no one is close to you; no one can accompany you or help you when the time comes. When you die, nothing accompanies you but your *kamma*. Whomever you call your relatives remain here, but your *kamma* continues to follow you from one life to another. You are not in possession of anything but your own *kamma*. It is your only companion.

Kammapaṭisaraṇā: their deeds are their refuge.

Refuge is only in one's own *kamma*. Wholesome *kamma* provides a refuge; unwholesome *kamma* produces more suffering. No other being can give you refuge. When you say "*Buddhaṃ saraṇaṃ gacchāmi*" (I take refuge in the Buddha), you understand fully well that a person by the name of Gotama the Buddha cannot give you refuge. Your own *kamma* gives you refuge. Nobody can protect you, not even a Buddha. Refuge in the Buddha is refuge in the quality of the Buddha, the enlightenment, the teaching that he gave.

By following the teaching, you can develop enlightenment within you. And the enlightenment that you develop within you, that is your wholesome *kamma*. This alone will give you refuge; this alone will give you protection.

Yaṃ kammaṃ karonti—kalyāṇaṃ vā pāpakaṃ vā—tassa dāyādā bhavanti: Whatever actions they perform, whether good or evil, such will be their inheritance.

This should become clear to one who is on this path. This law of nature should become very clear. Then you will become inspired to take responsibility for your own *kamma*. Remain alert and on guard each moment, so that every action, physical or mental, is wholesome.

You may not be perfect, but keep trying. You may fall down, but see how quickly you get up. With all the determination, with all the inspiration, with all the encouragement, get up and try again. This is how you become stable in Dhamma.

(Dhamma Giri edition—November 2010)

The Factors of Enlightenment *(Bojjhaṅgas)*

S. N. Goenka

The following has been adapted from Goenkaji's discourse during the Satipaṭṭhāna course.

Words of Dhamma

Yo ca dhammamabhiññāya,
dhammamaññāya paṇḍito;
rahadova nivāte ca,
anejo vūpasammati.

Thoroughly understanding the Dhamma,
and freed from longing through insight,
the wise one rid of all desire,
is calm as a pool unstirred by wind.

—Itivuttaka 3–92

There are seven *bojjhaṅgas* (factors of enlightenment) that have to be developed to reach the final goal of full liberation. They are:

1. *sati* (awareness);
2. *dhammavicaya* (investigation of Dhamma);
3. *viriya* (effort);
4. *pīti*: (rapture);
5. *passaddhi* (tranquillity);
6. *samādhi* (concentration, absorption) and
7. *upekkhā* (equanimity).

The first *bojjhaṅga* is *sati*, awareness. Without it, further steps on the path cannot be taken. *Sati*, the objective observation of reality, is the most important factor because it must be continuously present from moment to moment with every other factor.

Dhamma-vicaya is the second bojjhaṅga. The word *caya* or *cayana* means "to integrate." Apparent, consolidated, integrated, illusionary truth creates delusion and confusion resulting in wrong decisions and actions. *Vicaya or vicayana* means to divide, dissect, disintegrate, separate, which is what Vipassana intends you to do. Initially *dhamma-vicaya* is intellectual. The body is analyzed as just four elements, with no "I" about it. The mind is just the four aggregates. One observes the six sense doors, their respective objects, the contact of the two and the process of multiplication. The intellectual clarity gained by this process gives guidance to start the actual practice of Vipassana and study the truth at the actual level. To become a factor of enlightenment, *dhamma-vicaya* must become an experiential investigation—direct experience of the phenomenon of arising and passing away at the level of sensation.

The third *bojjhaṅga* is *viriya* (effort) as in *sammā-vāyāmo* in the Noble Eightfold Path. Great effort is required, but the effort is not to react, to let things just happen. Even if you have been victorious in 1,000 battles against

1,000 warriors, this inner battle of non-reaction is more difficult because the old habit is to do something, to react. Some pressure is necessary to drill a hole in a precious gem, but too much pressure will break it. It is a middle path. As you keep practising with *sati, dhamma-vicaya*, and *viriya*, the impurities go away, and you experience the fourth *bojjhaṅga*, pīti: rapture. You have to be careful. If you develop attachment to this free flow of pleasant vibrations throughout the body, if you look for it and cling to it, it is no longer a *bojjhaṅga*. If the understanding of *anicca* remains—that this is still the field of mind and matter, of arising and passing—then *pīti* becomes a factor of enlightenment.

After this, the meditator experiences *passaddhi*: a state of deep tranquility and calmness. The mind becomes extremely peaceful, quiet, and tranquil. Again the meditator may have the false impression that this deep peace, never experienced before, is liberation. Just as *pīti*, can become a bondage if not used properly, in the same way, *passaddhi* can also become a bondage. You understand that it is only a midway rest-house: the final goal is still far away. You can check that the six sense doors are still functioning: open your eyes, or listen. You are still in the field of arising and passing. You have not transcended the field of mind and matter.

Thoroughly examine this *passaddhi*, this deep, tranquil, calm experience. Although difficult to grasp, a subtle oscillation remains, and this sensation is called *adukkhamasukhaṃ* (neither pleasant nor unpleasant). In *pīti*, the experience was pleasant; now it is just peaceful, and the danger is that *anicca* is not experienced. Detachment from craving towards pleasant sensation or aversion towards unpleasant sensation is much easier than detachment from this feeling of peace. You must be very attentive, with a very sharp mind, feel the subtle oscillation, check the six sense doors, and keep understanding that this experience is *anicca*. If you are aware of the very subtle oscillation, arising and passing, then it becomes a *bojjhaṅga* and gives you the strength to move further. Your experience grows.

There is often a question about *adukkhamasukhaṃ* or neutral sensations. The Buddha did not mean the initial, surface sensations which are neither pleasant nor unpleasant. That is totally different and causes craving and aversion because people get bored with it, lose interest, and want something else. Their experience has become stale. They want something more or new, something they don't have. This is their old habit pattern.

The next enlightenment factor is *samādhi*—concentration or absorption. *Sammā-samādhi* takes us beyond all the planes of existence and results in full liberation from the bondage of birth and death, and from every type of suffering. It is practised with *sampajañña*, the awareness of the mind-matter phenomenon and the realization of its nature of arising and passing. With the practice of *sammā-samādhi* (with *sampajañña*), one after the other, the meditator attains the fruit of *sotāpanna*, *sakadāgāmī*, *anāgāmī*, and *arahant*. Thus, *samādhi* becomes an enlightenment factor.

Upekkhā—equanimity is the seventh factor of enlightenment. Like *sati*, it must be present from the beginning to the end, at every step. Whichever other factor is being developed, awareness and equanimity must always be present.

When the *bojjhaṅgas* are practiced properly, they increase and become perfect and when each is perfect, enlightenment is perfect. This is the whole process of Vipassana.

(Dhamma Giri edition—January 2008)

Maṅgala Sutta—Discourse On Welfare

Vipassana Research Institute

Sometimes known as the 'vinaya' for householders, the Maṅgala Sutta is very popular among the followers of the Buddha. Two traditional opening verses that give some background are often chanted, explaining that devas and men had been discussing for a long time what was a true maṅgala. The canonical text begins with "Evaṃ me sutaṃ" and tells us the immediate context for the sutta. The sutta is found in Khuddaka-nikāya, Sutta Nipāta, II. 4. Goenkaji's morning chanting of this sutta on the ninth day of the 10-day Vipassana course begins with the Buddha's answer to the question put to him.

Words of Dhamma

Pamādamanuyuñjanti,
bālā dummedhino janā;
appamādañca medhāvī,
dhanaṃ seṭṭhaṃva rakkhati.

The foolish and ignorant
sink into negligence;
but the wise one guards heedfulness
as the highest wealth.

—Dhammapada 26

Yaṃ maṅgalaṃ dvādasahi,
cintayiṃsu sadevakā;
sotthānaṃ nādhigacchanti,
aṭṭhatiṃsañca maṅgalaṃ.

For 12 years [men] along with devas
pondered, "What is welfare?"
But they did not arrive at the
38 welfares that bring happiness.

Desitaṃ devadevena, sabbapāpavināsanaṃ;
sabbaloka-hitatthāya, maṅgalaṃ taṃ bhaṇāmahe.

The Lord of the devas [the Buddha] taught [that which] destroys all evil,
for the benefit of the whole world: let us recite those welfares.

Evaṃ me sutaṃ—

Thus have I heard—

Ekaṃ samayaṃ bhagavā sāvatthiyaṃ viharati jetavane anāthapiṇḍikassa ārāme. Atha kho aññatarā devatā abhikkantāya rattiyā abhikkantavaṇṇā kevalakappaṃ jetavanaṃ obhāsetvā yena bhagavā tenupasaṅkami.

At one time the Blessed One was dwelling in Sāvatthi at Jeta's grove, the monastery of Anāthapiṇḍika.
Then, indeed, when the night was well advanced, a certain female deva of surpassing beauty, illuminating the whole of Jeta's grove, approached where the Buddha was.

Upasaṅkamitvā bhagavantaṃ abhivādetvā ekamantaṃ aṭṭhāsi.
Ekamantaṃ ṭhitā kho sā devatā bhagavantaṃ gāthāya ajjhabhāsi:

Having arrived there and respectfully saluting the Blessed One, she stood to one side.
Standing to one side the deva addressed the Blessed One in verse:

Bahū devā manussā ca, maṅgalāni acintayuṃ;
ākaṅkhamānā sotthānaṃ, brūhi maṅgalamuttamaṃ.

Many devas and men have pondered on welfares, yearning for happiness.
Please explain what is the highest welfare.

Bhagavā etadavoca:

The Buddha replies:

Asevanā ca bālānaṃ, paṇḍitānañca sevanā;
pūjā ca pūjanīyānaṃ, etaṃ maṅgalamuttamaṃ.

Avoidance of fools, the company of the wise, honour where honour is due—this is the highest welfare.

Patirūpadesavāso ca, pubbe ca katapuññatā;
atta-sammāpaṇidhi ca, etaṃ maṅgalamuttamaṃ.

A suitable place of abode, the merit of past good deeds, right aspirations for oneself—this is the highest welfare.

Bāhusaccañca sippañca, vinayo ca susikkhito;
subhāsitā ca yā vācā, etaṃ maṅgalamuttamaṃ.

Great learning and skill, well-mastered discipline, well-spoken words—this is the highest welfare.

Mātā-pitu-upaṭṭhānaṃ, puttadārassa saṅgaho;
anākulā ca kammantā, etaṃ maṅgalamuttamaṃ.

Serving one's parents, caring for spouse and children, a peaceful occupation—this is the highest welfare.

Dānañca dhammacariyā ca, ñātakānañca saṅgaho;
anavajjāni kammāni, etaṃ maṅgalamuttamaṃ.

Generosity, a life of Dhamma, caring for relatives, blameless deeds—this is the highest welfare.

Āratī viratī pāpā, majjapānā ca saṃyamo;
appamādo ca dhammesu, etaṃ maṅgalamuttamaṃ.

Ceasing and shunning evil, refraining from intoxicants, vigilance in the Dhamma—this is the highest welfare.

Gāravo ca nivāto ca, santuṭṭhi ca kataññutā;
kālena dhammassavanaṃ, etaṃ maṅgalamuttamaṃ.

Respectfulness, humility, contentment, gratitude, listening to the Dhamma at the proper time—this is the highest welfare.

Khantī ca sovacassatā, samaṇānañca dassanaṃ;
kālena dhammasākacchā, etaṃ maṅgalamuttamaṃ.

Forbearance, accepting guidance, beholding saintly people, discussion of the Dhamma at the proper time—this is the highest welfare.

Tapo ca brahmacariyañca, ariyasaccāna-dassanaṃ;
nibbānasacchikiriyā ca, etaṃ maṅgalamuttamaṃ.

Ardent practice, a life of purity, witnessing the Noble Truths, experiencing *nibbāna*—this is the highest welfare.

Phuṭṭhassa lokadhammehi cittaṃ yassa na kampati;
asokaṃ virajaṃ khemaṃ, etaṃ maṅgalamuttamaṃ.

When faced with the vicissitudes of life, one's mind is unshaken, sorrowless, stainless, secure—this is the highest welfare.

Etādisāni katvāna, sabbatthamaparājitā;
sabbatthasotthiṃ gacchanti, taṃ tesaṃ maṅgalamuttamaṃ.

Having acted in this way, everywhere invincible, they go everywhere safely—that is the highest welfare.

The Highest Welfare

The Buddha's teaching was not merely for monks and nuns, but also for householders, many of whom used to come to him to learn Dhamma. One group came and said: "Sir, we are not prepared to become monks or nuns; we have to live as householders. Will the technique work for us? Can we also get liberated?"

He replied, "Certainly, it is a technique for all." Monks and nuns do not have any worldly responsibilities. So they can give their whole life to this purpose, and the results come sooner. Householders cannot avoid their multifarious responsibilities towards their family members, relatives, and society but the teaching also works for them. The Buddha gave a discourse to this group, explaining how to live a wholesome life. He listed 38 welfares to be acquired by a family man or woman, each higher than the last. When he came to the highest, he said:

"Facing the vicissitudes of life the mind is not shaken; it is without grief, without impurity, without insecurity: this is the highest welfare."

Everyone has to meet vicissitudes in life but the mind should not get agitated; it should remain stable and balanced. Then there is no crying, no unhappiness, no impurity nor any feeling of insecurity in your mind. One always feels secure because one is on the path of Dhamma; nothing can go wrong. This is the highest welfare: equanimity with all the vicissitudes of life.

S. N. Goenka
(adapted from the Day 8 discourse.)

1. The eight worldly vicissitudes (lokadhammā) are: lābha (profit) and alābha (loss), yaso (fame) and ayaso (ill repute), pasaṃsā (praise) and nindā (criticism), sukha (pleasure) and dukkha (pain).

(Dhamma Giri edition—April 2000)

The Importance of Daily Meditation

S.N. Goenka

The following is a condensed translation of a discourse given by Goenkaji to some 5,000 old students in Nagpur, India, on October 8, 2000.

My dear Dhamma sons and Dhamma daughters: I am very happy that we have sat together and practiced pure Dhamma. Meditating together is of great importance.

Sukho buddhānaṃ uppado.
Sukhā saddhammadesanā.
Sukhā saṅghassa sāmaggī.
Samaggānaṃ tapo sukho.

Happy is the arising of the Buddhas in the world.
Happy is the teaching of pure Dhamma.
Happy is the coming together of meditators.
Happiness is meditating together.

Two thousand six hundred years ago, Gotama the Buddha arose in this country and taught pure Dhamma, bringing great happiness to the world. People started living in accordance with the teaching. They started meditating together just as we have done today. There is no greater happiness than this. When Dhamma brothers and sisters sit and meditate together, our practice is strengthened because the meditation of others is strong and the entire atmosphere is charged with Dhamma. Whenever possible, meditators should have joint sittings at least once a week.

Every meditator has to develop the strength to face the ups and downs of life. To do this, it is necessary to meditate one hour in the morning and evening daily, to meditate together once a week, and to take a 10-day course at least once a year. Then you will keep progressing on the path. Householders face many difficulties and obstacles. Even those who have renounced the household life tell me that they are not able to meditate regularly. But we must not give up! In spite of all difficulties we must meditate daily, morning and evening.

To keep the body healthy and strong, we do physical exercises, such as yoga, jogging or walking; otherwise our bodies will become weak and diseased. It is even more necessary to keep our minds healthy and strong; we should not allow them to become weak or diseased. We live in a complex and stressful world. When our minds are not strong, we lose our balance and become miserable. Sometimes meditators come to me and say: "I have stopped meditating. What can I do? I am too busy!" This is a feeble excuse. We give food to the body three or four times a day, do we not? We don't say, "I am such a busy person, I don't have time for food today." The meditation that we do every morning and evening makes the mind strong. When we forget this, we harm ourselves. Even when we have a very heavy workload, we must do this mental exercise.

Those who have not learned this meditation are unfortunate. But those who have received this benevolent teaching and are not using it are even more unfortunate. It is a great good fortune to be born as a human being. Only a human being can eradicate mental defilements from the depth of the mind. This work cannot be done by animals, birds, reptiles, insects or other lower beings. Even a human being cannot do this work if he or she does not practice this technique. Suppose someone is born as a human, finds this wonderful technique, learns to use it, benefits from it and still discontinues the practice—what a misfortune! Suppose a bankrupt person finds a treasure, then discards it and becomes bankrupt again; a starving person receives delicious food, discards it and becomes hungry again; a sick person finds medicine, discards it and becomes sick again—very unfortunate, indeed! We should never make this mistake.

You have attained a human birth. You have come in contact with this wonderful Dhamma. You have developed faith in this technique because you have benefited from it. And yet you have stopped meditating. Do not be heedless. You are not doing anyone a favor by meditating twice a day. You are not doing your teacher a favor; you are doing yourself a favor. When someone starts feeling sensations on the body, understand that the door of liberation has opened. A person who cannot feel sensations on the body is unfortunate; the door of liberation has not opened for them. When one learns to remain equanimous towards the sensations, not only has the door opened but one has entered and started walking on the path of liberation.

At the time of death some sensation will arise, and if we are not aware and react with aversion, we will go to the lower planes of existence. But a good meditator who remains equanimous towards the sensations at the time of death will not go to a lower plane. This is how we make our own future. Death can come at any time. We do not have an agreement with death that it should come only when we are ready. With Dhamma, we are ready whenever it comes. Vipassana is a priceless gem that can liberate us from the cycle of birth and death. It will improve not only this life but future lives, leading ultimately to full liberation from all suffering.

Some may say, "But we do not have time, we have so much work." These are poor excuses for squandering an invaluable jewel. When there is sorrow, despair or dullness in daily life for whatever reason, this technique will help. *Vedanā samosaraṇā sabbe dhammā*—Whatever arises in the mind (dhamma) flows together with sensations. Mind and body are interrelated. When a defilement arises in the mind, some sensation will arise in the body. This is the law of nature. A meditator understands that there is a defilement in the mind and observes sensation in the body. One practices this thoroughly, not just once or twice but again and again. Every sensation is impermanent; the defilement connected to it is also impermanent. When we observe sensations, the defilements become weak and drain away—like a thief who enters a house and, finding that the master of the house is awake, runs away.

Such a great benefit! No matter what defilement arises, whether lust, egotism, envy, fear or anything else, we will not be overpowered. We have learned the art of living. Negativities will keep occurring throughout our lives, for this reason or that. We have a very effective weapon in the sensations. No enemy will be able to overpower us; we are the masters. Vipassana is the technique to make us our own masters.

You have come on the path of Vipassana. Understand that you have received an invaluable jewel. Now you must meditate regularly to be happy and peaceful for the whole life.

(International edition—July 2004)

The Snare of Māra

The following is an extract, edited and condensed, from one of the discourses for a long course. In it Goenkaji refers to Māra, meaning the forces opposed to liberation—a kind of personification of one's own negativities.

It is easy to develop the faculty to feel bodily sensations but more difficult to maintain perfect equanimity toward them, understanding that they are all impermanent, *anicca*.

This is the most important aspect of the practice. Unless you develop the understanding of *anicca* at the level of bodily sensations, liberation is far away. The Buddha kept saying that if there is a sensation and, along with it, craving or aversion, *nibbāna* is far away from you. *Vedanā* and *taṇhā*, *vedanā* and *taṇhā*: so long as these come together, there is only *dukkha-samudaya-gāminī paṭipadā*—a path that multiplies your misery, that generates misery for you. The fire and the fuel, the fire and the fuel: you can't escape the burning. You have to understand at the experiential level, "Look, this is fire; look, this is fuel. And look, if more fuel is given to the fire, I will not escape the burning." With this understanding, one will try not to feed the fire. If you do not give more fuel, then whatever fuel is already there will sooner or later be consumed. When no new *saṅkhāra* of craving or aversion is given, the old *saṅkhāras* will automatically be consumed.

You can't do anything about the old *saṅkhāras* but you can certainly stop creating new ones. Once you do, the old ones will automatically be burned away little by little. A time will come when there will be no more *saṅkhāras* of the past because you have stopped creating new ones. The law of nature is such that when you stop creating new *saṅkhāras* you are on the path of liberation, *nirodha-gāminī paṭipadā*. The Buddha called it *dukkha-nirodha-gāminī paṭipadā*, the path to eradicate all miseries; and he has also called it *vedanā-nirodha-gāminī paṭipadā*, the path to eradicate all *vedanā*. In other words, by walking this path one reaches the stage where there is no more *vedanā* because one experiences something beyond mind and matter. Within the field of mind and matter there is constant contact, because of which there is *vedanā*, whether pleasant, unpleasant or neutral. To be free of *vedanā* is to be free of misery. And the only way to be free of *vedanā* is to stop giving new fuel to the fire. Let it burn out. It is so simple and yet so difficult.

In spite of understanding everything at the intellectual level, at the actual level deep inside there is a tendency to cling to pleasant sensations. And that is the real danger. It is relatively easy to free yourself from aversion toward unpleasant sensations but it is very difficult to be free of craving and clinging toward pleasant ones.

You must explore the truth of the entire field of *vedanā*. As you work, you encounter unpleasant gross sensations, and initially you react with aversion because of the old habit pattern. Then you realize, "Look, there is a reaction toward unpleasant sensations." You keep training your mind: "This is impermanent, this is impermanent. I have experienced so many unpleasant sensations in the past and none of them remained forever. They all arose and sooner or later they passed away. How can the one that has come now remain forever?" In this way, understanding with experience the characteristic of *anicca*, you train your mind not to react. To some extent you are successful.

Then the experience changes and you reach the stage of total dissolution, with no solidity anywhere; you observe a free flow of very subtle vibrations, an experience that is extremely pleasant. Without your realizing how or when, you start clinging to this, thinking, "Oh wonderful! This is pleasant; this is good." Then you recall the words of your teacher or the Buddha: "Oh no, this also is impermanent, impermanent." But a part of your mind still clings to it.

To judge whether you are clinging or not, you have to examine yourself when the free flow passes away. What happens then? Do you feel dejected, disappointed, defeated, depressed, as if you have regressed? If any trace of such feeling is present, it shows that there was clinging. Even after you first experience dissolution, from time to time unpleasant sensations keep coming. At that time you must examine yourself: "Now that these gross sensations have come again, is a part of my mind still craving for the dissolution I experienced some time back?" If the thought arises, " I must get it again, I must get it again!" then certainly there is aversion toward the unpleasant sensations and craving for pleasant ones; you are not coming out of the old habit pattern. Strive to come out of it. When a pleasant sensation arises and even a part of your mind starts relishing it, no matter how slightly, at that time wisdom should arise: "Oh dangerous! This is a truly frightening situation. This is Māra's snare. This is what has been happening for millions of lives."

At a very superficial level, a vision, a sound, a smell, a taste, a touch or a thought appear to be pleasurable. But one knows, "Indulging in such pleasures is a bondage; one must be free of them. One should not become entangled in pleasures." But with the practice of Vipassana, it becomes clear that whatever one calls pleasure is nothing but a pleasant sensation on the body. Whatever the outside object—whether a vision, a sound, something tangible, a smell, a taste or a thought—along with it there occurs a very pleasant sensation on the body. One understands, "This is what I used to call pleasure. And its opposite as well is only apparently an outside object; actually there is unpleasant sensation on the body. Reacting to sensations is a game I have been playing all my life and for countless lives in the past."

Now you find that in the name of Vipassana you are playing the same game. What's the difference? Now too, when you experience a free flow of very subtle sensations, you think, "Oh, very pleasant!" And when it disappears you feel depressed, as if you have lost ground. When it returns you feel you are progressing: "Now I've got it again!"

You have heard this before and understood it at the intellectual level. But examine yourself. If you are still playing the same game your understanding is very superficial; you have not grasped Dhamma properly—

liberation is far, far away. As the Buddha very emphatically said, if there is a sensation and, along with it, craving or aversion, *nibbāna* is far, far away.

Understand his words of warning, especially when you encounter a situation of very pleasant, subtle sensations. This is a very dangerous, even frightening, situation. Understanding this, you will want to disentangle yourself. It becomes impossible for you to relish it. It is so dangerous, so frightening; what is there to relish? Instead one feels disgusted: "What is there in this pleasant sensation?" Only then does one make progress on the path toward *nibbāna*.

So long as the relishing persists, so long as one is not disgusted with the relishing, so long as one does not see any danger in the relishing, one is far, far away from *nibbāna*. That is why it is so important to work with the bodily sensations properly. You have started feeling sensation. Good! But how are you feeling it? Is *saññā* [perception] still working in the same mad way, or has it changed into *anicca-saññā*? Do you understand what Māra's snare is? Are you deepening that understanding?

A story. A parrot came to stay in the hermitage where a bhikkhu meditated, a very peaceful place with many fruit trees. The bhikkhu tried to teach the parrot, saying, "Oh parrot, there is danger here. A hunter will come and scatter some grains; you will be attracted to them. He will throw his net; you will be caught in it. A great danger. You must be very careful. The grains that he scatters are very dangerous. Because of them you will be caught in the net. A great danger. Oh parrot, the hunter will come. He will throw some grains. You will be attracted toward the grains. He will throw his net and you will be caught. Be careful. Oh parrot, be careful!"

The parrot learned to repeat these words. It would keep on reciting, "Oh parrot, be careful! Oh parrot, be careful! The hunter will come and scatter grains. Don't be attracted to them. He will throw his net and you will be caught. Be careful! Be careful!"

And exactly as the bhikkhu had warned, one day the hunter came and scattered some grains. The parrot was attracted to them and the hunter threw his net, ensnaring the parrot. The hunter caught hold of the parrot, which kept on reciting the same words: "Oh parrot, be careful! The hunter will come. He will scatter grains. He will throw his net. Be careful, be careful!"

A Vipassana meditator who relishes the grains of the hunter becomes entangled in Māra's net. And these pleasant sensations on the body are the grains. This is Māra's snare. When you start relishing them, you are caught. Yet you imagine that, because you are practicing Vipassana, you are becoming liberated, you are approaching the experience of *nibbāna*. Instead you are running in the opposite direction.

This is how the wheel of misery keeps revolving. It always starts with pleasant sensations and with craving toward them. Aversion simply follows. One is not entangled in Māra's snare by the unpleasant sensations. So long as you have craving and clinging for pleasant sensations, you will have aversion toward the unpleasant. The root is your craving for the pleasant.

And when free flow occurs you face a dangerous situation. This is the stage at which a subtle craving will start. At the surface of the mind, at the conscious, intellectual level, you will keep saying, "This is *anicca, anicca*." But deep inside you will start clinging to the experience. You will behave exactly like the parrot that keeps repeating, "Oh parrot, be careful; oh parrot, be careful!"—even after he has been caught because of his craving for the grains scattered by the hunter. You have craving, and as long as the craving exists you cannot come to the end of *vedanā*.

This craving must go away. You must learn to stop relishing the pleasant sensations. You must discern the danger in them; you must recognize that this is a frightening situation. And you must understand that you have to get out of it. A feeling of disgust arises toward the pleasant sensations themselves: "What is really pleasant here? I have been caught in this snare in countless lives in the past, and I continue to be caught in it in this life as well."

A pleasant sensation appears to be pleasant, but it is really suffering because it enmeshes one in the old habit of relishing it, of clinging to it. It is *dukkha*, it is bondage. As the Buddha said, "*Yaṃ kiñci vedayitaṃ, taṃ pi dukkhas-miṃ*—Whatever sensation one is experiencing, it is actually *dukkha, dukkha, dukkha*." As long as there is *vedanā* there will be *dukkha*, because the process of multiplication of misery is operating. The fire is burning, and you are giving it fuel. Let the fire be extinguished. Then you will come to the end of *vedanā*, the end of suffering.

(International edition—July 2000)

The Practice of *Mettābhāvanā* in Vipassana Meditation

This article was presented as a paper to the Seminar on Vipassana Meditation held at Dhamma Giri in December 1986.

Words of Dhamma

Ahaṃ avero homi, avyāpajjho homi,
anīgho homi, sukhī attānam pariharāmi.
Mātā pitu ācariya, ñāti samūhā
averā hontu, avyāpajjhā hontu,
anīghā hontu,
sukhī attānam pariharantu.

May I be free from ill will; may I be free from cruelty; may I be free from anger; may I keep myself at peace.
May my mother, my father, my teacher, my relatives, the whole community be free from ill will, free from cruelty, free from anger; may they keep themselves at peace.

Sabbe sattā, sabbe pāṇā,
sabbe bhūtā, sabbe puggalā,
sabbe attabhāva pariyāpannā,
sabbā itthiyo, sabbe purisā,
sabbe ariyā, sabbe anariyā,
sabbe manussā, sabbe amanussā,
sabbe devā, sabbe vinipātikā,
averā hontu, avyāpajjhā hontu,
anīghā hontu,
sukhī attānam pariharantu.
Sabbe sattā sukhī hontu,
sabbe hontu ca khemino.
Sabbe bhadrāni passantu,
mā kinci pāpamāgamā,
mā kinci dukkhamāgamā,
mā kinci sokamāgamā.

May all creatures, all living things,
all beings, all individuals,
all persons included,
all women, all men,
all noble ones, all worldlings,
all humans, all non-humans,
all celestial beings, all those in states of woe
be free from ill will, free from cruelty,
free from anger;
may they keep themselves at peace.
May all beings be happy;
may they all be secure.
May they all see good fortune;
may no evil befall them,
may no suffering befall them,
may no sorrow befall them.

(Pāli verses traditionally recited during the practice of *Mettā*.)

The practice of *mettābhāvanā* (meditation of loving kindness) is an important adjunct to the technique of Vipassana meditation—indeed, its logical outcome. It is a technique whereby we radiate loving kindness and good will toward all beings, deliberately charging the atmosphere around us with the calming, positive vibrations of pure and compassionate love. The Buddha instructed his followers to develop *mettā* so as to lead more peaceful and harmonious lives and to help others do so as well. Students of Vipassana should follow that instruction because *mettā* gives us a way to share with all others the peace and harmony we are developing.

The commentaries state: *Mijjati siniyhatī'ti mettā*—"That which inclines one to a friendly disposition is *mettā*." It is a sincere wish for the good and welfare of all, devoid of ill will. *Adoso'ti mettā* —"Non-aversion is *mettā*." The chief characteristic of *mettā* is a benevolent attitude. It culminates in the identification of oneself with all beings, a recognition of the fellowship of all life.

To grasp this concept at least intellectually is easy enough, but it is far harder to develop such an attitude in oneself. To do so some practice is needed, and so we have the technique of *mettābhāvanā*, the systematic cultivation of good will toward others. To be really effective though, *mettā* meditation must be practiced along with Vipassana meditation. So long as negativities such as aversion dominate the mind, it is futile to formulate conscious thoughts of good will, and doing so would be a ritual devoid of inner meaning. However, when negativities are removed by the practice of Vipassana, good will naturally wells up in the mind; and emerging from the prison of self-obsession, we begin to concern ourselves with the welfare of others.

For this reason, the technique of *mettābhāvanā* is introduced only at the end of a Vipassana course, after the participants have passed through the process of purification. At such a time meditators often feel a deep wish for the well-being of others, making their practice of *mettā* truly effective. Though limited time is devoted to it in a course, *mettā* may be regarded as the culmination of the practice of Vipassana.

Nibbāna can be experienced only by those whose minds are filled with loving kindness and compassion for all beings. Simply wishing for that state is not enough: we must purify our minds to attain it. We do so by Vipassana meditation; hence the emphasis on this technique during a course.

As we practice, we become aware that the underlying reality of the world and of ourselves consists of arising and passing away every moment. We realize that the process of change continues without our control and regardless of our wishes. Gradually we understand that any attachment to what is ephemeral and insubstantial produces suffering for us. We learn to be detached and to keep the balance of our minds in the face of any experience. Then we begin to experience what real happiness is: not the satisfaction of desire or the forestalling of fears but rather liberation from the cycle of desire and fear. As inner serenity develops, we clearly see how others are enmeshed in suffering, and naturally this wish arises, "May they find what we have found: the way out of misery, the path of peace." This is the proper volition for the practice of *mettābhāvanā*.

Mettā is not prayer; nor is it the hope that an outside agency will help. On the contrary, it is a dynamic process producing a supportive atmosphere where others can act to help themselves. *Mettā* can be omni-directional or directed toward a particular person. In either case, meditators are simply providing an outlet; because the *mettā* we feel is not 'our' *mettā*. By eliminating egotism we open our minds and make them conduits for the forces of positivity throughout the universe. The realization that *mettā* is not produced by us makes its transmission truly selfless.

In order to conduct *mettā,* the mind must be calm, balanced and free from negativity. This is the type of mind developed in the practice of Vipassana. A meditator knows by experience how anger, antipathy, or ill will destroy peace and frustrate any efforts to help others. Only as hatred is removed and equanimity is developed can we be happy and wish happiness for others. The words "May all beings be happy" have great force only when uttered from a pure mind. Backed by this purity, they will certainly be effective in fostering the happiness of others.

We must therefore examine ourselves before practicing *mettābhāvanā* to check whether we are really capable of transmitting *mettā*. If we find even a tinge of hatred or aversion in our minds, we should refrain at that time. Otherwise we would transmit that negativity, causing harm to others. However, if mind and body are filled with serenity and well-being, it is natural and appropriate to share this happiness with others: "May you be happy, may you be liberated from the defilements that are the causes of suffering, may all beings be peaceful."

This loving attitude enables us to deal far more skillfully with the vicissitudes of life. Suppose, for example, one encounters a person who is acting out of deliberate ill will to harm others. The common response—to react with fear and hatred—is self-centered, does nothing to improve the situation and, in fact, magnifies the negativity. It would be far more helpful to remain calm and balanced, with a feeling of good will even for the person who is acting wrongly. This must not be merely an intellectual stance, a veneer over unresolved negativity. *Mettā* works only when it is the spontaneous overflow of a purified mind. The serenity gained in Vipassana meditation naturally gives rise to feelings of *mettā*, and throughout the day this will continue to affect us and our environment in a positive way.

Thus Vipassana ultimately has a dual function: to bring us happiness by purifying our minds, and to help us foster the happiness of others by preparing us to practice *mettā*. What, after all, is the purpose of freeing ourselves of negativity and egotism unless we share these benefits with others? In a retreat we cut ourselves off from the world temporarily in order to return and share with others what we have gained in solitude. These two aspects of the practice of Vipassana are inseparable.

In these times of violent unrest, widespread malaise and suffering, the need for such a practice as *mettābhāvanā* is clear. If peace and harmony are to reign throughout the world, they must first be established in the minds of all the inhabitants of the world.

Questions and Answers

Are there forces that support us as we develop our pāramīs (wholesome qualities)?

Certainly—visible forces as well as invisible ones. For example, people tend to associate with those of similar interest, background or character. When we develop good qualities in us, we naturally attract people who have those qualities. When we come in contact with such good people, naturally we get support from them.

If we generate love, compassion and good will, we will get tuned up with all beings—visible or invisible—that have these positive vibrations, and we will start getting support from them. It is like tuning a radio to receive waves of a certain meter band from a distant broadcasting station. Similarly, we tune ourselves to vibrations of the type we generate; and so we receive the benefit of those vibrations.

It is not a matter of seeking the intervention of a more powerful being to achieve one's desires. You have to work hard, with the understanding that your work will enable you to benefit from the good vibrations of others. As the saying goes, the Lord helps those who help themselves.

Will mettā get stronger as samādhi (concentration) gets stronger?

Without *samādhi* the *mettā* is really no *mettā*. When *samādhi* is weak the mind is very agitated, and it is agitated only when it is generating some impurity, some type of craving or aversion. With these impurities, you cannot expect to generate good qualities, vibrations of *mettā*, of *kāruna* (compassion). It isn't possible. At the vocal level, you may keep on saying "Be happy, be happy," but it doesn't work. If you have *samādhi* then your mind is calm and quiet, at least for that moment. It is not necessary that all the impurities have gone away; but at least for that moment when you are going to give *mettā*, your mind is quiet, calm, and not generating any impurity. Then whatever *mettā* you give is strong, fruitful, beneficial.

Is the generation of mettā a natural consequence of the purity of mind or is it something that must be actively developed? Are there progressive stages in mettā?

Both are true. According to the law of nature—the law of Dhamma—as the mind is purified, the quality of *mettā* develops naturally. On the other hand, you must work to develop it by practicing *mettābhāvanā.* It is only at a very high stage of mental purity that *mettā* is generated naturally, and nothing has to be done, no training has to be given. Until one reaches that stage, one has to practice.

Also, people who don't practice Vipassana can practice *mettābhāvanā.* In such countries as Burma, Śri Laṅka and Thailand, *mettābhāvanā* is very common in every household. However, the practice usually is confined to mentally reciting "May all beings be happy, be peaceful." This certainly gives some peace of mind to the person who is practicing it. To some extent good vibrations enter the atmosphere, but they are not strong.

However, when you practice Vipassana, purification starts. With this base of purity, your practice of *mettā* naturally becomes stronger. Then you won't need to repeat these good wishes aloud. A stage will come when every fiber of the body keeps on feeling good for others, generating good will for others.

Muditā and *kāruna* naturally follow as one develops *mettā. Mettā* is love for all beings. *Mettā* takes away the traces of aversion, animosity and hatred toward others. It takes away the traces of jealousy and envy toward others. What is *muditā* ? When you see other people progressing, becoming happier, if your mind is not pure, you will generate jealousy toward this person. "Why did they get this, and not I? I'm a more deserving person. Why are they given such a position of power, or status? Why not I? Why have they earned so much money? Why not I?" This kind of jealousy is the manifestation of an impure mind. As your mind gets purer by Vipassana and your *mettā* gets stronger, you will feel happy when seeing others happy. "All around there is misery. Look, at least one person is happy. May he be happy and contented. May he progress in Dhamma, progress in worldly ways." This is *muditā* , sympathetic happiness. It will come. Similarly, when you find somebody suffering, *kāruna* automatically arises if your mind is pure. If you are an egocentered person, full of impurities, without the proper practice of Vipassana, without *mettā*, then seeing someone in trouble doesn't affect you. You don't care; you are indifferent. You try to delude yourself saying, "Oh, this fellow is suffering because of his own karma. How can I do anything about it?" Such thoughts show that the mind is not yet pure. If the mind becomes pure and *mettā* develops, hardness of heart cannot stay; it starts melting. You see people suffering and your heart goes out to them. You don't start crying; that's another extreme. Rather, you feel like helping such people. If it is within your means, you give some tangible help. Otherwise, at least you help with your vibrations: "May you be happy. May you come out of your misery." Even if you have no material means to help somebody, you always have this spiritual means.

(International edition—December 1991)

The Gift of Dhamma

Goenkaji has often talked about the gifts of dāna, the mental volition of the giver and the many ways to give dāna. He talks about the supreme gift of Dhammadāna, the transmission of the Dhamma in its pure form from teacher to student through the generations. In addition he points out that, even for those who are not teachers, there are ways to share in the giving of Dhammadāna. Following is a selection of his words on this topic, drawn from various articles and talks.

Dhammadāna

From a talk given by S.N. Goenka on January 15, 1976, on the occasion of the founding of Dhamma Thalī, Jaipur, Rajasthan.

The taste of Dhamma surpasses all other

tastes. Other tastes do not quench craving, they increase it. Only the taste of Dhamma puts an end to all craving. It quenches it. Hence it is the best.

The gift of Dhamma surpasses all other *dāna*. Giving *dāna* towards a persons worldly needs, although beneficial, gives a temporary benefit—a limited benefit. But the gift of Dhamma gives enormous benefit, boundless benefit. By this *dāna*, from whatever misery one becomes freed, this freedom is forever. From whatever bondage one becomes freed, this freedom is forever. Hence the *dāna* of Dhamma is greater than any other *dāna*.

The *dāna* of Dhamma is given by teaching the Dhamma. As well, any contribution we make in any manner towards spreading the teaching of the Dhamma is *dhammadāna*. Therefore whatever contribution one makes towards having a meditation center built, for organizing and maintaining it, serving courses or providing other requirements is all *dhammadāna*, the *dāna* that is superior to all other *dana*.

If we give food, the benefit is that the hunger of the recipient is appeased. And in return, the law of nature, or Dhamma, will automatically help appease our hunger when we are hungry. This is a benefit. Similarly, whatever other worldly *dāna* we give, the resultant fruits will be of similar nature. They will give worldly benefit.

When we help a person to come out of craving, aversion and ignorance, the resultant fruit is not ordinary because the *dāna* is not ordinary. The *dāna* of Dhamma is supramundane. Its resultant fruits are also supramundane. It is a *dāna* that will assist us in coming out of all worldly bondage.

When we contribute towards this great cause, the kind of help we give is not significant. What is important is the volition with which we give. We should give with a Dhamma volition, thinking, I have this facility, this capacity, this resource. I shall contribute so much of it for the well-being of people. May there be true well-being. Whatever well-being may be achieved by various other kinds of *dāna*, in comparison, the well-being achieved by this *dāna* is boundless. There cannot be a better way to use my capacity, my resources, my wealth. When we give *dāna* with this Dhamma volition, we pave the path of our own progress. Whatever obstacles we face in our meditation, our practice, are the result of our own past *kamma*. Because we helped another person to become liberated, the resultant fruit will help us to overcome the obstacles we face. All the hindrances to our liberation will be removed.

What greater delight could this land have than if even one person gets liberated sitting in a cell or cave on this land, if even one person realizes *nibbāna* meditating on this land? What greater rapture could this land experience? What greater welfare could this land aspire to?

This land shall be venerated. When construction work takes place, it will cause hardship to the visible and invisible beings here. This will happen. But the work has begun with wholesome volition, with *dhamma-dhātu*. The land has been venerated, all its inhabitants have been venerated; they will be happy.

Something constructive, beneficial and good will take place here. The people who work here should generate good will towards all the visible and invisible beings whenever they work. May no being knowingly be killed.

We should not knowingly cause hardship to any being.

The good of all, the welfare of all should be the volition. And if unknowingly some hardship is caused, then may those who suffer share our merits, our good deeds, the Dhamma accumulated by us. May they also be happy.

Make sure all work is done with such feelings of good will. Work shall be done with a pure mind. The land is pure, the meditators who work are pure, their minds are pure. The wealth that flows in is pure. The results will be pure, they are bound to be pure.

The Dāna of Financial Support

It is an enormous gift of *Dhammadāna* to contribute financially to creating and maintaining a meditation center where the pure vibrations of Dhamma will support a meditator. In the 10-day discourses, Goenkaji tells the story of Anāthapiṇḍika, a multimillionaire in the days of the Buddha. This person was actually named Sudatta but he received the title Anāthapiṇḍika because he gave *dāna* so generously.

The title *Anāthapiṇḍika* comes from *anātha*, meaning those who are very poor and *piṇḍika*, meaning one who gives food. Because he gave so much food to all the hungry people, this was his title. He lived in Sāvatthi, which was the most populous city in India in those days. But there were branches of his business throughout the country and even beyond, in different countries. And he had a rule that wherever his office or branch was, nobody should go hungry, people should be given food. But still he didn't know Dhamma.

One day he came into contact with Buddha. That means, he came into contact with Dhamma, Vipassana. By practicing, he purified his mind and experienced a dip in the first stage of *nibbāna*. For the first time he experienced the truth beyond mind and matter and became altogether a changed person.

The purpose of giving a donation is not to build one's ego but rather to deflate it, to dissolve it. He now thought: All this money that has come to me is because of my good karmas from the past that have ripened now. It must be used for the good of others. Of course, as a householder, I must make use of it for my own maintenance, for the maintenance of all those who are depending on me. But the rest of it must go for the good of others, for the good of others. He now understood this.

The good of others, what is the real good of others? I give food to a hungry person. I should give; this is good. But the next day, this person is hungry again. I give water to a thirsty person, but after some time again he becomes thirsty. I give medicine to a sick person but he may contract another disease, or suffer a recurrence of the same disease. I may give clothes to a naked person but after some time the clothes become worn out, torn, and again he is naked. I am not helping people to come out of all their miseries. If they get Dhamma, if they get this wonderful technique of Vipassana oh, they can come out of all their misery! They can become totally liberated from misery, misery that they were encountering for life after life, life after life. They can come out of it. Dhamma should go to each and every suffering person. Besides all this giving of material *dāna*, this *dāna* is most important, the *dāna* of Dhamma is the highest *dāna*.

This man went to Buddha, who at that time was living in Rājgirī. *Anāthapiṇḍika* paid respects to him, and asked, Sir, why not come to Sāvatthi? A large number of people live there. All are miserable, rich or poor. If you have a meditation center there, many people will benefit, sir. Please come.

Buddha smiled, so he understood that Buddha had agreed. He came back home to look for a center, a place where Buddha could start teaching Dhamma to the people. A meditation center should not be in the midst of the city, with much noise and disturbance. It should not be so far away that people cannot go there. Looking for a proper place, peaceful and yet not very far from the city, he came across a garden, a park. It was very calm, very quiet, very congenial for meditation. And he inquired: Who is the owner of this park?

He came to know that the owner was Prince Jeta. He went to him and said, "Sir, I want to buy your park." But the prince became angry, replying, "I am not looking to sell my park. It is for my own amusement. I won't sell it."

"Please, sir, I have to buy it, at any price."

Just to get rid of him, the prince said, "You know the price of this land? You have to spread gold sovereigns over the entire land. This is the price."

"The deal is done. I will spread gold sovereigns." He brought cartloads of sovereigns, and started spreading them.

When the prince saw what *Anāthapiṇḍika* was doing he said, "Have you gone mad? No land can be this valuable. What are you doing?"

Anāthapiṇḍika replied, "No, I am not mad. This land is going to become so valuable. Buddha is going to come here and teach the wonderful Dhamma. All my wealth is nothing compared to what is gained if one person gets Dhamma, gets Vipassana, and comes out of misery. And I know that not one but thousands upon thousands of persons will benefit."

"Very well," said the prince, persuaded. "Let the rest of the price be my donation. The land is yours."

In this place *Anāthapiṇḍika* built a meditation center where 10,000 people could live, where they could stay and meditate, learning Dhamma.

His volition was to serve others. He had been giving *dāna* even previously, before he learned Dhamma. Now his *dāna* was to help more and more people get the benefit of Dhamma. He was giving, not to inflate his ego but to dissolve it, just to serve others.

Later, because of some karmas of the past, for a short time this multimillionaire lost all his money. When he had been wealthy he would come to the center every morning and evening to meditate. And as a householder, he understood, I should not go to the center empty-handed. I must offer something for the meditators. Every time he came, he brought something for the meditators. Now he was a pauper; he had nothing to bring. Then something came to his mind. Behind his house, he had a small garden. In that garden he had accumulated fertile soil from different parts of India. Now he took two handfuls of that soil. He came to the center and put it at the foot of a tree, saying, May this tree grow, and under its shade may someone get Dhamma, may someone be able to meditate.

Whether the gift is a handful of soil or millions of rupees, it makes no difference; it is the volition that counts. After some time, *Anāthapiṇḍika* regained his wealth and started giving donations as before. But he understood, whatever I give, the amount is immaterial. My volition must be a Dhamma-volition. I give for the good of others, for the benefit of others, not expecting anything in return.

The Dhammadāna of Service

From a talk given by Goenkaji to Dhamma servers at Dhamma Giri in June 1986, and printed in For the Benefit of Many.

What is the purpose of Dhamma service? Certainly not to receive board and lodging, nor to pass the time in a comfortable environment, nor to escape from the responsibilities of daily life. Dhamma servers know this well.

Such persons have practiced Vipassana and realized by direct experience the benefits it offers. They have seen the selfless service of the teachers, management and Dhamma servers, service that enabled them to taste the incomparable flavor of Dhamma. They have begun to take steps on the Noble Path, and naturally have started to develop the rare quality of gratitude, the wish to repay this debt for all that they have received.

Of course, the teacher, management and Dhamma servers gave their service without expecting anything in return, nor will they accept any material remuneration. The only way to pay back the debt to them is by helping to keep the Wheel of Dhamma rotating, to give to others the same selfless service. This is the noble volition with which to give Dhamma service.

As Vipassana meditators progress on the path, they emerge from the old habit pattern of self-centeredness and start to concern themselves with others. They notice how everywhere people are suffering: young or old, men or women, black or white, wealthy or poor, all are suffering. Meditators realize that they themselves were miserable until they encountered the Dhamma. They know that, like themselves, others have started to enjoy real happiness and peace by following the Path. Seeing this change stimulates a feeling of sympathetic joy, and strengthens the wish to help suffering people come out of their misery with Vipassana. Compassion overflows, and with it the volition to help others find relief from their suffering.

Dāna of Right Thought, Speech and Actions

The following message by Goenkaji discusses the opening of the first center in Europe, Dhamma Mahī. It was written for publication in Nouvelles de Vipassana, the French edition of the Vipassana Newsletter, appearing in June 1988.

The hour of Vipassana has struck in Europe. For many years, devoted students in France and neighboring countries have worked hard to make the Dhamma available to others. Now, with the purchase of a center, those efforts of so many students are coming to fruition. I am deeply pleased to see the good results of your work.

The establishing of a center marks a new stage in the growth of Dhamma. It is important to understand its significance.

A center for Vipassana meditation is not a commune where members of a sect can live in isolation from the outside world, according to their own peculiar rules. It is not a club designed for the enjoyment of its members. It is not a temple in which to perform religious ceremonies. It is not a place for socializing.

A center is, instead, a school which teaches one subject: Dhamma, the art of living. All who come to a center, whether to meditate or to serve, come to receive this teaching.

To ensure that the Dhamma is offered in its strength and purity, you follow the discipline of all centers. The more carefully this is maintained, the stronger the center will be.

Many ordinary activities are forbidden by this discipline, not because there is anything wrong in them but because they are inappropriate at a center for Vipassana meditation. Remember, this is the only place in your country where one can learn this type of Vipassana. The discipline is a way of preserving this unique purpose of *Dhamma Mahī*; guard it carefully.

The foundation of the edifice of Dhamma that you will construct here is *sīla* (moral conduct). As you know, undertaking *sīla* is the essential first step in a Vipassana course since, without it, meditation will be weak. It is equally essential that all who serve at a center keep the Five Precepts as carefully as possible. The rule of Dhamma has been established at *Dhamma Mahī*. From now on there should be no killing on this land, no stealing, no sexual activity, no wrong speech, no use of intoxicants. This will create a calm and peaceful atmosphere conducive to the work of self-purification.

With the firm base of *sīla* , the practice of self-purification can proceed. Keep in mind that this is the most important task at the center, first, last and always. All who come to serve at the center, even for a few hours, must not neglect their duty to meditate here as well. By doing so, they strengthen the Dhamma atmosphere and give support to other meditators.

This is not, of course, the only place in Europe at which meditation and the teachings of the Buddha are practiced; but it is the only place devoted to this particular transmission of the teachings, to this particular form of Vipassana. See that the center is kept at all times specifically for this purpose.

The final essential part of the technique is *mettā* and this too must be practiced by all who come to the center, whether to sit or serve. For your meditation and service to be beneficial, you must perform it joyfully, selflessly, and lovingly. Whatever task you undertake, do it with the volition that by your action all beings may be happy. Whenever welcoming others to the center, whether meditators or visitors, do so with *mettā*. Permeate this land with vibrations of love and good will, so that all who come here feel that they have entered a sanctuary of peace.

The Dhammadāna of Meditation

From a talk given on March 14, 1982 at Dhamma Thalī to inaugurate construction of its pagoda.

There are so many ways to help. One can help physically. One can help by speaking. If someone has wealth, then one can help financially. These are essential; however, the best way to help is by meditating.

The more that old students meditate on this land, the more their efforts will become instrumental in the welfare of many. During the lifetime of Sayagyi U Ba Khin there were so many of his students who had reached the stage of *nibbāna* and could experience it whenever they wished to, for as long as they wished to. One could ask, how did they become free of their debt to the Dhamma, the center and their teacher? Others might give *dāna* of physical effort, or wealth or other kinds of help to become free of their debts. But for such good meditators, it is proper that at least once a week they visit this place and sitting in some cell for an hour, they enter *nibbāna*. That is such a great service. The whole center will become suffused with those Dhamma vibrations. The Dhamma strength of the vibrations generated by each meditator will depend upon how much he or she has meditated and what stage has been attained, but all right effort will benefit those who come to the center.

Building meditation cells for students is in itself a very meritorious act. However, it is much more meritorious for every meditator to come here once a week to meditate. This is the *dāna* of our meditation. It is the *dāna* of our meditative vibrations that will purify the land, will ripen it, thereby making it easier for future students to gain more with less effort. Each person has to put in effort, has made an effort to fight the defilements within. However, if the environment around is charged with Dhamma vibrations, the effort becomes easier. If the vibrations at the center are impure they hinder progress, making it more difficult for the student to face the defilements within. They prevent the student from working properly. If students receive the protection of pure Dhamma vibrations, they gain great strength, great help.

Meditators should generate *mettā* within. By coming and meditating, we certainly benefit ourselves. We cannot say how many others will also benefit by our meditation, will gain from our work. For centuries people will benefit. People will automatically become attracted to a place where Dhamma vibrations arise. So long as the Dhamma is maintained in its pure form, people will come. For centuries people will come, meditate and benefit.

(International edition—November 2003)

Gain the Strength of Dhamma

S. N. Goenka

The following is a condensed and edited version of a discourse given by Goenkaji on the concluding day of the Satipaṭṭhāna course.

When you join a *Satipaṭṭhāna* course, the technique remains the same. You have been participating in a number of courses, practising the same technique: observing eight precepts, developing your *samādhi* with the awareness of respiration, and then developing your *paññā* with the awareness of the sensations and equanimity with the sensations—that means equanimity at the deepest level of the mind. This is what you had been practising in all your courses and this is what you have practised now.

The only difference—and a very important difference—is that in this course you are working with the direct words of the Buddha. You were able to listen to those words and to understand those words at the intellectual level—and also at the actual level because you were practising. One gets more inspiration, one gets more confidence, and one works more diligently, more seriously.

This is the advantage of coming to a course like this: the essence of Dhamma becomes clear.

The more one practises, understanding the teaching properly at the intellectual level and at the level of *paññā*, wisdom—the clearer the essence of Dhamma becomes. There is no confusion about it. One starts giving importance to the essence of Dhamma and starts applying it in life.

Merely coming to a course doesn't help if you don't apply it in your life. It is applied Dhamma which gives all the fruits, all the benefits. Coming to a course is certainly not an escape from the responsibilities of life. One goes to a hospital to regain one's health. One does not stay in the hospital all the time. Similarly, one does not come to a Vipassana centre to escape from the responsibilities of life.

Gain strength, and then make use of this strength to face all the vicissitudes of life. The vast majority of you are family men, family women, having responsibilities of the family, and of the society. Dhamma will give you the strength to face these responsibilities and to live ideal lives.

Anyone who comes and practises Dhamma has a dual responsibility. One responsibility, of course, is to liberate oneself from all the miseries and to start living a very happy, harmonious, peaceful life.

Another big responsibility is to live the kind of life that will become an example to others. Of course you cannot please everyone else but you have to be careful that you do not harm anyone. You don't do anything which will hurt others and you start living a life which gives inspiration to others.

If people see a Vipassana meditator living a life full of misery and tension, they will hesitate to come to a Vipassana course: "Look, this is a product of Vipassana meditation. If I am also going to become like this, what is the use of my spending 10 days at a course?" You become a barrier for others to take Dhamma.

On the other hand, if someone sees a person's life changed for the better, if they see this person is now living a better life, facing various situations calmly, they will feel: "Wonderful. This person is developing such good qualities." They will be inspired to take a course.

When someone comes to a course, the first to benefit are the members of his family. When one person comes to a Vipassana course, practises properly, and changes for the better, then the members of his family see this change and start coming to courses. Once they start practising Vipassana, there is a great improvement in the family.

Whenever there is misunderstanding or ill will among members of a family, if they sit together for Vipassana, one hour in the morning and one hour in the evening, followed by a few minutes of *mettābhāvanā*, they get up smiling. The entire atmosphere of the family changes. The tension is gone and cordiality prevails. The family becomes an ideal family.

When one family becomes an ideal family—happy, peaceful, and harmonious—this attracts the members of other families. They start coming to Dhamma. One family after another practises Dhamma, until the whole community starts enjoying peace and harmony. Gradually, the whole nation will start experiencing peace and harmony. Eventually, the whole world will start experiencing peace and harmony. It all starts with the individual.

So every individual who comes to a Vipassana course has a great responsibility, a dual responsibility: "My life must change now, not only for my good, but for the good of so many." After 25 centuries, Dhamma has arisen once again. One feels, "I'm so fortunate that I have come in contact with Dhamma. Otherwise, in the name of Dhamma, I would have been involved in rites, rituals, philosophical beliefs and dogmas—in different sectarian entanglements. Now I have received the universal Dhamma. I am so fortunate. And the time has ripened for Dhamma to spread throughout the world. What can I do? How can I help?"

One may give service, contributions, assistance in different ways. But the best help is to be an example, a good example of Dhamma. This will generate inspiration in people's minds so that they will also walk on the path of Dhamma: "Look this person has started living such a peaceful, harmonious, and wonderful life. Why not I?" This is the biggest service.

As this course comes to an end, the students have been purifying the mind and dissolving the ego. They start developing two rare qualities. One quality is: "How can I help others without expecting anything in return? How can I be helpful so that more and more people come on the path and come out of their misery?" One's only satisfaction is to see others happy, peaceful, harmonious, without any expectation in return.

The second quality is a feeling of gratitude. One feels gratitude towards Gotama the Buddha. After his enlightenment, he did not just liberate himself—he started distributing it to others with infinite love and compassion. And he trained others:

Caratha bhikkhave cārikaṃ,
bahujanahitāya, bahujanasukhāya,
lokānukampāya...

Go forth, O bhikkhus,
for the good of many, for the happiness of many, out of compassion for the world...

The purity of the tradition was maintained from generation to generation. After five centuries it was lost in the country of its origin, though other countries maintained it for a longer time. Fortunately the neighbouring country of Myanmar maintained it for 25 centuries. This is why you have it now. So a feeling of gratitude naturally arises.

Some students come and express their feeling of gratitude towards their guide. But the only way to express one's gratitude is to get established in Dhamma, to get ripened in Dhamma. There cannot be a better way to express the feeling of gratitude. A father or a mother becomes happy and proud if their child surpasses them. In the same way, your Dhamma guide feels happy and satisfied when he finds: "These people who have taken Dhamma from me are developing so well. May they surpass my ability!"

So get established in Dhamma. It will be so good for you and good for so many others. Many others will take inspiration from your life. The revival of Dhamma has just started. You are fortunate to be born in a period when the Dhamma has arisen again, and is spreading around the world. May you become an instrument for the spread of Dhamma, for the good of so many, for your own good and also for the good of so many!

You are fortunate to get a human life. You have come in contact with Dhamma and have started practising Dhamma. All these factors are very fortunate. Now grow in Dhamma, glow in Dhamma, get ripened in Dhamma so that more and more people get inspiration and start walking on the path of Dhamma; more and more people come out of their misery and enjoy real peace, real harmony, real happiness.

May all of you grow in Dhamma, may all of you glow in Dhamma. May all of you live a Dhamma life, good for you and good for others; beneficial for you and beneficial for others.

(Dhamma Giri edition—February 2008)

Fulfilling the Teaching of the Buddha

S. N. Goenka

The following is a condensed and edited version of a discourse given by Goenkaji on Day 41 of a 45-day course.

You have to live Dhamma very seriously, to make best use of this valuable human life. You come to courses to eradicate as much impurity as possible and also to understand Dhamma more deeply. As layers of ignorance are eradicated, the Dhamma becomes clearer and you think, "Oh, this is Dhamma!"

There cannot be any doubt about Dhamma. The teaching of the Buddha becomes so clear. Here is a person who is teaching Dhamma not to establish a sect of believers in a particular philosophy. Not at all. The Buddha is the Compassionate One. Out of compassion he teaches Dhamma so that people can come out of misery. He has himself come out of misery by practicing Dhamma, not merely by believing in the theory of Dhamma. Such a person would never give emphasis to mere belief. His entire emphasis will always be on the creative part of Dhamma, the practice of Dhamma.

The Buddha said that throughout his life he taught only two things: suffering (*dukkha*) and the total eradication of suffering (*dukkha-nirodha*). That's all he taught. How will establishing a sect eradicate *dukkha*? How will establishing a belief in a particular philosophy eradicate *dukkha*? A Buddha is not interested in all those things. He is interested only in actual *dukkha nirodha*. All his teaching is directed only towards the actual eradication of *dukkha*.

But these two things, *dukkha* and *dukkha-nirodha*, logically become four. To understand *dukkha*, you must understand *dukkha samudaya*, how *dukkha* arises. To realize *dukkha-nirodha*, you must understand *magga*—the way, process or path leading to the eradication of *dukkha*. Thus we have the Four Noble Truths.

Now what if the Buddha had been interested only in the theory of these four truths: "Oh people of the world, understand there is *dukkha*, understand that craving is the cause of *dukkha*, understand that there is total eradication of *dukkha* and understand that there is a way to the total eradication of *dukkha*."? If all his teaching had ended there, he would have been no different from any other teacher of those days or later times.

But that was not his interest. He had become the Buddha not by mere belief in these four truths. He knew that just accepting the Four Truths does not help. One has to do something about them—in Pali language, this is *kicca*, to be done or put into practice. Then one can say, as the Buddha did, "I have done what is to be done about these Four Truths. The work is done—*kataṃ*."

However good a philosophy may be, however true it may be, it will not help people to come out of their misery unless the *kicca* becomes *kataṃ*. Each individual must do whatever has to be done concerning the Four Noble Truths.

This is why a Buddha never teaches mere philosophy, and anyone who makes the teaching a philosophy does not benefit from it. Each person must work as the Dhamma intended, as the Buddha intended. And however much they succeed in doing what must be done concerning these four truths, to that extent they have come out of their misery.

For the First Noble Truth of *dukkha*, what has to be done? Explore the entire reality of it, the totality of it—*pariññeya*. If even a small part is left out, you have not explored it all. You can say you have explored the totality only when you have transcended the field of suffering and gone beyond it. And transcending *dukkha* is *dukkha-nirodha*, the eradication of misery.

At the same time, exploring *dukkha* involves observing the Second Noble Truth of *dukkha-samudaya*, the arising of misery. You observe, "Look how *dukkha* starts!" And by understanding that, you keep on eradicating the tendency of the mind that is responsible for the arising of *dukkha*. You observe until no more *dukkha* arises; you have done what is to be done concerning the Second Noble Truth.

And how did you do it? How did you reach the stage of *dukkha-nirodha*? Every step you have taken to explore the entire field of *dukkha* is part of the process through which you have passed, the path over which you have walked. You have walked step by step over the entire path. You have accomplished the Fourth Noble Truth, the truth of the path leading to the eradication of suffering.

By doing what is to be done concerning the First Noble Truth, you automatically do what is to be done concerning the other three. And how do you do what is to be done concerning the first? How do you explore the entire field of *dukkha*? You start experiencing *dukkha*, you start feeling *dukkha*. In the language used by the Buddha, the words are *vedanā*, *anubhāvana*. You must feel it. You must experience it. You are not here simply to play an intellectual game. You start observing sensations.

The exploration started with *dukkha-vedanā*—unpleasant, gross sensation. As you understood in detail its reality by feeling it, you also understood that there is an ingrained tendency to react with aversion toward this unpleasant sensation. And it also becomes clear that every time you react with aversion, you become more miserable. Every reaction of aversion brings misery. You realize, "Oh, there is an unpleasant feeling in the body, and I am reacting with aversion. That means I am making use of my misery to multiply misery. Instead I must make use of this misery to come out of misery." And it becomes clear that if you do not react, you do not multiply misery. You understand, "Oh, the best thing is for me not to react."

Working in this way with unpleasant sensations, sometimes you succeed in not reacting and sometimes you fail. The old habit pattern keeps on overpowering you at times and you react with aversion. Then you remember that there shouldn't be any reaction of aversion and you have a few moments when you do not react. This is how you start your work. Exploring the field of *dukkha* at the level of unpleasant sensations, you are experiencing *dukkha*, the First Noble Truth.

Then a time comes when the unpleasant sensations turn into *sukha-vedanā*—pleasant sensations—partly because some *saṅkhāras* have been eradicated and partly because this is the law of nature. From time to time changes naturally come, whatever the reason may be. You have started experiencing pleasant sensations, subtle vibrations.

Now, if your understanding of Dhamma is not very clear, you won't know what to do. The old tendency of reacting to the pleasant sensations with craving will start overpowering you, and you will keep on reacting. You will think, "This is wonderful! The unpleasant has gone, now the experience is pleasant. I am free from misery. Dhamma has worked, I am liberated! Look, there are pleasant sensations, everything is good." And you are generating craving, craving.

But as the unpleasant sensations sooner or later turn into pleasant ones, the pleasant sensations eventually turn unpleasant. This is the law of nature. Someone who understands properly will think, "Look, because I developed clinging to the pleasant sensations, when unpleasant sensations arise again I become more miserable than I was in the first place. Oh, my aversion toward unpleasant sensations is the result of my clinging toward pleasant sensations." The more one clings to pleasure, the more one generates aversion toward pain.

In daily life also, when something desirable happens, you become elated and develop attachment to it. And when it passes away and something undesirable happens, you become depressed. Because you have developed attachment to the desirable, you are bound to have aversion toward the undesirable. Now it is becoming clear at the depth of the mind, where the sensations are experienced. Then wisdom starts arising with the experience: "Every time I react with craving toward the pleasant sensations, I am sowing seeds of misery, nothing but misery. I am allowing myself to be overpowered by ignorance. This is misery."

Because the pleasant sensations reinforce the tendency to react with craving, actually they are misery. This is more dangerous than unpleasant sensation, which is obviously *dukkha*. When experiencing the unpleasant, it is easy to remember that any aversion will be harmful; one thinks, "I'd better observe, I'd better wait, I'd better remain equanimous." But when the pleasant experience comes, one reacts blindly. Instead one should realize, "Oh, this is a dangerous situation. This pleasant sensation is also *dukkha*."

With this realization, one starts coming out of the habit of reacting with aversion toward the unpleasant and craving toward the pleasant. Gradually one changes the habit pattern of the mind and keeps working. When many of the *saṅkhāras* have gone away, one starts experiencing calm, quiet and tranquil feelings.

What you call unpleasant sensation is no longer there. But what you call pleasant sensation also is no longer there. The pleasant sensations came like the flow of a river, or like waves on the sea, or like strong electric currents. There is no such thing happening now—just calmness, tranquillity and a very subtle oscillation. This is what the Buddha called *asukhamadukkha-vedanā*, neither *sukha* nor *dukkha*. It is not the so-called neutral sensation you experienced when you first started meditating. That was a superficial sensation that you eventually found boring; you developed aversion toward it.

But now you do not become bored; you wish to remain immersed in the experience. You think it is wonderful because it is so peaceful and quiet. And so a new danger arises. First was the danger of reacting with aversion toward unpleasant sensation, then the danger of reacting with craving toward pleasant sensation. Now there is the danger that ignorance will overpower you. You think, "Ah, this is what I wanted. I've got it now. This tranquil, peaceful experience is *nibbāna*." In fact you are mistaken. Yes, you are nearing *nibbāna*, but the experience of tranquillity is still within the field of mind and matter, the sensory field.

If wisdom arises, one recalls, "Look, this is still not beyond mind and matter. There is an oscillation going on. There is *anicca*." And this very subtle oscillation disturbs you. It disturbs the feeling of quietude, tranquillity, and you think, "Oh this is misery."

Only when you realize this can you come out of suffering and experience something beyond it. Otherwise you remain stuck at this stage, as someone might become stuck with the free flow of subtle vibrations. The gross, unpleasant sensation is *dukkha*. The pleasant sensation is *dukkha*. And this subtle oscillation, which is neither pleasant nor unpleasant, this stage of tranquillity is also *dukkha*.

Then the words of Buddha become clear: "*Yaṃ kiñci vediyatiṃ taṃ dukkhasmiṃ*: Whatever sensation you experience is of the nature of *dukkha*." You have to realize this reality. When you do, you transcend it and experience the stage of *dukkha-nirodha*, the cessation of suffering. Then one can say, "*Pariññāta*—I have explored the entire field of *dukkha*."

And how have you explored the entire field of *dukkha*? By exploring the entire field of *vedanā*. When the Buddha says that you must explore the entire field of *dukkha*, he also says that you have to explore the entire field of *vedanā*. When he says that you must walk on the Noble Eightfold Path to come out of *dukkha*, he says you have to do so by exploring the entire field of *vedanā*: "*Tissannaṃ vedanānaṃ pariññāya ariyo aṭṭhaṅgiko maggo bhāvetabbo*—You have to practice the Noble Eightfold Path to explore the entire field of these three *vedanās*, pleasant, unpleasant and neutral."

Similarly, when the Buddha tells you to

practice the four *satipaṭṭhānas*, he says, "*Tissannaṃ vedanānaṃ pariññāya cattāro satipaṭṭhāna bhāvetabbo*—You have to practice the four *satipaṭṭhānas* by exploring these three *vedanās*." Without exploring the entire field of *vedanā*, you cannot explore the entire field of *dukkha*. You can not fulfill even the First Noble Truth and can never fulfill the other three.

With all four *satipaṭṭhānas*—observation of the body, observation of sensation, observation of mind and observation of mental contents—you must keep on understanding the arising and passing of *vedanā* at the experiential level, from moment to moment. With all four *satipaṭṭhānas*, the Buddha emphasized the importance of exploring the entire field of *dukkha* at the level of *vedanā*. Without it, there is every possibility of clinging to some experience. You cannot transcend all sensory experiences unless you understand that every sensory experience is *dukkha*.

Thus everything taught by the Buddha must at a deeper level be with *vedanā*. This is true even of what is normally thought of as the preliminary step of observing *sīla*, the moral precepts—that is, abstaining from unwholesome actions of body and speech. For example, a situation has arisen where there is a strong likelihood that you will break a particular *sīla* by killing, or stealing, or performing sexual misconduct, or speaking lies and deceiving others, or becoming intoxicated. But you stop, you refrain from doing that. You are able to stop because you observe sensations in the body. Then you are not merely working at the surface of the mind. You are not merely restraining your physical and vocal actions. You are working at the deep mental level as well.

The urge to break a *sīla* originates because of the sensation that arises, pleasant or unpleasant. And because of this particular sensation, the volition in turn arises to do something physically or vocally that is not in your own interests or the interests of others.

However, when you are with sensation, you are working at the deepest level of the mind. And you are following the instructions of the Buddha to explore the entire field of *vedanā*. And as with *sīla*, when you practice *samādhi*, developing concentration, you have to remain aware of the sensations, pleasant, unpleasant or neutral. And when you develop your *paññā*, wisdom, you have to be aware of sensations. *Sīla, samādhi, paññā*—entire practice of the Buddha's teaching must be with the awareness of sensation.

If you remain aware of sensation and understand that it is arising, passing, arising, passing, you will eventually reach the stage of *nirodha*. You will be able to say, "*Kataṃ buddhāna-sāsanaṃ*—The Buddha's teaching, what he wanted me to do, has been done completely. *Natthi dāni punabbhavo'ti*—there is no new life for me. I have finished, I have done what the Buddha intended me to do, what the Dhamma intended me to do."

Work diligently, intelligently, understanding Dhamma, understanding the pitfalls. Keep working hard to become firm in Dhamma and attain real happiness.

Bhavatu sabba maṅgalaṃ—May all beings be happy!

(International edition—December 2007)

The Purity of Dhamma

S.N. Goenka

The following has been translated and adapted from Goenkaji's article in the March 2010 issue of the Hindi Vipassana Patrika.

To understand why the pure teaching of the Enlightened One was lost in India, we must look at the last 2,000 years of Indian history. Until then there were people who had practised the teaching and experienced its goal; they were fully liberated or had reached one of the stages on the way to full liberation. Later, however, forces opposed to the Dhamma gained strength and sought to undermine its purity. Many bhikkhus were killed. Many others left India. Almost all the monasteries were destroyed, and the few remaining ones could not maintain the purity of the teaching. The contamination spread eastward to Myanmar, reaching the capital of Pagan.

Suttantesu asantesu,
pamuṭṭhe vinayaṃhi ca,
tamo bhavissati loke,
suriye atthaṅgate yatā.

When the words of Dhamma go unheard
and its practice is forṣaken,
The world becomes dark
just as when the sun sets.

—A.N. Aṭṭhakathā 1–1–130, Dutiyapamādādivaggavaṇṇanā)

In southern Myanmar, news reached the arahant bhikkhu Dhammadassi of what had happened in the north of the country. He decided to go himself to Pagan. There he met King Anawrahta and explained to him the pure teaching of the Buddha. Seeing with new eyes, the king put an end to the degraded practices and re-established the purity of the Tipiṭaka and Vipassana. This was approximately 1,000 years ago.

At an earlier time, in the reign of India's Emperor Asoka, Dhamma envoys had carried the pure words of the Buddha as well as the technique of Vipassana to different countries. One of these was Suvaṇṇabhūmi, now southern Myanmar. There the custom started of memorising the entire Tipiṭaka or a section of it to maintain the actual words of the Buddha. At the same time people continued to practise what the Buddha had taught by maintaining the Vipassana technique in its pristine purity.

Envoys went as well to Śri Laṅka, in this case the son and daughter of the Emperor Asoka himself. In that country the entire Tipiṭaka was first written down to ensure its preservation, and for many generations the pure Vipassana technique was also maintained.

The benefit of these actions could be seen in more recent times when scholars from different countries attended the councils convened in Myanmar, to once again verify the text of the Tipiṭaka. In the 19th century, they caused the text to be inscribed on stone tablets; in the 20th century, they published the text in book form.

Suttantesu rakkhite sante,
paṭipatti hoti rakkhitā,
paṭipattiyaṃ ṭhito dhīrā,
yogakkhemā na dhaṃsati.

When the words of the Teaching remain secure,
the practice remains secure.
The courageous person who practises persistently
does not fail to be liberated.

—A.N. Aṭṭhakathā 1–1–130, Dutiyapamādādivaggavaṇṇanā

From Dhammadassi onward to the time of Ledi Sayadaw, the pure technique of Vipassana was preserved in northern Myanmar, although among only a few. This is indeed very fortunate for us. Ledi Sayadaw had a strong belief that 2,500 years after the Buddha, the Teaching would again arise and Vipassana would spread far beyond the monasteries where small numbers practised it. This was why Ledi Sayadaw decided to train not only bhikkhus and bhikkhunīs but also lay followers in Vipassana. He appointed Saya Thetgyi, a farmer, as a teacher of Vipassana. In turn, Saya Thetgyi appointed Sayagyi U Ba Khin, because of whom Vipassana and the words of the Buddha have become available in India and around the world.

Since Vipassana is universal and non-sectarian, people from all sects are drawn to it. No one has objected to the technique. The Buddha's Vipassana teaching has been respectfully accepted everywhere. In the past 40 years, people of more than 80 countries have offered support for the benefit of many. There are more than 1,000 assistant teachers and over 150 permanent centres, aside from courses held at rented sites. Nearly 1,200 junior assistant teachers hold children's courses at various places. The discourses and instructions have been translated into close to 60 languages for use in Vipassana courses.

So far as the words of the Buddha are concerned, modern technology has made it easy to preserve their purity. But there remains the possibility that inappropriate changes would be made to the technique of Vipassana. My teacher, Sayagyi U Ba Khin, was very insistent that the Buddha's pure tradition should be maintained. Therefore, it is now our responsibility to keep alive this technique in its pure form, as imparted by Sayagyi. The same discourses and instructions have been used at Vipassana courses in India and all over the world for 40 years. Everywhere they have been wholeheartedly accepted. Therefore it would be unwise to change what has been accepted so universally. But if anyone sees a problem with some part of the teaching, the proper thing is to bring the matter to the attention of the Principal Teacher, so that he may consider it and do whatever is required.

Sayagyi U Ba Khin said that wherever Vipassana is taught, no other practice should be added however good it appears to be, since it might gain importance at the expense of the pure Dhamma. We have carefully followed this instruction for the past 40 years.

Nevertheless, well-intentioned people have sometimes tried to add something to the teaching of Vipassana. In some cases it was a specially healthful diet at courses. Sometimes it was the actual provision of medical guidance by renowned physicians who were meditators. Sometimes it was the introduction of forms of religious observance. Sometimes it was the addition of physical exercises. Sometimes it was extra discourses to the students, beyond what has been recorded for use in the course. In one case it was an offer to teach yoga to students after a course. In another case it was an offer to provide acupressure treatment at a centre.

The people who wanted to make these changes were all sincere and well intentioned. And they had good ideas. But what each was suggesting had no place in a Vipassana course.

Vipassana is a technique of self-observation for the purpose of liberating the mind from suffering. That is all. That is everything.

Therefore it is the responsibility of all sincere Vipassana meditators to keep the technique secure and not allow anything to be mixed with it, however good the addition might seem to be. This is how the Wheel of Dhamma will keep turning for generations, for the benefit of one and all.

May all be happy!
May all be liberated!

(Dhamma Giri edition—March 2010)

Discovering the Buddha in the Tipiṭaka

The following article is a condensed extract from Goenkaji's foreword to the new edition of the Pāli Tipiṭaka being published by the Vipassana Research Institute. The Tipiṭaka is the literal recording of the words and teachings of the Buddha. It is divided into three Piṭakas (literally, baskets): Vinaya Piṭaka (the monastic discipline), Sutta Piṭaka (the popular discourses), and Abhidhamma Piṭaka (a compendium of profound teachings elucidating the functioning and interrelationship of mind, mental factors, matter, and the phenomenon transcending all of these). The first volumes of this work appeared recently in Devanāgarī script, and versions in Roman script will follow—as will a book-length introduction by Goenkaji.

All of the Tipiṭaka is saturated with the noble and sacred personality of the Buddha. The material body (*rūpakāya*) of the Buddha was one appealing aspect of his personality; it possessed the 32 signs of a great man and radiated incomparable peace and beauty, pleasing for all to behold. But the other aspect of his personality was the unparalleled body of the Dhamma (*dhammakāya*), which was suffused with complete enlightenment, perfect wisdom, moral behavior, right understanding, and compassion.

A Tathāgata or Buddha is a fully liberated being (*arahata*), having destroyed all the enemies, his impurities. He has attained perfect enlightenment (*sammā sambodhi*). He is full of wisdom (*vijjā*) and is well established in the practice of morality and concentration (*caraṇa*). He is "well-gone" (*sugato*) because of his pleasant physical, vocal, and mental activities. He is the knower of the entire universe (*lokavidū*) understanding completely the mundane as well as the supramundane: *nibbāna*. He is peerless, without equal or superior (*anuttaro*). He directs untrained people to the right path, as a skilled charioteer manages untrained horses (*purisa damma sārathī*). He is the Teacher of gods and humans (*satthā devamanussānaṃ*). He is Lord (*bhagavā*), having destroyed attachment, antipathy, and ignorance. Because of all these special qualities, he is different from others: he provides enormous welfare for the world.

The entire Tipiṭaka is permeated with the nectar of the Buddha's Dhamma body. The Tipiṭaka contains the mellifluous sound of the Ganges of Dhamma arising from the Dhamma-kāya. It is suffused with the invaluable essence of emancipation. At every turn the Dhamma is illuminated, the Dhamma which is clearly expounded (*svākkhāto*), which takes us directly to the truth, helping us to leave behind all illusory imaginations (*sandiṭṭhiko*). It gives concrete, visible fruits here and now to those who follow the path (*akāliko*). It summons us to realize the truth (*ehipassiko*). With every step, it takes us to the highest goal of *nibbāna* (*opaneyyiko*), and is worth experiencing personally by every intelligent person (*paccattaṃ veditabbo viññūhī'ti*).

Such is the noble Dhamma: universally beneficial to all; free from sectarianism; acceptable to all people, from all countries, in any age. The entire Tipiṭaka helps us savour this sweet nectar of Dhamma. The Tipiṭaka also illumines the inspiring *sāvakasaṅgha* (the community of accomplished disciples), who drank deeply the ambrosial words of the Buddha. The Saṅgha clearly demonstrates that in Dhamma there is no place for blind faith, emotional devotion, or the logician's hair-splitting intellectual acrobatics.

The Dhamma is immensely practical. One who follows it becomes a righteous practitioner (*suppaṭipanno*), upright practitioner (*ujuppaṭipanno*), wise practitioner (*ñāyappaṭipanno*), and proper practitioner (*sāmīcippaṭipanno*) on the way to liberation. One becomes noble (*ariyo*) by attaining one of the four stages of liberation. Such a noble person is worthy of devotion, reverent salutation, honor, and offerings.

We are inspired to follow the path of Dhamma by beholding in the Tipiṭaka the *sāvakasaṅgha*, saintly persons who included both lay people and renunciants. Their pronouncements about their practical realizations hearten and thrill us, raising goose bumps and electrifying our practice of Vipassana.

Not only is the ancient spiritual and philosophical landscape of the India of 25 centuries ago brought to light in the Tipiṭaka, but a vivid spectrum of the historical, geographical, political, and cultural conditions of the times is also provided. The Tipiṭaka opens a window onto the administrative, educational, commercial, and industrial customs of the Buddha's times. It sheds light on both social and individual conditions, in the urban as well as rural life of ancient India. The India of 2,500 years ago comes alive in the Tipiṭaka.

Although the wisdom expounded by the Buddha apparently disappeared from India, in reality it has flowed through subsequent Indian literature. Sanskrit, as well as Hindi and other regional literature, is full of the benevolent teachings. Words of the medieval saints of India are suffused with the wisdom of the Buddha. The influence of the Buddha's contribution is not confined to Indian thought; the deep impact of his teaching is also visible in the spiritual thought and literature of the rest of the world. Therefore the Buddha's words have a special significance for the human race even today. The stately grandeur of the Buddha's teaching is verdant forever. It is the perennial forerunner of the resurrection of fallen human values. What could be more relevant in this age of moral degradation, with its inevitable result of downtrodden people afflicted with terror?

A study of the Tipiṭaka will correct some of the prevalent misconceptions about the Buddha. One is that, since the Buddha was a recluse, his followers were also recluses, and his teachings were therefore meant for recluses only, not for lay people. Examination of the Dhamma literature will totally dispel such myths. The reality is that the Buddha was very popular among the masses in his lifetime; his lay devotees outnumbered monks and nuns. He was nearly as popular among the recluses and ascetics of his day as he was with the lay people of northern India.

During the rainy season the Buddha would stay for three months in one place. He often spent this time near densely populated towns such as Sāvatthi or Rājagaha, so that more people might take advantage of his presence and teachings. After these retreats, he would undertake Dhamma wanderings in the villages, towns, and cities situated in the land of the Ganges and Yamunā rivers in northern India. He disseminated the Dhamma and gave guidance in the technique of Vipassana to hundreds of thousands of people.

Wherever he went, crowds of people gathered to see him and listen to his discourses. At the same time, many people would come to meet him alone. Impressed by his benevolent speech, lay people would invite the Buddha and his monks to accept their offerings of meals at their homes. Again they benefited from his teachings. The recluses of the day used to come to him for religious discussions and sometimes for debates, but the majority of his visitors were lay people. A detailed account of his relationship to the people is conspicuous in this literature.

The Buddha delivered thousands of Dhamma discourses, from the time he attained enlightenment until he passed away 45 years later. Inspired by the pure Dhamma, not only recluses and ascetics but lay people from every tradition, every belief, every profession, every class came to him and profited by walking on the path of Dhamma. Whether kings, queens, princes, generals maidservants, royal servants and their children, physicians, philanthropists, ascetics, beggars, wanderers, wealthy housewives, courtesans, sweepers, high or low caste—whoever came into contact with the Buddha and took a dip in the Ganges of Dhamma by practicing Vipassana was totally changed, totally rectified. Their suffering was eradicated.

Another prevalent misconception about the Buddha is that he taught how to gain release from the cycle of repeated existences, but he ignored the everyday concerns of the individual and the family. It is held that he was indifferent to political and social problems. Study of the Tipiṭaka reveals that he was cognizant of and sensitive to worldly problems. While it is true that he gave the majority of his discourses to monks, explaining the topic of the ultimate truth, nevertheless he delivered numerous discourses to his lay followers addressing mundane concerns. He dealt with all aspects of lay life. He gave instructions concerning the mutual duties of parent and child, wife and husband, master and servant, teacher and student, friend and friend, king and subject. These are refreshing, relevant, and beneficial even today. The advice given to the Licchavīs, for the maintenance of adequate protection of their republic, are a model for any republican government of modern times. Similarly, his teachings are equally valuable for other administrators. In the tradition of his teachings it is said: "The king should protect his subjects in the same way as he protects his own children (*Rājā rakkhatu dhammena attano va pajaṃ pajaṃ*)."

Inspired by such words, the emperor Dhammarāja Asoka established a righteous administration which was unique and unparalleled in human history and worthy of emulation. His reign shines like a luminous pillar of light in the administrative history of India, indeed of the entire world.

Yet another major misconception about the Buddha is that he lay undue emphasis on suffering in his discourses. Some people have commented that his teaching is primarily about suffering and is therefore negative and pessimistic, full of despair and inclining towards apathy. With the publication of this literature, these misconceptions will be corrected. It will become evident that there is no comparable literature which inspires confidence in, and provides solace to, people who are sunk in abject suffering and despair.

Truly a patient is discouraged when told that his or her disease is incurable. But if someone makes the patient aware of the disease, discovers its primary cause and offers a way of removing the cause by pointing out a medicine which can totally eradicate the disease, this is a blessing for the patient. What could possibly be a source of greater hope and solace for the patient than this?

It is exactly the same with the Buddha's explanation of suffering. However bitter it may be, suffering is a universal truth in the lives of beings. It cannot be denied. The Buddha not only revealed the fundamental truth of suffering, he made its cause crystal clear and he thoroughly delineated the simple, easily acceptable art of living of Vipassana, consisting of the Eightfold Noble Path. This art of living is not merely a philosopher's theoretical or intellectual exposition; it is an entirely pragmatic, proven path, which gives visible results here and now to those who practice it. It gives hope to those who are discouraged and mired in suffering. It grants peace and happiness in both the mundane and supramundane fields of life.

The teachings of the Buddha completely uproot the discrimination of caste and the pollution of communalism. Relief from these poisons is a pressing need in India as well as the rest of the world today. Their removal will help bring much-longed-for peace and happiness.

The Buddha's discourse to the Kālāmas of Kesamutta is the first declaration of human rights and is a beacon for all humanity, enunciating the principle of freedom of thought. All his teaching is free from blind faith and corrupt clericalism. It is completely empirical, impartial, and dedicated to intellectual rigor. Therefore it is universally acceptable.

Practitioners of Vipassana who read these texts may feel as if the Exalted One has understood their difficulties and has given instructions which are for them alone—as if the Buddha is personally exhorting them with deep understanding and love. The publication of such ambrosial words will prove a great boon to them. May the publication of the words of the Buddha and the other Pāli texts be helpful and beneficial to all. May the dawn of peace, happiness and liberation arise for all the readers.

For information on how to order the Tipiṭaka publications, either in Devanāgarī or Roman Pāli, contact Vipassana Research Institute. See ***www.vri.dhamma.org*** or ***www.pariyatti.org***

(International edition—June 1994)

The entire Tipiṭaka is now available on the Internet at ***www.tipitaka.org***. *There are also online Pāli courses. See, for example,* ***www.pariyatti.org***. *Pāli workshops and study courses are provided from time to time in various locations worldwide (for example see* ***www.vridhamma.org***).

SECTION TWO

MESSENGER OF DHAMMA

Messenger of Dhamma—Introduction

This section is devoted to S.N.Goenka's life story and contribution to the spread of Dhamma in modern times.

Many of the articles are autobiographical: recalling his early years and enduring affection for Burma; the intriguing chain of events which led to his sitting a Vipassana course and apprenticeship in Dhamma service with his meditation teacher Sayagyi U Ba Khin; his return to India in 1969 and how Vipassana became re-established in the Land of the Buddha and then from 1979 onwards, through his energetic travels abroad to give courses and public talks, how Dhamma gradually spread worldwide.

When commentators praise his personal role in this process, Goenkaji consistently replies that he is merely an instrument of Dhamma, repaying a debt of gratitude for release from misery to U Ba Khin and undertaking a responsibility on his behalf. Since 1982 Goenkaji has been appointing assistant teachers from among mature old students to help him with this Dhamma mission. Leading by example, he insists that to be effective Vipassana must always remain true to its principles, a pure, universal teaching free from any commercial influence. Courses in this tradition are funded only through the grateful donations of past students. They are staffed by volunteers who give their time and skills to help others learn a technique from which they themselves have benefited. So the Wheel of Dhamma turns. Without the backing of any professional organisation or publicity, Vipassana has spread like wildfire these past 40 years as people from every background and part of the globe continue to respond to the time-honoured invitation *Ehi passiko*—Come and See!

Sixty Years Are Over

In India, the sixtieth birthday is regarded as an important milestone in life. Traditionally this is the age at which one is supposed to lay aside all worldly responsibilities, in order to devote oneself completely to spiritual matters. The following article by Goenkaji appeared early this year on the occasion of his sixtieth birthday in the Hindi-language newsletter published from Dhamma Giri. It has been translated and adapted for Western students.—Editor

Words of Dhamma

Sutvā tathā ye na karonti bālā
Caranti dukkhesu punappunaṃ te.
Sutvā tathā ye paṭipattiyuttā
Bhavanti te saccadasā sapaññā

Those who hear the truth but do not act according to it are fools,
Bound to face suffering over and over again.
Those who hear the truth and also practise it
Become ones who see the truth with their own wisdom.

—Apadāna 137, 138

Sixty years are over. How many are left in the incessant running from birth to death cannot be known. When I look back on the past, the heart feels a glow of contentment despite all the ebbs and flows, all the vicissitudes of life. Many images of past years come to mind, some of them very vivid.

Grandfather's Blessing

In Mandalay, the old capital of Burma, a boy was born and grew to the age of six or seven years under the kindly, protecting shadow of his grandfather, then over 70 years old. The grandfather was a master of the popular Rajasthani poetic form called dohā—rhyming couplets. He had an inexhaustible supply of such verses at the tip of his tongue. Many of them moved the boy greatly, and left a deep impression on his mind.

In the early morning the grandfather would dress in traditional Rajasthani style, in snowy white dhoti and kurta and light pink turban. Then he set out for his morning walk, with the little boy often keeping him company. On his way out the door, as he reached for his walking stick, he would tenderly recite the following verse:

Come, oh friend! My legs are weak,
so I must lean on you.
To the temple, stepping safe and slow!
Time has brought fulfillment of
my mother's loving wish,
Her blessing given many years ago.

Sometimes he would explain the verse to the boy: "When I was your age, my mother used to bless me by saying, 'May you grow old! May you have long life!' And now her blessings have come to fruition. Look, now I am a staggering old man!" And he would chuckle at his own infirmity.

One day the grandfather fell sick, and his condition deteriorated. As he lay on his sickbed, a verse sprang from his smiling lips:

"Oh king of the forest! Now we must part,"
Cried the leaf to the tree as it fell.
"The merciless wind will bear me away;
Forever I bid you farewell."

What helplessness! Leaves wither and fall regardless of their wishes, and can never return to the tree. Decay and death are bound to come; this is the reality of impermanence. We have no mastery over the situation; it is beyond our control. What powerlessness! How miserable to be separated from what is dear to us! *Anicca, anattā, dukkha*—the verse is full of Dhamma.

One night everyone in the household kept vigil through the night. The little boy also stayed awake, sitting by the bedside of his beloved grandfather. As dawn approached, the condition of the old man worsened. Carefully he was taken from his bed and laid on the floor, so that he might die in accordance with the venerable Hindu tradition, lying on the breast of Mother Earth. The adults tried to shoo away the boy, but he refused to budge, and kept his eyes fixed on his grandfather. The old man's breathing became intermittent. Suddenly he opened his eyes and all the family bowed to pay their last respects to him, the little boy along with the others. He saw his grandfather smile at him. Then the old man raised his hand in blessing and breathed out—the breath never to return. His hand stayed raised in benediction.

A decorated bier was prepared, and the body laid on it, covered by a costly embroidered shawl. Still the hand remained upraised. And so the bier was carried to the funeral ground, with the boy following behind. According to Hindu custom, children are not usually permitted to attend cremations, but the boy insisted on coming to witness the last rites of his grandfather. As flames enveloped the shroud-wrapped body, still the hand remained lifted in benediction.

The ashes were scattered in the nearby sacred Irrawaddy River. The family returned home and resumed their lives, but ever after the boy felt the hand of his grandfather raised over his head in protection and blessing. At the tender age of seven, he had witnessed old age, disease, and death, and he had seen how a saint faces all these: with smiling acceptance and love. A seed of Dhamma had been planted in his mind, waiting for the proper time to sprout.

Devotion and Defilements

The boy continued growing in the bosom of his family. The atmosphere of his home was deeply pious. Both his parents were steeped in the Hindu devotional tradition, and from them the boy learned to chant daily prayers to the deities, and also to recite the Bhagavad Gīta. Eagerly he joined in the ceremonies of worship in the family temple.

In his schooling as well, he was exposed to the best of the Hindu tradition. Every morning his tutor, who lived in the house, sweetly sang poems of various saints. The boy listened intently, with his heart melting. Tears flowed from his eyes, and he sang with his tutor, totally absorbed in the melody. He also began reading stories of the saints and their devotees, and was deeply moved by them. The sweet stream of devotion flowed through him, lending beauty to his life. On Sundays he would also go to a nearby temple of a reform Hindu group *(Arya Samaj)*, where he was deeply impressed by the programs of social reform.

After some time he was transferred to a high school run by the Sikh community. There and in the nearby Sikh temple, he learned to appreciate more deeply the beauty and wisdom of the saintly tradition of India.

Being of keen intelligence, the boy excelled in his studies, regularly leading his class. However, scholastic success started to inflate his ego. The process, begun at an early age, continued unchecked for years.

At 16 he finished secondary school with high honors, and was offered a government merit scholarship to continue his studies. The award further strengthened his ego, although he did not actually make use of it. Instead he entered the family business, and was married at the age of eighteen. And now he found that despite his immersing himself in devotional practices, he had become a prey to overwhelming anger and passion, even in his adolescence. These defilements continued to grow as he approached maturity, and he suffered from the agitation they generated in him.

Business Success

During the Second World War Burma was occupied by Japanese forces, and the youth came to South India, along with the other members of his family. Although still in his teens, he now started to achieve great success in business, which strengthened still more the demon of ego within him. After the war when he returned to Burma, his success became even greater. He soon became a leader of the Indian community in Burma. Whenever an honorary position needed to be filled in virtually any field—religious, educational, industrial, commercial, literary, cultural, or social—automatically his name was thought of. This achievement of status and honors served only to increase his ego, and therefore his misery. At the same time his anger and passion continued to grow. These three enemies kept invading his mind, and he was powerless to resist them.

As his inner problems kept multiplying, his devotion also kept deepening. At literary gatherings he would recite religious poetry and give discourses, profoundly moving his audience and himself. At home as well he would chant for long periods, becoming dissolved in devotion. At times he would implore his deities to free him from the defilements which caused him so much misery. But all his chanting, his tears and remorse did not help. He remained miserable and kept others miserable.

At this time in his life he had an opportunity to make a thorough study of Indian philosophy, of the Gīta and the Upanishads. He would give public lectures on the Vedanta, explaining the nuances of Sthita Pragya—the nature of one who is established in wisdom—and examining subtle aspects of the detachment described in the Gīta. His words would hold the audience spellbound, but after he returned home many a time he would weep at the absence of established wisdom in him, at his own lack of actual detachment. No matter how carefully he explained them, the words remained mere words for him. Neither devotion nor intellectual games could put an end to his defilements. These kept growing, rendering him more and more unhappy.

Thus outside he enjoyed success in every worldly field, but he suffered deep turmoil within.

Vipassana—a Path to Happiness

In such a pitiable state, at the age of 31 this unhappy young man encountered that great saint, Sayagyi U Ba Khin, and received from him the precious gift of pure Dhamma, the blessing of Vipassana. The shell of ignorance was broken, and the ego started to dissolve. Now a new life lay before him, rich in inner fulfillment. Even the first 10-day course was enough to obtain great benefits. These increased with continued practice and began to spread beyond him, affecting positively all those around him. The Ganges of Vipassana started flowing in his family, bringing with it peace, happiness, and harmony.

Having found the essence of real Dhamma, he emerged from the unhealthy tendency to devotionalism and emotionalism, from sterile intellectualizing and philosophizing. The attachment to sectarian views was shattered. The light of Dhamma began to illumine every aspect of his life. With Vipassana he was able to uncover and uproot the sources of the anger, passion, and ego which had kept him so unhappy. The more he was freed of these defilements, the more he enjoyed real peace.

Fourteen long years were spent in the cool and pleasant shade cast by this noble Dhamma personality. These years also brought great changes in the mundane field. He achieved still further success in business and industry, but within he had a rarer treasure—equanimity. This mental balance stood him in good stead when suddenly all business and industry in Burma were nationalized. Overnight his worldly position changed dramatically. But the jewel of Dhamma was within him, and now revealed its worth. His mind remained completely unshaken, without a trace of animosity, with only good will toward those responsible for the change in his fortunes. The thought arose, "Good that I am relieved of the burden. Now I can devote all my time to strengthening myself in the practice and theory of pure Dhamma!" The mind stayed peaceful and therefore happy. Truly his worldly loss brought him greater gain: the chance to make more progress on the path, under the benevolent guidance of his Dhamma father.

Messenger of Dhamma

And then another period in his life unfolded. At the age of 45, this man came to India, his ancestral homeland, carrying with him the infinite blessings of his teacher. Despite initial obstacles, again the Ganges of Dhamma started flowing in the land of its source. People started coming forward to offer their help. A new family of thousands of Dhamma sons and daughters sprang up, not only in India but in so many other countries as well—as if the family members from past lives had gathered again to serve others in Dhamma. The way opened to restore to India its precious lost heritage of pure Dhamma. The way opened for its spread around the world.

On passing the milestone of 60 years, the mind looks not only to the past but also to the future. The royal road of Dhamma stretches straight ahead. The goal is clearly in sight. Every step on the path brings it closer, and also confers benefits here and now.

And in the mind a Dhamma volition arises: This ancient, precious treasure of India, carefully guarded for centuries in Burma, its foster home—may it now become a blessing to all people of its motherland, and to people of the entire world. May it become a blessing to all suffering beings throughout the universe. May the new generation take up the charge of this precious technique, and not only benefit themselves but also help others to benefit. May Vipassana meditation help suffering people everywhere throughout the world.

—Dhamma Traveler—S. N. Goenka

(International edition—July 1984)

Forty Years of New Life

S. N. Goenka

40 Years of New Life first appeared in the Hindi language newsletter, Patrika, in the autumn of 1995, marking the fortieth anniversary of Goenkaji's beginning the practice of Vipassana. This article has been translated and adapted from the original.

Words of Dhamma

Buddhaṃ saraṇaṃ gacchāmi	I take refuge in the Buddha
Dhammaṃ saraṇaṃ gacchāmi	I take refuge in the Dhamma
Saṅghaṃ saraṇaṃ gacchāmi	I take refuge in the Saṅgha
(Ti-ratana saraṇa)	(Refuge in the Triple Gem)

The first 10 days of September 1955 were the most precious of my life. Sitting at the feet of the supremely compassionate householder-saint, Sayagyi U Ba Khin, I learned the pristine art of observing the truth within. It was a great fortune, an exalted *pāramī* (wholesome deed) of some past life that had borne a priceless fruit. I could never have dreamed that these sacred moments would happen. It was a new birth.

Reborn in Dhamma

My first birth had taken place 32 years earlier. Now I was truly twice-born! This second birth was indeed a worthy birth. Like a bird born of its mother encased in a shell, my first birth was shrouded in the darkness of deep ignorance. A bird's second birth is its true birth—when it breaks the eggshell and emerges into the light. Just as the little bird blinks its eyes when it emerges from its shell into the sunlight, so was I astounded when the dark layer of ignorance was penetrated for the first time and I glimpsed the rays of true understanding. Indeed, the darkness of ignorance is darker than the absence of light within an eggshell or the womb.

Hitherto I had not even remotely perceived the truth within. Yet how well I experienced it in those 10 days! This perishable, material body which had always seemed so solid and heavy—now its every atom trembled and came alive. Yet a still greater achievement was that I found a simple and scientific method of eradicating mental defilements. By realizing the true relationship between the body and mind, the shackles of those deep-rooted mental defilements now began to disintegrate. I had read or heard about the highly-valued stages of meditation practice, and now I was experiencing them. My heart overflowed with gratitude toward my Teacher, Sayagyi U Ba Khin.

After returning home I practiced Vipassana every morning and evening without a break, despite the acute demands of my busy schedule. This brought about fundamental changes, and profound gratitude toward my revered Teacher deepened immensely.

Vipassana became a part of my life. The mind that had burned incessantly in the fires of passion, anger and ego now experienced a rare spiritual peace and calm. Where it had been plagued by the constant tension of myriad domestic, business and social responsibilities, my mind was now enriched by happiness and health. Vipassana did not draw me away from my worldly responsibilities, rather it gave me renewed energy to dispassionately fulfill them. Consequently, my capacity for work increased significantly.

For years I had been immersed in serious scriptural studies and steeped in sentimental devotional practices, tremulously praying to the deities my family worshipped. Despite these practices, deep-seated defilements remained. But now they began to weaken due to this simple and natural process of meditation. My heart overflowed with thankfulness.

Beyond Rites and Rituals

Since my childhood I had been conditioned by beliefs about our family deity. Although it was taught that Lord Buddha was the ninth and most evolved incarnation of the god Vishnu, his teachings were portrayed as oriented toward magic; they were considered unfit for true believers. These beliefs were stumbling blocks which caused me to hesitate joining my first course of Vipassana.

But I had also heard that the Buddha was deeply compassionate. As a child I had read the story in which his cousin Devadatta wounded a swan with an arrow and how young Gotama compassionately saved it. I had also observed that the people of Myanmar (Burma) were so simple, straightforward and guileless. A question arose in my mind: If the Buddha's teachings were wrong, then how could his followers be such decent people?

Confounding my mind still further were blind beliefs that I had clung to since childhood. Some came from one of my uncles who held a high position in my father's firm. He was much older than me and a Sanskrit scholar. He had read the scriptures extensively and his frequent weapon in an argument was: "The scriptures say so." Immersed in rites and rituals, he prayed and worshipped for four or five hours every day. His daily chants were impressive; from a young age they inspired me to recite important scriptural passages for which I am grateful to him. I enjoyed these daily morning recitations; the words reverberated in my mind long afterwards. My entire family was deeply devoted to the gods Vishnu, Krishna and Shiva. My chants further strengthened this inherited devotion.

My uncle was extremely strict. Though he did not oppose Lord Buddha, he strongly opposed his teachings. I, on the other hand, often visited the famous Mahāmuni (Buddhist) temple in Mandalay with my grandfather, and felt very peaceful there. My uncle often said to me, "The old man has become senile, but you are still young and should refrain from taking the wrong path." But I continued to visit the temple even after my grandfather's death. The peace and cleanliness of Buddha's temples attracted me. I knew nothing about meditation then, but whenever I visited the Mahāmuni temple I felt very calm.

I finally joined a Vipassana course after speaking with Sayagyi U Ba Khin. His explanations, given with deep compassion and *mettā* , allowed me to understand how blemish-free this meditation practice is. In the very first course I realized how false and misleading was the centuries-old propaganda against the Buddha's teachings!

I now saw clearly: What can be wrong in practicing a meditation which is based on universal truth and can bring this wild, unruly mind to one-pointed concentration? What, indeed, can be wrong in establishing the mind in wisdom and knowledge based on one's own experience—a mind that hitherto had depended on somebody else's wisdom? Can anything be wrong in learning the art of leading a new life, the result of a mind cleansed and purified from defilements, and filled with *mettā* (loving kindness), *karunā* (compassion), *muditā* (sympathetic joy) and *upekkhā* (equanimity)? I had read and heard about the importance of these subtler qualities since childhood. Now I felt: If someone teaches the experiential aspects of the eternal truth—which had only been described in empty rhetoric—then how can these teachings be considered false, illusory or magical? I found the Vipassana practice faultless.

I then decided to read the Buddha's words, thinking that perhaps I'd find something false or misleading lurking there. But as I read the scriptures I saw with increasing clarity that Dhamma was sublime and pure, beneficial to one and all.

In those days I used to come to India to visit established ashrams (centers for spiritual practice) and meet various religious leaders. I wanted to determine if I had, perhaps, started walking on a wrong path, if I had become entangled in a delusion. I also sought to learn: If Vipassana was a proper path, how could I progress beyond what I had already learned? Alas, after these explorations, I felt certain that India had become spiritually poorer since losing the sublime knowledge of the Buddha's teaching.

India's neighbor Myanmar is truly blessed in having preserved these priceless jewels in their pristine purity: not only Vipassana meditation, but the original Buddhist scriptures which were lost due to our Indian ancestors' lack of wisdom. I now clearly understood the way in which misinformation had been propagated all over India, whereby Buddha was praised but his teachings were denounced. I was saddened and dismayed when I realized how the educated classes of India had been duped and so lost our country's ancient, timeless, priceless treasure. It was time for the country to awaken.

Wisdom through Meditation

Besides my daily practice of meditation, I visited my revered Sayagyi at his center in Yangon every Sunday morning at 7:00 for group meditation and I continued to go deeper in Vipassana *paññā* (experiential wisdom) by taking at least one 10-day course a year. At times I also undertook longer, more intensive retreats. Gradually I came to realize the true purpose for human existence. The reality of the senses at the mental and physical levels, their universal characteristics of *anicca* (impermanence), *dukkha* (suffering) and *anattā* (ego-lessness), became increasingly clear experientially. I could see the truth as obviously as a piece of fruit held in my hand.

The state of total dissolution that I had experienced so naturally and effortlessly in my first course had created the illusion that this was indeed the permanent, eternal, absolute state; whereas in reality, this dissolution was nothing but physical and mental sensations, clearly within the realm of *anicca* (arising and passing away).

Subsequently, when I experienced even subtler realities and their concomitant states of deep peace and sublime bliss and joy, I realized the importance of experiencing these states with increased alertness. This is essential to prevent the seeker from getting stuck in this elevated but illusionary experience, which is still in the field of mind and matter. The meditator must clearly perceive whether this blissful state is one of heightened awareness of the senses, or the experience which transcends the senses. In this experience beyond the senses, the senses do not work; if this has not happened, then one is still in the field of mind and matter. With deepened awareness, I experienced rising and falling in this profoundly subtle realm also. Without the awareness of *anicca*, this state would have trapped me with the illusionary thought of "me, my, mine," and "permanent, eternal, absolute soul." That is why it is vital to remain totally aware of the reality of this experience.

Gratitude for the Teaching

Through practicing constant awareness and experiencing the various stages on the path to total liberation, all doubts were gradually dissolving. At every step, the sublime purity and spiritually beneficent aspects of Dhamma manifested themselves. Naturally my heart overflowed with feelings of gratitude, gratitude toward Gotama the Buddha who, despite tremendous hardships, rediscovered the technique of Vipassana which had been lost for aeons—the only technique which leads to mental purification and total liberation. Not only did he seek out the path and liberate himself, but with boundless compassion he shared it with one and all.

Deep gratitude flows toward the unbroken tradition of Teacher-student, diligently maintained in India and thereafter in Myanmar, which preserved the basic tenants of this knowledge in total purity. Gratitude flows toward my Dhamma father, Sayagyi, who taught me Vipassana with such compassion, and firmly established me in the theoretical and practical aspects of pure Dhamma.

When I survey the last 40 years of my new life on the path of Vipassana, my heart brims with deep satisfaction and joy. In the worldly sphere, during these 40 years, there have been so many ascents and descents, so many springs and autumns, so many turns of the tide. But the daily practice of Vipassana never failed to help me to develop equanimity in all situations.

My life is fulfilled. From the abundant compassion of my respected Teacher, I have received incomparable sustenance, and I continue to receive it in such abundance! The rejuvenating medicine of Dhamma gives me confidence to move firmly on. It continues to benefit me so much and uplifts so many others also. Pondering this, a spark of gratitude toward my respected Teacher rekindles in my heart.

The river of Dhamma that started flowing 25 centuries ago through the efforts of the supremely compassionate Buddha—may it spring forth once again in the current era due to the efforts of my deeply revered Sayagyi. May it liberate all those who are enchained, who are tired and thirsty, who are in pain and sorrow. May it benefit all, may it uplift all, this wish of goodwill flows from my heart.

Having experienced and appreciated the Buddha's teaching, deep like the ocean, broad like the vast earth and high like the Himalayas, I feel very comfortable in accepting, practicing and passing it on in its pristine purity. There can be no question of practicing or teaching anything but this wonderful Dhamma. Dhamma is *paripuṇṇa*—it is complete, there is nothing to add. And it is *parisuddha*—so pure, that there is nothing to be removed.

Jo guruvara milate nahīn
Dharama Gaṅga ke tira,
to basa Gaṅgā pūjatā
pī pātā nā nīra.

Had I not found my Teacher
on the banks of the Ganges of Dhamma,
I would have kept worshipping the river
but not have drunk its water.

Mere arjita puṇya meṅ
bhāga sabhī kā hoya.
Isa maṅgalamaya Dharma kā,
lābha sabhī ko hoya.

May the merits I have acquired
be shared by one and all.
May this munificent Dhamma
benefit one and all.

Ao logo jagata ke
calen Dharama ke pantha.
Isa patha calate satpurusha
isa patha calate santa.

Come, people of the world!
Let us walk the path of Dhamma.
On this path walk holy ones,
on this path walk saints.

—Hindi Dohas by S.N. Goenka
(International edition—September 1996)

Farewell Dhamma Brother

S. N. Goenka

Words of Dhamma

Phuṭṭhassa lokadhammehi,	When faced with life's vicissitudes,
cittaṃ yassa na kampati;	one's mind is unshaken
asokaṃ virajaṃ khemaṃ	free from sorrow, impurity, or fear
etaṃ maṅgalamuttamaṃ.	—this is the highest welfare.

—Khuddakapatha 5–12, Maṅgalasutta

"How extraordinary!" Speaking in his customary soft voice, Dr. Om Prakash repeated, "It is really extraordinary. I have seen so many people die, but never like this." He was referring to my aunt and adoptive mother, Rami Devi. Truly, her illness and death were extraordinary. At the age of 75, about 15 days before she died, she was chatting with Illaichi Devi (Mataji) and happened to remark that for several months she had felt constant pain in her abdomen. She was able to endure it and remain equanimous, but she mentioned the fact in passing.

At once I called our doctor and my close friend, Dr. Om Prakash, who had become an inseparable part of the family. He examined my mother and then, taking me aside, he said, "It might be cancer of the liver. The signs all clearly point toward this diagnosis, except for one fact: in such a case the pain is intolerable, and the distressed patient keeps crying and weeping. No person could suffer from the pain of this cancer for months and not so much as mention it to anyone. Even now your mother is so peaceful. I shall have to investigate further."

Two days later, Dr. Om Prakash came with Col. (Dr.) Min Sein, a well-known doctor in Rangoon. After examining Mother, the colonel said much the same thing: "All the signs suggest an advanced stage of cancer. But the patient is so peaceful, so free from distress; it is difficult to accept that she is suffering from cancer. We shall have to carry out further tests before making a diagnosis."

After they left, Illaichi Devi asked Mother, "What is the pain like that you feel?" The reply astonished everyone; Mother said, "It is much more severe than the excruciating pains of childbirth. But what is the use of crying? I observe the pain with equanimity. After all, isn't this what Guruji [Sayagyi U Ba Khin] taught us to do?"

Mother was an outstanding Vipassana meditator. At the meditation center of my revered Teacher, only one 10-day course was held each month, starting on the first Friday of that month. Ever since she had started walking on the path of Vipassana six or seven years before, there had not been a single course in which Mother had not taken part. Just recently she had completed a special 30-day course. Her equanimity had become so established that there was no possibility of her giving way to lamentation.

After many tests, both doctors concluded that it was definitely cancer and that it had already advanced to the terminal stage. They believed that Mother had only a few days left. Any kind of treatment would be useless and would only increase the suffering. Nevertheless, they continued with palliative care.

At 3:00 a.m. on her last night, Mother told the nurse that the time of her death was approaching, and she asked for her children to be called. We all went to her room. I immediately telephoned Dr. Om Prakash. He had not yet gone to bed; just two hours before, he had been called out to see another patient who was dying. Even so, he came at once. I also called Sayagyi, and fortunately he too came with Mother Sayama.

Dr. Om Prakash checked and could not find a pulse. Mother had only a few minutes left. Shortly before her death, she said, "I want to sit up." Dr. Om Prakash advised against it, saying, "It would be better for her to keep lying down. The pain will worsen if she sits up." But Mother insisted and, understanding this as her last wish, I supported her so that she could do as she wished. To our astonishment, she made the effort to sit up cross-legged and started meditating. Truly this was remarkable Dhamma strength.

A few minutes before, her pulse had been undetectable, and now she was sitting cross-legged and meditating! To reinforce her resolve in meditation I said, "*Tai mā, anaissā, anaissā'—Aunt/Mother, anicca, anicca,*" pronouncing the word as they do in Burmese. She lifted her right hand and, touching the top of her head, said, "Yes, son, *anaissā, anaissā.*" Then she lowered her hand. She looked at me, she looked at Dr. Om Prakash, she looked at Sayagyi and Mother Sayama, and then she looked upward and breathed her last.

The sight of such a death had astonished Dr. Om Prakash. It was about 4:20 a.m. Mother's body had been removed from the bed and placed on the floor, in accordance with Indian custom. We would have to wait for the others to arrive before the funeral could take place. Relatives living in Rangoon and other members of the community would arrive by 8:30 a.m. In the intervening hours, all of us, including Dr. Om Prakash, remained in a sitting room nearby. We kept talking of this unusual death.

Finally the hour of 8:30 a.m. approached, when we would proceed to the cremation ground. Before the body was placed on the bier, it would have to be bathed and dressed in new clothes. Illaichi Devi went to Mother's bedroom to perform this task, but she returned immediately and startled us all by saying that Mother was still alive. Dr. Om Prakash said, "How can this be?" Illaichi Devi explained that Mother's body was still soft and warm, unlike a dead body.

We all went to Mother's room with Dr. Om Prakash. He examined the corpse carefully and said that though Mother was certainly not alive, it was true that the whole body was still warm. Her face was exceptionally tranquil and illuminated by some divine radiance. It seemed as if she was in deep sleep. And this was the moment when Dr. Om Prakash remarked, "How extraordinary!" There was no doubt that she was dead, but what marvel was this? I was at a loss for words.

We performed the funeral ceremony and returned home. Everyone in the family was a Vipassana meditator, and so no one cried. I meditated most of the time to maintain a Dhamma atmosphere. By early evening all the Vipassana meditators in the city had assembled for a one-hour group sitting. Sayagyi and Mother Sayama were also present. After the hour, other members of the community who were not Vipassana meditators came and, with Sayagyi's permission, I gave a one-hour Dhamma discourse. Immediately afterwards, Dr. Om Prakash came to me and said that he wished to sit a course. "Tell me when the next course will be held," he requested. It was scheduled to be held after about 15 days. I assured him that I would inform him well in advance. The next day, again there was a Dhamma discourse in the evening. Again at the end, Dr. Om Prakash came to me and said, "The next course will not be held for some days; I wish to sit as soon as possible." Sayagyi was standing nearby. Seeing the strong Dhamma impulse that had arisen in Dr. Om Prakash, he agreed to hold a course immediately. We were astonished that Sayagyi would conduct a course for just one person, but he directed me to come to the meditation center on the following day with Dr. Om Prakash.

The next day Dr. Om Prakash came to the meditation center himself. I also arrived there on time, and two other people joined the course. After the giving of Ānāpāna, I returned home and Sayagyi went to his office. As usual, he returned to the center in the evening, and later came to my home for the group meditation. On completion of the Dhamma discourse, Sayagyi told me that Dr. Om Prakash was making excellent progress. I was very pleased to hear this.

The next morning I received a summons from Sayagyi: "Your friend is endowed with abundant *pāramī*. After only one day of Ānāpāna, he is for ready Vipassana. Come immediately; he must be given Vipassana now." I went to the center for the giving of Vipassana to Dr. Om Prakash, and once more returned home. Sayagyi came again for the evening meditation and discourse. He was very happy, saying that after only one day of Vipassana, Dr. Om Prakash had attained the state of *bhaṅga* [dissolution] and was now working at a very deep level.

The next morning he called me again and said, "Come at once. The progress of your friend is extraordinary. It seems that he has abundant *pāramī* of many lives. He has reached close to the state of *nibbāna*. He will have to be given the necessary instructions now." Overwhelmed with great joy and wonder, I went to the center and took my seat near Sayagyi. Dr. Om Prakash was given the requisite instructions. There was no limit to my happiness when he immediately experienced *nibbāna*, the state transcending the senses. Sayagyi was also happy. He examined him closely and found that all the signs indicated this was the state of *nibbāna*. What limit could there be to my happiness! My dear friend had entered the stream of liberation, had become a *sotāpanna*, an ariya [noble person].

My first contact with Dr. Om Prakash was at a public meeting in Rangoon after the Second World War in 1947. We were immediately drawn toward each other.

Fortunately the friends whom I met socially were good people and I had affectionate relationships with all of them. But of them all, Dr. Om Prakash was closest to me. We used to work together in various fields. In the post-war period, we re-established the All-Burmese Hindi Literature Society, and branches opened in many places throughout the country. A symposium on Hindi literature was organized every week in Rangoon. Hindi colleges were established for the Society's primary, secondary and post-secondary levels of study, and many students took part. Work was also done on exchanges between Burmese and Hindi literature. Hindi textbooks were written and published. The Indo-Burmese Cultural Center was established, and through it many cultural programs were organized. Together, both of us set up an orphanage and took responsibility for its management. Thus, after working together in several public service activities, now we had the opportunity to dedicate ourselves in the field of Vipassana.

Dr. Om Prakash had also treated me for my migraine headaches. When other medications proved ineffective, he started giving me morphine injections. But he himself worried that I might become addicted to morphine, and so he urged me to go abroad for treatment. "Even if you do not find a cure for your migraines," he said, "you will at least free yourself from dependence on morphine. You will certainly find some other effective painkiller abroad." Heeding his suggestion, I traveled to many countries for treatment, but in the end I returned disappointed. Dr. Om Prakash shared my concern. Subsequently, when I joined a Vipassana course and became free from my disease, he shared my happiness.

But when I started taking repeated courses, meditating daily and attending group meditation every Sunday at the center, he became worried that I might become a Buddhist, an atheist. He often tried lovingly to dissuade me. I would explain to him, "With the deep influence of the *Arya Samaj* [a Hindu reform movement—Ed.], I cannot be trapped in any blind belief. I have examined the teaching of the Buddha very objectively on the basis of experiential truth, and I have found it to be completely faultless. For centuries, erroneous conditionings had led the people of India to shun the stainless teaching of the Buddha. I myself was a victim of this false propaganda. But now I have found by experience that there is no trace of blemish in this teaching. I am amazed that this pure, invaluable technique of India became lost in the country of its origin." I do not know what effect my words had on him, but after my mother's death his immense *pāramī* were awakened and he became eternally dedicated to this technique.

I came to India in 1969, and Vipassana courses started to be held here. But Dr. Om Prakash stayed in Myanmar for some years longer. Even after he passed through some extremely painful experiences, his mind was not tinged with bitterness. He did not even report the misconduct of certain officials to the president of the country, who had been his classmate in college. His mind continued to be full of *mettā* and equanimity. Vipassana was his bulwark. Even before, his nature had been calm and stable. Now Vipassana made it more so. After some years he came to India and became engaged in Vipassana activities.

He had been one of the leading doctors in Myanmar but, because of his generous nature, he used to practice medicine in a spirit of service. He did not charge any fixed fees. He gladly accepted whatever payment the patient offered after regaining health. He took nothing from many poor patients. Instead, to some he used to give free medicines. This was his natural disposition. After coming to India, whenever he was in Delhi, he regularly served two hours a day at the *Arya Samaj* free clinic; the rest of the time he devoted to the service of Vipassana. Even at the age of 87, he traveled to different places and conducted courses with unflagging enthusiasm, outdoing those much younger than himself. He also went abroad on several occasions.

Recently, he again visited America to conduct numerous courses. His itinerary brought him to Los Angeles, with the next stop to be Kansas City, followed by courses at *Dhamma Kuñja* (near Seattle) and *Dhamma Sirī* (near Dallas). While in Los Angeles, however, he suffered a stroke. When brought to the hospital, he explained his condition to the attending doctors with complete lucidity, but while doing so he entered a coma. He was in this state in the intensive care ward for some days. During this time I myself was on a Dhamma tour of Southeast Asia. When I reached Singapore, I received the news of his illness. I telephoned and gave him *mettā* , but his son-in-law, Dr. Soni, who was then with him, said that there was no physical sign by which it could be said that the *mettā* was effective. He said, "His brain is not functioning at all, and so no sense organ is functioning." I was very sad to hear this. But a few minutes before death, he seemed to regain his sense of hearing. Tapes of dohās and Dhamma discourses were being played continuously nearby. His son, Dr. Rajiv, said that near the end his eyes opened slightly, his lips moved a little and he seemed to be looking at something above. Then his breathing started becoming slower—only nine breaths in one minute. His respiration gradually kept slowing until he peacefully breathed his last. His face was glowing with a divine radiance. From this we may conclude that the inner consciousness had really been present all along, but he had been unable to make any physical movement though he may have wanted to. In the end his Dhamma strength arose, his eyes opened, and his lips moved, proof that the inner consciousness was awake.

When I returned to Mumbai after a long Dhamma tour of seven countries, I saw that among the pile of papers awaiting me was a letter he had written on August 26. In it he described his journey up to Los Angeles, gave details of future courses and asked for *mettā*.

His Dhamma service was most effective. Many Vipassana centers were eager to have courses conducted by him. In America as well, people awaited him with great eagerness. But midway in the journey he departed and attained a great promotion. The people were kept waiting. After reading his letter, I drew a deep sigh and spontaneously these words came forth:

Baḍe gour se sun rahā thā zamānā,
tumhi so gaye dastān kahte kahte!

The world was listening very intently, but you fell asleep while narrating the story!

The world Vipassana family is increasing day by day, but my Dhamma brothers are dwindling in number. How many now remain who received the teaching directly from Sayagyi U Ba Khin? This Dhamma brother also carried out his mission: "*Anta samaya taka dharma ki, seva hoti jaya*—Let me serve the Dhamma until my final moment."

I was extremely fortunate to have such a Dhamma brother.

The ideal that Dr. Om Prakash set for all Vipassana meditators and teachers will serve as a beacon in the future. This inspiration will bring welfare to many, happiness to many. India will regain its ancient glory and dignity, leading to immense welfare for the entire world.

Incomparable Refreshing Tranquillity

Once, while on a Dhamma tour of North India, I stayed at Dr. Om Prakash's residence in Delhi for two days. He gave us his own bedroom and slept in another room nearby. The morning after our arrival, I meditated together with him on the bed in his bedroom. Near the end of the one-hour sitting, suddenly an incomparable *nibbānic* cooling tranquillity emanated from him and spread throughout the room. On completion of the sitting he said with great humility, "Meditating with you today, I have become blessed. I experienced incomparable refreshing tranquillity." I replied, "You know best about your own experience, but after experiencing your *nibbānic* cooling tranquillity I have become truly blessed!"

(International edition—September 1998)

1989: A Double Milestone

Words of Dhamma

Dhammo dhajo yo viya tassa satthu,
dassesi lokassa visuddhimaggaṃ,
niyyāniko dhammadharassa dhārī,
sātāvaho santikaro suciṇṇo,
dhammaṃ varantaṃ sirasā namāmi,
mohappadālaṃ upasantadāhaṃ.

The Dhamma, that is like the Teacher's banner, showing to the world the path of purity, leading to liberation, upholding those who uphold it, well-practiced, leads to happiness and peace. To the most excellent Dhamma I bow my head, cleaver of delusion, calmer of fiery passion.

—Namakārasiddhigāthā

The year 1989 marks a double anniversary in the spread of the Dhamma. It is now 20 years since S.N. Goenka left Burma to begin teaching Vipassana meditation in India, and 10 years since he began teaching in the west.

Goenkaji has often told the story of how he came to India in July of 1969. The immediate reason was to help his ailing mother by conducting a Vipassana course for her benefit. In addition, however, Goenkaji's teacher Sayagyi U Ba Khin had long wished to travel outside of Burma, to re-introduce the Vipassana technique in India and bring it to countries where it had never before been practiced. In this way he hoped to fulfill the prophecy that 2,500 years after the time of the Buddha, the Dhamma would experience a resurgence and spread around the world.

On one occasion U Ba Khin had accepted an invitation to teach abroad, and had fixed dates for courses in India and America. In the end, however, travel restrictions prevented him from leaving Burma. For this reason he saw Goenkaji's visit to his mother in India as an opportunity to fulfill the traditional prophecy. In a formal ceremony he authorized his student as a teacher of Vipassana meditation, and shortly afterward Goenkaji embarked for India.

Naturally, Goenkaji shared his teacher's hopes. He was eager to serve his mother and father as well as other people who wished to learn Vipassana meditation. At the same time he did not realize that the journey on which he was embarking would last decades. He knew few people in India, and regarded Burma as his beloved homeland. He confidently expected to return there within a few months.

The Wheel of Dhamma had started turning again, however, and Goenkaji had to extend his stay in India indefinitely in order to meet the surprisingly strong demand for Vipassana courses. With at first virtually no old students and organizational support to help him, he traveled from one end of the country to the other, giving courses in rented sites and gradually laying the foundation for the rebirth of Vipassana in India. His efforts have borne abundant fruit: today there are four Vipassana centers in India, and tens of thousands of meditators from every walk of life.

Re-establishing the practice of Vipassana in India was still only a part of his mission. Another part was to help it spread around the world. From the very beginning people from western countries had joined Goenkaji's courses, and many of them were eager to see courses held in their own lands. One of these students—a woman from France—invited Goenkaji to come and conduct courses in her country. Goenkaji explained that he had taken a decision for the first 10 years to confine his teaching to India, so as to build a firm base there for the spread of Vipassana. But he promised that France would be the first western country where he would hold courses. "Come back and ask me again when 10 years are over," he said.

In fact there was a second reason that kept Goenkaji in India. When he had left Burma in 1969, he was issued a passport valid only for travel to India. Because his family was originally from there, he could of course easily receive Indian citizenship, and would then be able to travel freely. But he was reluctant to sever his links with the land that had given him birth and Dhamma. For this reason he made repeated requests to the Burmese authorities to grant him travel endorsements for other countries. If after 10 years he had still not received a positive response, he would accept the inevitable and change his nationality for the sake of the Dhamma.

The years passed quickly, filled with Dhamma work and achievement. As they approached their end, the same student again contacted Goenkaji, this time with a formal invitation from the European Federation of Yoga Teachers, to conduct courses under their auspices in France. Goenkaji accepted their invitation, and students in other western countries made plans for further courses to follow the ones in France.

The problem of his passport still remained, however; the Burmese government had not given him permission to travel outside India. At last Goenkaji decided to apply for Indian citizenship, although he knew that this action might be viewed as disloyal by some Burmese, and might bar him from ever returning to his motherland. He could only hope that one day the Burmese government would realize that he had acted in a noble cause: to make the jewel of Dhamma, long preserved in Burma, more widely available in the world. Finally, in June 1979, he became an Indian citizen. He received his new passport hours before his departure for France.

On July 1, Goenkaji's first course in a western country began at Gaillon, in Normandy, France. The site was a chateau that had been converted into a luxurious vacation hotel; the Yoga Federation customarily held meetings for its members in such luxurious accommodations. Quite a few old students who had sat with Goenkaji in India came for the course. Most of the students were members of the Yoga Federation and there was almost no management; cooking was done by the hotel staff. The discipline was much laxer than at centers in India.

Language presented a major problem. Taped French translations had been made of Goenkaji's discourses, but the recording quality was not good enough to use for a large group. As for the meditation instructions, no French versions existed. The only way to proceed was with the help of old students who acted as interpreters: Goenkaji would speak a few sentences in English, and the interpreter would repeat them in French. Interpreting is always a stressful task; to perform it in the context of a meditation course was all the more difficult. The students had to work in teams, one relieving the other when the pressure became too great.

There were other difficulties, not all unexpected. Any major advance in the spread of the teaching of liberation, Goenkaji explained, is bound to encounter obstacles. Overcoming these was a way of gaining strength. Gradually a meditative atmosphere was established, and participants in the course were able to appreciate the technique of Vipassana.

At the end of this first course, Goenkaji stayed overnight in Paris. Like most tourists, he asked to visit the Eiffel Tower. His purpose, however, was not to admire the view from the top, but to distribute *mettā* to all the inhabitants below.

A second course followed at Plaige, near Lyon in central France, after which Goenkaji flew to Montreal, Canada, to conduct his first course in North America. Unlike the courses in France, this was organized and managed by a team of Vipassana meditators. The site was a boarding school in the suburbs of the city. Approximately 185 people participated from all parts of the North American continent. Many of them were old students who had started meditating with Goenkaji in India in the early 1970s, but had not been able to sit with him since. Despite a heat wave and extremely limited outside walking areas, the meditators worked hard, and Goenkaji was very pleased with the course.

Next Goenkaji traveled to Britain for two consecutive courses, again organized by meditators and attended by people from all over Europe. At these courses the evening talks were videotaped for the first time. Although the tapes have never been widely used, they marked the first time Goenkaji's teaching had been recorded in this way.

The entire tour covered two months during which five courses were held in three countries with over 640 participants. More important, however, the 1979 tour laid the groundwork for the spread of Vipassana in western countries.

Meditators developed the skills to plan, manage and (perhaps hardest of all) cook for large courses at rented sites. They also began to form the organizational structures that were necessary for offering regular course programs and for founding centers. The work of translation of the teaching into other languages and of recording Goenkaji's words both received fresh impetus. It became clear that all these tasks, and many other related ones, can and must be undertaken by dedicated old students wishing to help others experience the benefits of Vipassana meditation.

Most important, the 1979 tour gave renewed inspiration to western meditators. For those who served, it was deeply moving to see their efforts assist in the transmission of the teaching in their homelands. For many, the tour was a chance to meditate again with their Dhamma Father, and to revitalize their practice. For all, it demonstrated that the Dhamma is indeed universal, transcending cultural boundaries and offering a way out of suffering.

(International edition—September 1989)

Hail to Dhamma!

S.N. Goenka

The following is an abridged version of an article that appeared in the June 1989 Hindi-language Vipasyana Patrikā.

20 years have passed in the life's journey of a *Dhamma-dūta.* [envoy of Dhamma]. In 1969 my revered Dhamma Father formally conferred on me the great responsibility of teaching Vipassana meditation. For a number of years I had served and been trained by him as his assistant, yet still I doubted my fitness for the weighty task he had now given me. Compared to his great Dhamma stature, I felt like a pygmy. In addition, I would face the

problems of teaching in India. The very prospect made me nervous.

In ancient times the heartland of the Dhamma had been Northern India, then called Majjhimadesa or the Central Realm, and Burma was an outlying district to which the Teaching had not yet penetrated. This was the case in the days of Bhikkhus Sona and Uttara: when they travelled from India to Burma, they brought the Dhamma to a land that was foreign to it. Now the situation was completely reversed. Long ago the Ganges of the Dhamma had flowed from India into Burma; now the time had come for it to turn back in its course and fructify afresh its native land.

But the bitter fact was that Majjhimadesa had become a land foreign to the Dhamma. There Gotama the Buddha and countless fully enlightened ones before him had discovered Vipassana, the beneficent path of liberation; from there this teaching had repeatedly spread around the world. Yet in our time this very land—indeed all of India—was void of Vipassana. Where every member of each household—man and woman, young and old, servant and master—had once practiced Vipassana daily, now not only the practice but even the word "Vipassana" had become unknown. What, I asked myself, could I accomplish in such a country? How could I possibly be successful?

Being myself of Indian descent, I knew well the rites and rituals, sectarian practices and philosophical views in which the people of the land of my forefathers were enmeshed. And even if some were willing to lay these aside, practical problems still remained. How many would agree to leave their homes, families and jobs for 10 days in order to join a Vipassana course? Who would arrange accommodations, provide meals and take care of all the other physical needs of participants? Where would the money come from for expenses? In a country where I was a stranger, who would cooperate with me and give me support in my task?

Rightly or wrongly, thousands of such questions kept churning in my mind. The thought of going as a *Dhamma-dūta* to the ancient land of India, the home of countless saints and fully enlightened beings, filled me with exaltation. At the same time I was besieged by doubts.

Recognizing the conflicting impulses in me, Sayagyi reassured me with words of love and confidence. "Certainly what you alone can do is limited." he said. "But do not think that you are going to India; through you I am going, the Dhamma is going. Dhamma will do its own work; who can stand in its way? Now the time has ripened for the Dhamma once again to arise. 25 centuries ago it transformed India by the practice of Vipassana. Now is the time for the second spreading of Dhamma, and it will start in India with Vipassana. Indeed the hour of Vipassana has struck. Because of your great *pāramī* of the past, you have been chosen by the Dhamma as its vehicle, and in this way you will be able to gain still further merits. Go with full confidence. The Dhamma will work."

Sayagyi's loving words and confidence in me provided sustenance for the journey ahead. I arrived in India filled with joyful anticipation, and I found that all began to happen as my had predicted. The Dhamma started working. Within my first month in India the first Vipassana course was arranged in the city of Bombay. Eleven days after, another was organized in Madras. After that the flow started, with courses one after the other up to today. The Wheel of Dhamma started rotating and will keep doing so long into the future.

Truly, Dhamma works in its own way; an individual is merely a vehicle. When in Burma, I had so many questions and misgivings about the difficulties I was likely to encounter. In fact difficulties did arise, but the Dhamma helped me to develop patience, equanimity and *mettā* to face them, and in time they were resolved. The Dhamma started helping. Its help was tangible at every step.

Place after place was offered for Vipassana courses: *dharmsalas* (rest houses for pilgrims), college or school buildings, the hostels of universities and research institutes, library buildings, rooms at a stadium, ashrams of saints such as Gandhi and Vinobha, huge buildings at pilgrimage centers, industrial buildings, the homes of wealthy people, tents in an open field, hotels, sanatoria, health centers, youth hostels, holiday camps, scout camps, a police academy, prison buildings, religious centers of Hindus, Buddhists, Jains, Christians and Muslims, royal palaces and crumbling ruins. It was as if all locks were broken, all gates opened to welcome the Dhamma. And how unfounded was the worry that no one in India would co-operate with a stranger like myself. What greater co-operation can there be than that of Dhamma? I have only two hands, but Dhamma has thousands. All these began to share in the noble task. Thousands of unknown people came forward. But how can I call them unknown? Who knows for how many lives they have walked with me on the path of Dhamma, acquiring merits along with me? Their support is the support of Dhamma itself. Dhamma is great; Dhamma is strong. Hail to Dhamma! Hail to the nature of Dhamma!

So much still remains to be done, but the events of the last 20 years give cause to hope for the rapid spread of Dhamma in the future. Since 1976 there have been 14 Vipassana meditation centers established in India, Nepal, England, France, America, Japan, Australia and New Zealand; still more are being planned. So many selfless meditators have gathered to offer free service at such centers, and approximately 100 male and female assistant teachers have assumed the responsibility of teaching Vipassana. These Dhamma servants receive no salary or other remuneration; all have their own means of support. They expect no material gain, no name or fame. Instead they perform their service so that more and more suffering people might experience the benefits they have found upon the path. Naturally they feel joy and satisfaction at the sight of people emerging from misery, and this happiness encourages them to work. Praiseworthy are these selfless Dhamma servants and teachers. Hail to Dhamma! Hail to the nature of Dhamma!

People of every background are being drawn to the bank of the Ganges of Dhamma to quench their thirst: the miserable inhabitants of luxurious skyscrapers in the great cities, people living in huts and even the homeless who sleep on the footpaths, have-nots of the lowest strata of society, professionals and urban intellectuals, illiterate villagers, people overwhelmed with pride at belonging to a high caste, people suffering from discrimination and from their own sense of inferiority at belonging to a low caste, Hindus, Muslims, Buddhists, Jains, Sikhs, Christians, Parsis, Jews, Indians and non-Indians. What is the miracle of Dhamma that attracts them? It is that people find here a simple scientific way to free themselves of mental defilements and thus achieve liberation from suffering. What greater benefit could one seek? What greater miracle could there be? May all people everywhere enjoy such benefit. May the Dhamma serve all for centuries to come. May the Dhamma help all the people of the world.

(International edition—September 1989)

Anecdote and Recollections

S.N. Goenka and others

The following passage is from the Vipassana Journal (India, 1985) in the section "Reminiscences," pp. 21–22.

Following the nationalization of trade and industry in Burma, many Indian residents there were left without means of livelihood, and therefore had to return to their native land. On leaving Burma they were forbidden to take any valuables with them. Nevertheless, to avoid the loss of their entire savings, many departing Indians would try to smuggle out valuables, particularly in the form of gems—rubies or other stones for which Burma is famous. In order to suppress such smuggling, Burmese customs inspectors were naturally more vigilant with departing Indians.

As I was preparing to embark for India at Rangoon Airport, I passed through the emigration check and came to the customs counter. The official there was very friendly, and jokingly asked whether I was carrying any valuables with me. "Yes," I replied, "I am carrying a gem." The official became nervous; though friendly to me, he was an honest man who would not neglect his duty. Therefore he searched all my belongings carefully without finding what he was looking for. I kept watching him with amusement. Finally I happily explained to the worried man, "My friend, the gem that I am taking from here will be used to pay back a debt of Burma to India. It originally came from India, and is sorely needed there today. By my taking it from here, Burma will not become any poorer. I am taking the jewel of the Dhamma."

The official laughed and said, "Please go ahead—take this gem with you! I am very happy that you will use it to repay this debt." And this is what I did, bringing Dhamma back to India in fulfillment of the wishes of my Teacher. According to the news I had from my friends in Burma, the official always felt very happy whenever he heard about the success of my work here.

Recollections

The following are from students who attended Goenkaji's first courses in the west.

July 1979 : Goenka's first course in France, at Gaillon. What wonderful memories. First of all, a magnificent site and perfect weather. But above all, in the sparsely furnished old barn, the wonderful discovery—like two plus two equals four—of Ānāpāna and then Vipassana, taught by this man who was at the same time so simple and so disciplined. We were about 60 people. We were all new to the technique, but so full of good will!

When the meditators came to sit before Goenka, I could hear their questions and his answers. For example, a lady said, "In the last sitting I had a pain in my heart. It was so sharp I thought I was going to die." Goenka replied, "Has it passed now?" "Yes." "Good," said Goenka. The woman seemed stupefied by this answer. Seeing this, Goenka added: "Why? Would you have liked it to continue?"

I lived intensely those 10 days, experiencing pain, tears, despondency, joy, deep inner silence, and moments of great happiness. I was 62 at the time. As a young man, I had been a Trappist monk for 13 years. When the course was over I said to myself, "Goenka has just taught me in 10 days what the Trappists could not teach me in 13 years!"

For years some of us had divided our lives between home, family and work in the west and the Dhamma in India. Of course there were meditation activities around the world, but they lacked the impetus of Goenkaji's presence. His first visit seemed like a new beginning, when anything might happen.

Students had to be warned not to create mob scenes by gathering to greet him at airports on arrival or departure. He wanted no undue attention. Still it was a thrill to watch him arrive in Paris—one of the first times I'd seen him in a business suit—accompanied by Mataji in sari, of course. He was smiling broadly, eager to begin the new stage of his work.

I had served on courses at *Dhamma Giri* and knew a little French, so I offered to help on the first course in France. I started by doing the usual things a course manager does: making signs and ringing bells for sittings. To my surprise, these awoke quite violent reactions; one day someone even hid the bell! Many of the members of the Yoga Federation had evidently joined the course without knowing much about it. They expected a pleasant holiday with friends in a deluxe hotel, with a few meditation classes thrown in. They were not at all prepared for such basic aspects of a Vipassana course as silence, cutting of contacts with the world outside, or regular attendance at group sittings. I kept running to Goenkaji to report on new breaches of discipline. The worse it got, the more upset I became.

In those days in India, Goenkaji used to alternate giving the Dhamma talks in Hindi in one course and in English in the next. Participants in Hindi courses were mostly Indians, while westerners made up the majority in English courses. It was noticeable that the discipline was looser on Hindi than on English courses; this was simply a cultural difference that we had to accept with a smile.

Now in France, Goenkaji reminded me of this. "Just pretend it's a Hindi course," he told me. The important thing for him was not that each rule be followed, but that the seed of Dhamma be planted.

Each evening of the course in Montreal, the managers would report to Goenkaji in his room on the day's events. He was in wonderful spirits, very pleased with the course, and bubbling over with stories and anecdotes. The new beginning in the west must have recalled to him his early days in India, and he reminisced about them. In those first courses when U Ba Khin was still alive, Goenkaji would report to him in detail on each course and each student's progress. Sayagyi was delighted at the large numbers coming to learn Vipassana. In one of those early courses there were 37 students. As Goenkaji told us, Sayagyi was very pleased: "An excellent number," he said; "37 for the 37 factors of enlightenment!" When the first course of 100 students was held, Sayagyi was still more pleased, and told all the visitors to his center in Rangoon about it. It must have seemed to him that, as he said, the hour of Vipassana had indeed struck. How happy he would have been to see hundreds of people around the world now coming to learn the Dhamma.

The Montreal course in 1979 was my first course with Goenkaji. I flew 3,000 miles to be there. The school where it was held was in what seemed to be a poor district of the suburbs. The exercise yard was about the size of a three-car garage. It was separated from the street by a chain link fence. Walking in it you felt like you were trapped in a small cage. The neighbors used to hang on the fence and watch us while we were walking. None of the meditators spoke—I felt like a monkey in a zoo. All the facilities were for kids: the water fountains were two feet high, the chairs were three to four size; the toilets and sinks were for people who are four feet tall. The meditation hall was a huge, miserably ventilated gymnasium. It was stifling hot; some of the people in the back rows where I was sitting passed out. Every day we heard the same sounds, of teenage residents of the neighborhood squealing their automobile tires. One day later in the course, on day six or seven when people were getting lighter, during a pause when the hall was quiet, we could distinctly hear someone jump into his car, slam the door, screech out of the driveway, brake suddenly, then crash into a trash can, which bounced down the street. The room erupted in a chorus of laughter.

There have only been two times in my sitting career of 11 years when I have felt the need to go to the teacher for guidance. One was on this course. I was experiencing intense rage. I was boiling with anger; I was murdering people in my mind. I didn't know what to do about it—I thought meditation was supposed to make you peaceful. I went to see Goenkaji. He was sitting in a beach chair, with his legs crossed. It pleased me to see him so casual. He listened and laughed and said, "Yes, yes, yes. This shows that the technique is working perfectly. You'll probably have some violent dreams." He was right. I did have violent dreams, and as a result of the course, that particular *saṅkhāra* of acute anger passed. I've had other problems, but I've never had anything like that happen again. I cleaned out a lot although I didn't realize it at the time. A big chunk of emotional trauma just stopped happening. I found the course in retrospect to be very healing.

Some friends of mine flew from the west coast to Montreal to sit Goenkaji's first course.

Montreal and this teacher from India seemed remote to me. When my friends returned, one of them said, "Goenka is a businessman. When I had an interview with him, he got straight to the point, and didn't let me dawdle in long-winded philosophizing. Since I'm a businessman too, that appealed to me." Another friend said, "It was one of the most significant steps I have taken. I think you should try it." Someone else warned, "The discipline was really rigorous." This scared me, and I had reservations about attending the course in California the following year. But I went, and happily completed the course. Rather than being the barrier I had feared, the strong discipline was an enormous help. It helped enable me to meditate deeply. I've been sitting every day since that retreat. It is miraculous to think back to those first western gypsy camps a decade ago, to reflect on how quickly and widely the Dhamma has spread since then.

(International edition—September 1989)

The Floodgates of Dhamma Open

S. N. Goenka

Sayagyi U Ba Khin, my revered Teacher, strongly believed that 2500 years after the Buddha's *mahāparinibbāna* (final passing away of Enlightened Ones), the second *Buddha-sāsana* (cycle of teaching) will start again in the land of its origin, and from there spread throughout the world for the boundless benefit of humankind.

Dhamma will again arise with the practice of Vipassana. For millennia, Vipassana was lost to India. But it was preserved in its pristine purity in Myanmar (Burma).

Close to the end of this 2500-year period, the historical Sixth Council was held from 1954 to 1956 in Yangon (Rangoon). It was during this time—from 1st to 11th September, 1955—that I got my Dhamma birth. I sat my first Vipassana course.

After benefiting me immeasurably for 14 years, Vipassana returned to India on 22 June, 1969, with the blessings of my Teacher. An interval of about 2,000 years had passed. In spite of all the self-doubts about my ability, Dhamma started to take root in India.

I am merely a medium. Dhamma is doing its own work. "The clock of Vipassana has struck," Sayagyi often said. "At this time, many people endowed with abundant *pāramitā* have been born in India and in the other countries of the world. The ticking of this Vipassana clock will attract these people towards Dhamma".

So it happened. Innumerable people from different countries, religions, beliefs started participating in courses. So too did leaders of various religions. All of them accepted this technique as their own; none of them felt that it was alien.

These initial Vipassana courses were taught only in Hindi since the majority of courses were held in North India. After a few months, a few westerners also started participating in these courses.

After giving the Dhamma talk in Hindi, I used to give them a five or ten-minute discourse summary and instructions. These students were very hard working and this brief guidance was enough for them to achieve surprisingly good results.

Gradually, words of praise of Vipassana spread amongst western travellers. A year later, a group of tourists staying at Dalhousie requested me to come there and conduct a course exclusively for them.

It was difficult for me. The entire course would have to be conducted in English. To talk a few English sentences of guidance and to clear their doubts would have been simple. But to give an hour-long discourse fluently in English, or to give long, inspirational instructions throughout the day, as I did in Hindi, was impossible for me.

In Rangoon, I used to read out a written speech whenever I had to give a talk in English as President of Chamber of Commerce and Industry, or at any important public function. I neither had the experience nor the ability to give a talk in English without reading from a text.

And a talk on meditation, in which I have to give English equivalents of technical terms of Indian spiritual traditions, was even more difficult for me.

So I expressed my inability to conduct a course in English and advised them to keep joining courses conducted in Hindi in small numbers. They argued that whereas Hindi-speaking students benefited greatly from the inspiring discourses and instructions, the foreign students were deprived of this benefit. Besides, they were convinced I knew enough English to conduct the course.

When I still refused, they contacted Sayagyi U Ba Khin and complained to him about me. "Sir, outside Burma, only one of your representatives is teaching this technique and he is not accepting our request", they told him. "Where can we go to learn this technique?".

Besides, in those days, one could not get a visa to Burma for more than three days. So they pleaded with Sayagyi that he should order me to conduct courses in English.

I was in Bombay, then. My revered Teacher telephoned me and ordered that I should go to Dalhousie to conduct that course. He told me with loving firmness : "You must go. Whatever English you know will be enough. You will be successful. Dhamma will help. All my *mettā* is with you." After getting such a powerful reassurance I went to Dalhousie .

I had nothing against going to Dalhousie. In fact, I had reasons to look forward to the trip. This would be my first course in the lap of the Himalayas. Sayagyi used to say : "Who knows how long in how many lives we have meditated in the serene caves of the Himalayas." That is why on reaching there, my mind was filled with rapture. My self-doubts began to melt.

The course started. For the first two days, while sitting on the Dhamma seat I experienced an inexplicable feeling of suffocation. As a result, I was unable to speak for more than 15 minutes the first evening.

On the second evening, I had to struggle to

speak for about 25 minutes. I felt suffocated again. Although, I found no cause for it in the surface layers of my mind, I felt that maybe the inferiority complex of having trouble speaking English was creating obstacles at the deepest level.

But the actual cause turned out to be something else. This was a small course with eleven students. It was conducted in a little bungalow called Shanti Kutir. The group sittings and discourses were held in a small room. The student who had invited me for the course lived in the adjacent room.

On the third day, I felt strong, impure, anti-Dhamma vibrations flowing from that room and polluting the adjacent meditation room.

With the pure vibrations of the Himalayas on the one hand and the powerful *mettā* of my revered Teacher on the other hand, I could not understand what could cause these anti-Dhamma vibrations.

That afternoon, when I went to that room to check the student, I was startled to see a human skull on his table. Nearby was a blood-stained kukri, [curved knife used by Gurkhas].

The student explained he was the disciple of some local tantric mystical cult. Only three nights ago he had gone to the cremation ground, and had made an animal sacrifice with this kukri as part of a tantric ritual. His guru had told him that his meditation would be very successful if he kept the skull and kukri close to him.

Now I understood the cause of the suffocating, negative vibrations pervading the meditation room. Only after much persuasion by me did he throw that kukri and skull in some cavern faraway. And only then was the anti-Dhamma force eliminated from Shanti Kutir.

That afternoon, I meditated on the Dhamma seat for a long time. The time for the evening discourse approached. I saw that the entire atmosphere, washed by the purifying waves of the breeze from the Himalayas, had become even purer with the *mettā*-filled Dhamma vibrations from my revered Teacher.

Just a few moments before the start of the discourse, Dhamma vibrations flooded my being through the top of the head . I began the discourse and I found I spoke English as fluently as I speak Hindi. I spoke for an entire hour.

After the five-minute break, I gave long instructions with the same fluency. I could see that all meditators—male and female—were absorbed in deep meditation. At 9:00 p. m., when the day ended, their faces were radiant. I was wonderstruck.

It was Sayagyi's *mettā* that gave me the Dhamma strength to turn what seemed impossible to possible. The first-ever Vipassana course in English became successful. What Dhamma desired happened.

After this, all courses were bilingual. Daily, I gave Hindi discourses in the morning and English discourses in the evening. Instructions too were bilingual.

More courses and courses with more students were conducted. The number of foreign students progressively increased. Courses in places like Bodhgaya, Kushinagar, Varanasi and Rajagir had almost only foreign students. Word spread to many Western countries. Groups of foreigners came to learn Vipassana. With courses often running full, many had to wait for the next course.

In a few years, thousands from about 80 countries came for Vipassana courses. Students came from neighbouring Śri Laṅka and Thailand. The time had come for the prophecy and Dhamma wish of Sayagyi to come true.

Vipassana will spread throughout the world. Perhaps that is why it became possible to conduct courses in English. Without this, Vipassana would not have spread among the people of foreign countries.

I felt contented. The Vipassana flood gates had opened and the infinitely beneficial Ganges of Dhamma also flowed to students outside India, to the world.

(Dhamma Giri edition—May 1997)

Fruition of *Sacca Adhiṭṭhāna* – Part One

S. N. Goenka *(An autobiographical narrative)*

In the early days of the spread of Dhamma, year after year, I continued to give Vipassana courses throughout India. Time passed. During this period the meditation centres of *Dhamma Giri*, *Dhamma Thali* and *Dhamma Khetta* were established.

By now the number of western students had increased greatly and they were very persistent in inviting me to teach Dhamma in their own countries. But what could I do? I was helpless because my Burmese passport was not endorsed to travel outside India. Even my appeal to General Ne Win had proved fruitless. Therefore I again contacted my good friend U Thi Han in Yangon but the government policy on passport endorsements had not changed during these past years. He advised me to take refuge in Dhamma, and make a Dhamma *adhiṭṭhāna* (strong determination). This was the only way left to be successful.

Pulls to the West

I saw that Vipassana was establishing roots in India, the country of its origin. Now it was necessary for me to take steps to fulfil the other Dhamma desire of my Teacher Sayagyi U Ba Khin: to spread the Dhamma around the world. For this purpose, I felt I had to go to foreign countries to carry on the Dhamma mission.

This apart, a situation occurred that caused great confusion in Western countries and drew my attention to the urgency to go there to spread the Dhamma, in its pristine purity, as taught by my Teacher. Some of my American students had taken a few Vipassana courses with me in India, and before getting fully ripened in the technique, out of over-enthusiasm, they had established a Vipassana centre in the USA.

Due to their own weakness in Dhamma, these students had very wrongly stopped giving due importance to *sīla*, the foundation for Vipassana. Secondly, they had made teaching the Dhamma a profession, a means of livelihood, and this is totally against the tradition of pure Dhamma teaching. Thirdly, they had started mixing Vipassana with other techniques, and had thus polluted and diluted the purity of Dhamma. Seeing all this, a great sense of urgency arose in my mind to go to the West to teach Dhamma with the purity intact.

In spite of the fact that the Prime Minister of the Myanmar government was a good friend, he was unable to give me endorsements for the countries I wanted to visit. So the only alternative left for me was to forgo my Myanmar nationality, accept Indian nationality, and acquire an Indian passport. Thus I could travel to any country in the world to teach Dhamma.

I hesitated for an emotional reason. It is true that India is the land of my forefathers and is also the holy land of all the Buddhas. Therefore I greatly respected and honoured this country. But Myanmar is my motherland and definitely there is a special honour for Myanmar in my heart.

There is a famous Sanskrit saying, "*Jananī Janmabhūmiśca Svargādapi Garīyasī*," which says honouring the motherland is far superior to honouring even the celestial world. And mine was a special motherland where I was born not only once, but twice: first, I emerged from the womb of my mother and secondly, I came out of the womb of ignorance by practicing Vipassana.

So, on one hand there was this emotional pressure not to give up Myanmar citizenship, and on the other, there was the call of duty to fulfil the Dhamma desire of my Teacher.

A few days of this tug-of-war in my mind passed. Ultimately I decided to accept my friend U Thi Han's suggestion and I made a Dhamma *saṅkappo* with the *adhiṭṭhāna* of *sacca kiriyā* (a strong determination made with the base of a statement of truth) as follows:

Sacca Kiriyā

"Whatever Dhamma service that I have given till now is totally free from any selfish interest and it has only been given with the sole motive of helping others. I have acted thus to fulfill the Dhamma wishes of my revered Teacher. May my Teacher feel free from the debt of Dhamma received from India. May I feel free from the debt of Dhamma I received from my Teacher. It is only with this motive that I have given Dhamma service. These are words of truth and with the strength of these true words I leave the decision to Dhamma. If Dhamma wants me to carry on my Dhamma duties only in India then may I remain a Myanmar citizen, and if Dhamma wants me to travel the world for the spread of Vipassana, then at the completion of 10 years of my Dhamma service in India, may I receive Indian citizenship."

When the end of this 10 year period was nearing, I submitted my application for Indian citizenship. I did this with the determination that if Dhamma wanted me to go around the world as an Indian citizen may it so happen.

At that time, the thought arose that the geographical boundaries between countries were merely for political and business purposes. Dhamma cannot have geographical barriers. Definitely, I am not changing my nationality for any political, commercial or financial gain. Even if I adopt Indian citizenship I will continue the same Dhamma work around the world. My motherland Myanmar and my ancestral holy land of India will both feel honoured with the credit of spreading Dhamma. One country is where Dhamma originated, and the other is where Dhamma has been preserved in its purity. May both enjoy this honour.

"My only aim is to spread Dhamma for the good and benefit of suffering humanity around the world. My love and feeling of gratitude and honour for my motherland will not diminish even a little by changing my nationality for this good cause."

An Obstacle Arises

After submitting my application to the Indian government, I was quite confident I would soon obtain the citizenship. But my experience was that whenever an important step was taken on the path of spreading Dhamma, an unexpected obstacle always raised its head. But the obstacle could not stand for long. The obstacle this time: I was informed, later, that my application was stuck in the Intelligence Department of the government of India.

I knew very well that some years before, the Intelligence Department had started making serious enquiries about myself and my activities. The Indian members of our family, specially two of my brothers and one nephew, were intensely involved in the Ananda Marga.

This organization was looked upon very suspiciously by the government of India as its activities were designed to gain political power by violent means. During the days of Emergency both of these brothers were put behind bars for a number of days. So it was natural that the government was suspicious that perhaps I too was indirectly working for Ananda Marga, while conducting the courses under the name of Vipassana.

I knew that the Intelligence Department of India had made exhaustive enquiries about my activities and a few officials had also interviewed me on this subject.

Some of them had even attended a 10-day course in disguise. One such high official had revealed his identity at the completion of the course he had attended. He had told me that he was highly impressed by my selfless service and had seen for himself how this non-sectarian technique was spreading for the good of others. He also revealed to me that a few junior officials had made enquiries and had reported that my work was free from any ulterior motive. Now he said he personally had been able to observe this and he was fully convinced that it was faultless and had no connection with the Ananda Marga movement.

But it was only at the time of my application for citizenship that I came to know that my file had not yet been closed in the Intelligence Office. Perhaps the top people in the Intelligence Department wanted to keep further watch on my activities for sometime. Or because, although I had totally retired from all commercial activities, my sons were doing business jointly with the members of the family who were followers of Ananda Marga. Maybe this was why they wanted to keep a watch on my activities for a few more years.

But in spite of this gloomy situation, I was fully convinced that because of the *adhiṭṭhāna* I had made, I surely would attain Indian citizenship and an Indian passport as soon as the period of 10 years service was completed. I could then freely go to foreign countries to teach Dhamma.

With this strong confidence I had given consent to my students in the West to arrange 10-day Vipassana courses in Gaillon, France, from the 1st to the 11th of July, in Plage, France, from the 14th to the 24th of July, in Montreal, Canada from the 26th of July to the 6th of August, and then in Godalming, England from the 9th to the 20th of August, and from the 21st of August to the 1st of September. Thus I had committed myself to five Vipassana courses in the West and sites had been reserved for them.

The biggest problem was the first course in Gaillon, France, where the meditators had booked a very costly youth hostel, and had paid the whole rent in advance. Most of those who had registered to join the course were from the higher strata of society. One of them, from Switzerland, was a diplomat. All of them had arranged their holiday to cover the course dates. If the course could not be given on schedule the organizers would have to face great difficulties.

What could be done? The anti-Dhamma forces had erected barriers to prevent the spread of Dhamma through the world—the Myanmar government was not able to give endorsements in my passport due to their strict policies, and the Indian government was not giving me citizenship. My application was stuck in Delhi. There seemed to be no hope. The only confidence I had was from the Dhamma *adhiṭṭhāna* that I had taken with the base of *sacca kiriyā*. I had great confidence that the forces of Dhamma would ultimately help.

(To be concluded. Dhamma Giri edition—August 1997)

Fruition of *Sacca Adhiṭṭhāna* – Part Two

***by S. N. Goenka** (An autobiographical narrative)*

This is the second and concluding part of this article. The first part was published in the Vipassana Newsletter dated August 1997.

Words of Dhamma

Dhammo have rakkhati dhammacāriṃ,
dhammo suciṇṇo sukhamāvahāti.
Esānisaṃso dhamme suciṇṇo,
na duggatiṃ gacchati dhammacāri.

Dhamma protects the person who lives a righteous life. When practiced in the right way, Dhamma is beneficial and brings happiness. Such a person is never born in a lower plane.

—Theragatha 303, Dhammikatthetagatha

What could be done? The anti-Dhamma forces had erected barriers to prevent the spread of Dhamma throughout the world—the Myanmar government was not able to give endorsements in my passport due to their strict policies, and the Indian government was not giving me citizenship. My application was stuck in Delhi. There seemed to be no hope. The only confidence I had was from the Dhamma *adhiṭṭhāna* that I had taken with the base of *sacca kiriyā*. I had great confidence that the forces of Dhamma would ultimately help.

The 1st of July—the day the first course was due to start in France—came nearer and nearer. Days passed. Just one week to go. There seemed to be no light at the end of this dark tunnel.

There was no possibility of getting Indian citizenship in time, and even if I did, it would be impossible to get a passport in time. There are many lengthy formalities to get a passport. It seemed I would have to cancel that first course in France, though I knew that it would be a great disappointment to my students, and they would also have to bear great financial losses. The worst part was that they would lose confidence in me. I had been telling them, "Believe me, the course will be held on schedule." But now, what could be done? In this situation, time was melting away.

My Dhamma *adhiṭṭhāna* had been: "When I finish 10 years of Dhamma service in India, may I get the opportunity to teach Dhamma beyond India." On the 22nd June, 1979, these 10 years were completed.

The 23rd, 24th, 25th, and 26th also passed away. A feeling of helplessness increased. Perhaps the Dhamma did not want to use me as a medium for the spread of the work around the world. "Well, leave it to Dhamma. Let it happen as Dhamma desires. If Dhamma wants me to limit my service to India, may it be so."

In this frame of mind, on the next day, the 27th of June, I got a call. It was a happy shock. A government official phoned to say that the citizenship papers for my wife, Mrs. Ilaichi Goenka, and myself, were ready. We were asked to go to the Metropolitan Magistrate in the Esplanade Court of Bombay, and receive our citizenship certificates. The next day we both went there and easily received our certificates.

Hurdles Safely Crossed

A great hurdle for the spread of Dhamma around the world was now crossed. But there was still the problem of getting our passports, and in such a short time of just two days this was an impossibility. We could not reach France in time for the first course.

Until now, we could not even apply for a passport. Now even if everything went rapidly, the passport would still take three to four weeks to be ready. But my mind was still not prepared to cancel the courses in France. I had left everything to Dhamma. "Let us see what Dhamma desires, and how Dhamma plans it to happen."

As we came out of the Magistrate's Office with our citizenship certificates we saw our travel agent standing there. He had passport application forms in his hands, and he asked us to fill them out, which we did then and there. We were of course happy to have our citizenship, but there was still a doubt whether the courses in France could be given. With this uncertainty we returned home to another pleasant shock. The travel agent phoned and said that because of instructions from above, the passports would be issued the very next day.

The 28th of June. The passports were in our hands. Now hope of conducting both the French courses increased. But yet, we needed a visa. By the time we received our passports, the French embassy was closed.

The 29th of June. Only one day left now. Even if we could get the French visa, we still needed visas for U.K. and Canada. And then there are so many other formalities to go through for an Indian citizen before leaving the country. All in one day? But look how Dhamma works. All the closed doors were miraculously opened.

Before the 29th of June was over, we had our French visas and had completed all the formalities required to leave the country. And our travel agent said that we may not need visas for the U.K. and Canada, as we were now citizens of a commonwealth country. Even if they were required they could be obtained from the respective embassies in Paris.

It was thus we could leave Bombay by a flight on the night of the 29th of June. On the 30th, we reached Paris. From there, we went by car to Gaillon and the course started on the 1st of July, just as scheduled.

After that, one after the other all the courses were conducted very successfully. With a feeling of great satisfaction and gratitude to Dhamma we returned home.

My confidence in Dhamma was strengthened by these wonderful events, and also my belief that I am only a medium—it is only Dhamma that is working. Dhamma has to choose some medium to get the work done.

How Dhamma Works

The mystery of receiving our clearance to travel in time became clear as we learned that my son Murari and his wife Vatsala had discussed my difficult situation with Mr. Radhe Shyam Murarka, who is the maternal uncle of Mr. Hari Prasad, Vatsala's father.

Mr. Murarka promised Murari and Vatsala that he would try to help me. I knew that Mr. Murarka was an important person in the Congress Party. He had been a member of parliament for a number of years and was always chosen to lead the Public Accounts Committee because of his expertise on the subject. He was a close friend of Shri Morarji Desai who was then the Prime Minister of India.

But in spite of all this, knowing fully well how slow the government machinery works, I was not confident that he could do much to help us in this matter. However, he took all the details of our case and went immediately to Delhi and met the Prime Minister, Shri Morarji Desai.

Shri Morarji Bhai called for our file from the Home Ministry, and saw that the Central Intelligence Department note on it, that they wanted to make further enquiries before granting me citizenship. Morarji Bhai said that under such circumstances, he was helpless.

Hearing this Mr. Murarka told him, "What further information will your Intelligence Department gain about this person? Do you think that we gave our daughter to his family without making any enquiries?" Hearing this the Prime Minister was dumbfounded. He immediately decided in favour of my application, and also gave instructions that all the formalities for my foreign travel should be completed in time.

It is so wonderful how Dhamma works, how Dhamma uses different people as mediums for different purposes.

Dhamma arose in the minds of my daughter-in-law, Vatsala, and my son Murari, and they went and met Murarkaji. Murarkaji got some Dhamma inspiration and went to meet the Prime Minister Morarji Bhai. Some Dhamma wisdom arose in Morarji Bhai and thus my Dhamma *adhiṭṭhāna* could be fulfilled.

These three Muraris, together, completed this Dhamma work which has proved so beneficial to people around the world. The Ganges of the pure Dhamma started flowing throughout the world as Vipassana.

So many thousands began experiencing the benefit of Dhamma. My son, Murari, and my daughter-in-law Vatsala had already learnt Vipassana, but I very much wanted Mr. Murarka and Shri Morarji Bhai to also take this *dhammadāna* for their liberation from the cycle of birth and death. But now both of them are no more.

The best that I can do is to send my deep *mettā* to them. May they both share all the merits that I acquire by spreading Dhamma in the world. May they both be happy, may they both be peaceful, may they both be liberated.

(Dhamma Giri edition—September 1997)

Seventy Years Have Been Completed

S. N. Goenka

Words of Dhamma

Nābhinandāmi maraṇaṃ,
nābhinandāmi jīvitaṃ.
Nikkhipissaṃ imaṃ kāyaṃ,
sampajāno paṭissato.

—Theragāthā, Sāriputtathera 54

I do not long for death nor do I desire to be alive. (When the time comes) I shall leave this body with mindfulness and insight into its impermanent nature at the level of sensation.

My life has seen 70 autumns. And who knows how many more are left? How can the ones that are left be best used? May this awareness be maintained.

On this occasion some beneficial words of the Buddha come to mind. The incident is of Sāvatthi, in Anāthapiṇḍika's Jetavanārama. It is night-time. A devaputta has come to meet the Buddha. He expresses his thoughts to the Buddha in the form of a gāthā of four lines:

Accenti kālā, tarayanti rattiyo
Time is passing, nights are passing.

Vayoguṇā anupubbaṃ jahanti
Life is gradually coming to an end.

Etaṃ bhayaṃ maraṇe pekkhamāno
Observing the fear of (approaching) death

Puññāni kayirātha sukhāvahāni
Perform meritorious deeds that yield pleasant fruits.

Someone has rightly said,

"Morning comes, evening comes,
Thus the end of life comes."

Do not let this priceless human life end in vain. Even if it is only out of fear of the approaching death, be engaged in meritorious deeds that yield pleasant fruit. If we perform unwholesome deeds, they will result in suffering for us. If we perform wholesome deeds, they will result in happiness for us. This is the unbreakable law of nature. Therefore it is better to do wholesome deeds rather than unwholesome deeds in order to avoid suffering and to enjoy happiness.

We do not know how long we have been crushed under the ever changing wheel of existence of worldly happiness and suffering, and for how long this wheel of worldly happiness and suffering will continue in the future. The Buddha discovered a simple and direct path to full liberation from this wheel of existence. He made it easily accessible to all.

He taught the liberation-endowing technique of Vipassana to the people, by the practice of which they could be liberated from the wheel of existence and attain the eternal, unchanging *nibbānaṃ paramaṃ sukhaṃ* meaning the ultimate happiness, the ultimate peace of *nibbāna*, which is much superior to worldly pleasures. But this is possible only after the habit of heedlessly running after the enjoyment of worldly sensual pleasures is broken. And this is just what Vipassana enables us to do. It breaks the habit pattern of multiplication of the *saṅkhārās* of craving and aversion which lie in the depth of the subconscious mind. It digs out the *saṅkhārās* of craving for pleasure and aversion towards suffering. It eradicates the longstanding habit of blind reaction. As long as craving for worldly pleasures remains, aversion will continue to arise towards worldly suffering and because of these two, the wheel of existence will continue to roll. Only when the wheel of existence breaks, can ultimate peace, which is supramundane, beyond the worlds, beyond the round of existence, beyond the field of senses, be attained. It was with this purpose that the Buddha taught the beneficial technique of Vipassana.

Hinting at this, upon hearing the above gāthā of four lines, the Buddha, changing its fourth line, said—

Lokāmisaṃ pajahe santipekkho
One who hopes for the ultimate peace should give up the desire for worldly happiness.

Only by the intensive practice of Vipassana can one eradicate this worldly desire. While practising Vipassana, a meditator should maintain awareness of one's impending death, but there should not be a trace of fear of death. Whenever death comes, one should be constantly prepared for it with a tranquil mind.

On the occasion of every birthday, a Vipassana meditator should certainly look back at the past. He should make a firm resolution that he will not repeat the mistakes he has commited in the past and that he will continue to perform whatever wholesome deeds he has done until now for the rest of his life. The most important wholesome deed of all is the practice of the liberating technique of Vipassana. This should not be neglected; it should be diligently practised. Do not postpone today's practice till tomorrow. Let these words of the Buddha constantly echo in your ears like a warning:

Ajjeva kiccamātappaṃ
Perform the work of meditation today itself. (Do not postpone it till tomorrow.)

Kojaññā maraṇaṃ suve
Who knows, death may come tomorrow.

It is not necessary to invite death, but when it comes, there is no need to be afraid of it. Let us be prepared for it every moment.

From time to time we should practise *Maraṇānussati* (contemplation about death). I have seen from my own experience that this is very beneficial. Sometimes while doing this, one should examine one's own mind, "If I die tomorrow morning, what will be the state of the last moment of this life? Will any longing remain, even though this desire may be to complete some Dhamma mission? Whenever the *saṅkhāra* of some excessive emotion arises in the mind, we should immediately practise *Maraṇānussati* and understand that, "If I die in the very next moment, what fearful direction will this excessive emotion give to this stream of becoming?" As soon as this awareness arises, it becomes easy for one to be liberated from this excessive emotion.

There is one more advantage of *Maraṇānussati* from time to time. The mind thinks, "Who knows how many lives I have been rolling in the cycle of existence? This time, as a result of some wholesome deed, I have obtained the invaluable life of a human being. I have come in contact with pure Dhamma. I have developed faith in pure Dhamma, which is free from meaningless rituals and philosophies as well as from sectarian barriers. What benefit have I derived from this?" When one makes an assessment of this, whatever shortcomings remain, one develops enthusiasm to correct them. Whether death will come tomorrow morning or after a 100 autumns, I do not know. But no matter how many days I have to live, I will use them to perfect my *pāramitā* with a contented mind and make my human life meaningful. Whatever results come, let them come; whenever they come, let them come then. I leave that to Dhamma. On my part, let me continue to keep making the best use of the remaining time of this important life to the best of my ability.

For this purpose, let these inspiring words of the Buddha be with us:

Uttiṭṭhe nappamajjeyya dhammaṃ sucaritaṃ care.
Arise! Live the Dhamma life with diligence.

May I keep living the life of Dhamma. The results will naturally be beneficial.

(Dhamma Giri edition—February 1998)

Forty Years of *Dhammadāna*

Forty years of *dhammadāna* have been completed. I recall a 45-year old man who left his beloved motherland, Myanmar, and came to India, the land of the Enlightened One. My Teacher, Sayagyi U Ba Khin, emphasized repeatedly that many centuries ago, India has gifted the invaluable gem of Dhamma to Myanmar. Myanmar is greatly indebted to India. It has preserved this noble teaching in its pristine purity. Unfortunately India has totally lost it. Now Myanmar has to repay this invaluable debt.

Sayagyi U Ba Khin wanted to come to India to revive the Vipassana technique that was lost in this country. However, he was unable to do so. Therefore, in the last week of June, in 1969, he appointed me as a teacher of this ancient tradition and gave me the responsibility of repaying this debt. I was taken aback. Though he had taught me the practice of Vipassana meditation as well as the Buddha's words and trained me to conduct Vipassana courses, I felt I was totally incompetent to fulfil this heavy responsibility.

Seeing my apprehension, Sayagyi exhorted me, "Why are you troubled? You are not going alone; I am accompanying you in the form of Dhamma. Many people with *pāramī* have taken birth in India and they will be attracted to you; they will be attracted to Dhamma. Dhamma will work on its own. 2500 years of the Buddha Sāsana have been completed. The time has ripened for the debt has to be paid back. Vipassana will be revived in India and this will be accomplished through you. So go without any anxiety."

I left for India two or three days later. However, I still felt anxious. Who would accept me as a Dhamma teacher? My appearance and attire were not that of a conventional spiritual teacher. I did not have saffron robes or long matted hair or fully shaven head or beard and moustache. I was an ordinary Burmese householder, who had brought the invaluable spiritual teaching from Myanmar. I was opposed to any pretence. I was disinclined to let go of my simple attire of the Burmese *loongyi* and *angyi* (over shirt). Who would accept me as a Dhamma teacher?

I arrived at my family home in Mumbai. None in my family had any inclination towards Vipassana. They were all following a different path that was incompatible with Vipassana. There was no hope of any support from them to organize a Vipassana course. How could the first course be organised? Where could it be organized? Who would organize it? Who would take part in the course? My mind became overwhelmed with disappointment, helplessness and sorrow.

It was the second or the third night in India. While I was sleeping, there was a sudden flash of light. As soon as my eyes opened, I thought, "Who is this 'I' who will organize a course? This is Dhamma's job. Dhamma will take care of itself."

Some friends and acquaintances came to visit me early the next morning. There was a discussion about conducting a Vipassana course. I asked, "Is a suitable place available to conduct a course? Even if it is available, who will organize the course and who will agree to sit for 10 days with me?"

On hearing this, one of the visitors, Dayanand Adukia said, "Do not worry. I shall arrange for the venue and I will manage the course". Hearing this, my close friend from Myanmar, Kantilal G. Shah said, "I will take part in the course and will also bring one or two of my friends."

Dhamma started working and the first course was organized. Dayanand Adukia managed the course and his son, Vijay Adukia, joined the course. Kantilal Shah and his friend, B. C. Shah, joined the course. And much to my pleasant surprise, my father and mother agreed to sit the course. A few other relatives also sat the course and the first course was successfully completed with 13 students. Dayanand Adukia managed the course very well. He and Kantilal Shah will always be remembered in the history of the revival of Vipassana in India.

As soon as the first course was completed, I went to Madras. I had a pleasant surprise there. My elder brother Bal Krishna and all his family members were deeply involved in a tradition opposed to Vipassana. Even then, out of affection for me, he organized many public talks and also organized a course. I felt blessed. Along with other family members, Shyamsundar, brother Chothmal's son, sat the course.

Some more courses were held in a guest-house in Mumbai. Then I went to northern India, where my friend and author, Shri

Yashpal Jain, arranged a course at a guest-house in Birla Mandir. Some more courses were organized in Northern India.

The 14th course was held in the Samanvaya Ashram at Bodhgaya in which were many bhikkhus and my old friend Anagarika Munindra. Delighted with his first experience of free flow of sensations, he wrote a letter to my Teacher who was in Rangoon.

Courses were held at different locations all over northern India and a few Western students took part in every course. I would explain to them separately, giving short discourses and instructions in English. They worked very seriously.

For the twentieth course, some Western students requested me to hold a course for them in English. I did not accept their request. I was teaching two or three Western students in the courses but felt that I did not have the ability to give discourses in English fluently. So I was not willing to conduct an entire course exclusively for foreigners. They complained to my revered Teacher at Rangoon. I received strict instructions from him that I should conduct a course for them. He said that Dhamma would take care of the barrier of language. I reluctantly went to Dalhousie to conduct a course. On the night of the first day, I gave a discourse for just 15 minutes, the second day for 30 minutes and from the third day onwards I gave an hour-long discourse, as fluently as the discourses in Hindi. I was surprised. This was due to the strength of Dhamma and the strong *mettā* of my beloved Teacher. The course was completed successfully.

After this course, in addition to Indian householders, bhikkhus and sanyasis, young men and women from abroad started participating in large numbers. I started conducting courses in Hindi and English. The number of Westerners in courses started growing. One among them was Daniel Goleman, who later became consultant to many American businessmen and industrialists. Joseph Goldstein and Sharon Salzberg also took part in some courses and later started teaching Vipassana in America.

The practice of *sīla, samādhi* and *paññā* started attracting others just as it has attracted me because it did not leave room for intellectual arguments and did not need acceptance of any sectarian belief. This pure scientific teaching started attracting everybody.

A large number of foreigners participated in some courses held at Dalhousie. An elderly Christian priest and two elderly nuns participated in one of these courses. They were happy that many hippies discontinued LSD and other intoxicants as well as sexual misconduct after practising Vipassana. But they wanted to find out whether I was converting their followers to Buddhism. After directly experiencing the benefits gained from the course, they were delighted. Mother Mary said, “Goenka, you are teaching Christianity in the name of Buddha.”

After this course, many Christian priests and nuns started participating in courses. Now, a course is held exclusively for them in Mumbai. More than 6,000 priests and nuns have benefited from Vipassana courses so far.

My friend, Shri Yashpal Jain and Vishnu Prabhakar attended one of the courses held at Dalhousie. Both of them were pleased with this teaching. Shri Yashpal Jain told Acaryashri Tulsiji, the Principal Teacher of Terapanth Saṅgha, about Vipassana and introduced me to him. Acaryashri Tulsiji was impressed and organized a course in Delhi for Acarya Munishri Nathmalji and other male and female disciples. All of them liked the purity of this teaching. As a result, he organized two courses in *Tulsi Adyatma Needam* of Ladnun, in which many of their male and female disciples participated and took benefit. After Acarya Tulsiji, the young Acarya Mahapragya (Munishri Nathmalji) became the Principal Teacher of Terapanth Saṅgha. He had already taken four courses in Vipassana. He made some modifications and started teaching it as *Preksha Dhyan*.

Sthanakvasi Sramansanghiya Chaturth Patdhar Acarya Dr. Shivmuniji and Munishri Amarendravijayji, Munishri Bhuvanchandraji, Munishri Parshwachandraji of Parshwachandragaccha Saṅgha had participated in many courses. However, there is no report of any of them making changes in the teaching of Vipassana. Along with Upadhyaya Amarmuniji, Sadhvishri Chandanaji, the manager of Virayatan, arranged a course at Rajgir and also at their second branch Naval Virayatan in Pune. Several other munis and sadhvis benefited from Vipassana and encouraged others to practise it.

Nirmalaji, Gandhiji's daughter-in-law, organized the 50th Vipassana course at Mahatma Gandhi Ashram, Wardha. Some of Gandhiji's followers participated in it. At the end of the course, I was taken to Vinoba Bhave's Ashram. He stated that he will accept Vipassana only if it benefits prison inmates. I accepted the challenge. However, due to the government's policy, a course could not be organized in the prison then.

Later, the first prison course was made possible by the efforts of Shri Ram Singhji, the Home Secretary of Rajasthan, who had participated in the 109th course. He relaxed the prison rules so that the courses could be conducted in the Central Jail of Jaipur. The beneficial results achieved in these courses paved the way for Vipassana courses in prisons all over the world. Kiran Bedi arranged several courses in Tihar Jail and a Vipassana centre was established there. Courses are being held in prisons of different countries. The Government of Myanmar has also allowed courses in prisons and centres have also been opened in two prisons there.

In India, in the initial seven to eight years, Vipassana courses were organized in guest-houses, schools, temples, educational institutions, vihāras (monasteries), churches, mosques, dargahs, etc. People attended these courses and followed all the course rules in spite of inconvenience. In 1976, Shri Sriram Taparia and Shri Ratilal Mehta organized the construction of Vipassana centres at Igatpuri and Hyderabad. After that, Vipassana centres were started all over the world.

During the first 10 years in India, 165 courses were conducted and 16,496 students participated in them. Munis, bhikkhus, sanyasis, priests, nuns; Hindus, Muslims, Jains, Sikhs, Christians, Jews, Parsis; Indians and foreigners; men and women; people of all races, and classes participated in the courses. They participated in courses conducted by an unknown person like me and presented me the wonderful opportunity to give Dhamma *dāna*, the gift of Dhamma. I am grateful to each one of them.

Some of those who participated in the courses learnt the technique partially and started teaching Vipassana after making some changes in it. I recall some who got distanced from me or started practicing some other form of meditation or discontinued practicing Vipassana. I am grateful to all of them because they spared their invaluable 10 days to attend the course. Many other students accepted Vipassana in its pure form and started spreading the light of Dhamma in India and abroad. I am deeply grateful to them too.

Till now, 147 Vipassana centres have been opened in India and abroad. Nearly 2,000 trained teachers are holding regular courses as well as courses for children in English, Hindi and other languages all over the world. The teaching in my words has been translated into 58 languages and courses are held in all those languages. I am grateful to all these teachers, course organizers and Dhamma servers. Today, nearly 80,000 people are benefitting every year from about 1600 courses held all over India and abroad. The numbers are increasing every year. It is thanks to them that the Global Vipassana Pagoda has come into existence. Shri Subhash Chandra and his family have donated the land and meditators and others have worked together to construct the Pagoda.

The Enlightened One said, "*Sabbadānaṃ dhamma dānaṃ jināti*—the gift of Dhamma exceeds all gifts." *(Dhammapada 354, Taṇhāvaggo)*

I brought this invaluable gem to India. However, if no one had accepted this Dhamma dana from me, if they hadn't spared ten days of their life to learn this technique from me, how could I have earned this supreme merit? Therefore, I am grateful to each and every one of them.

In addition, they proved right this ancient belief: On completion of 2500 years of the Buddha Sāsana, the pure Dhamma will return to the India, the land of its origin; the people here will accept it and then it will spread all around the world.

Therefore, I feel indebted towards them and I wish to meet all of them again so that I can voice my deep gratitude to them. I wish that any meditator who knows anyone who has done any Vipassana course with me in the first ten years (1969 to 1979), invite him or her to the Gratitude Gathering on Sunday, 17 January, 2010 at Global Vipassana Pagoda, Gorai (Borivali), Mumbai.

(Dhamma Giri edition—August 2009)

SECTION THREE

IN THE FOOTSTEPS OF THE BUDDHA

In the Footsteps of the Buddha—Introduction

Goenkaji repeatedly emphasises the need for respect and devotion with proper understanding towards the Buddha and Vipassana teachers from the past. This should not be done through rites or rituals or in the belief that some external force will do something for us. As meditators, we have to liberate ourselves from various kinds of suffering. But the Buddha and all who are deeply established in Dhamma show the way. How else would we have received such a gem in our lives? For this we should be grateful, drawing inspiration from their qualities and example and walking the same path ourselves.

In 2002 Goenkaji was invited to address an international conference arranged to mark Vesākha, the day of Gotama the Buddha's birth, enlightenment and passing away. The talk, reprinted here in full, draws on his personal experience of Vipassana as someone originally from another spiritual tradition who became convinced of the teaching's universal, rational, pragmatic and scientific nature. He encourages all who value the Buddha's teaching to put aside sectarian differences and unite to establish peace and harmony where ignorant hatred and extremism frequently prevail.

Goenkaji and his wife Mataji have led pilgrimage visits for old students on a number of occasions to sacred sites in India and Burma. The articles included here often describe these events through the eyes of pilgrimage participants. The significance of pilgrimage here goes far beyond a spiritual sight-seeing trip. Together and individually one has the chance to sit at locations where a fully enlightened person, the Buddha himself, and other highly developed Dhamma teachers have meditated. For this reason the pilgrimage experience is frequently profound, leading to a deepening of one's understanding and practice.

The Meditation Now tour of North America and Europe in 2002 was Goenkaji and Mataji's most recent visit to Western countries. Despite encroaching age and personal discomfort, the Principal Teachers undertook an extensive trip giving introductory talks in public halls and to the media and conducting short courses for old students. The final article in this section captures a flavour of this remarkable tour. A full account can be found in "The Caravan of Dhamma" (VRI publications 2004). DVDs of some talks given during the tour are available through ***www.vridhamma.org*** and an extensive list of podcast talks is also available through ***www.pariyatti.org***

Buddha: The Super-Scientist of Peace–Part One

S. N. Goenka

This address by S. N. Goenka was delivered at the United Nations on the occasion of Vesākha, the full moon day of May, which is celebrated each year as the day marking the birth, the enlightenment and the passing away of Gotama the Buddha. In 2002, Goenkaji was touring North America during the month of Vesākha, teaching Dhamma and giving public addresses in 35 cities over a period of nearly four months.

Venerable monks and peace-loving friends:

I thank the United Nations and the organizers of this magnificent Vesākha celebration, especially the Myanmar and Śri Laṅkan delegations, for the opportunity offered to me to address this distinguished gathering.

One feels so sorry when one looks at what is happening in the world. Man has become the enemy of man. There is no personal enmity; people are being killed only because they belong to a particular sect or community, a particular ethnic group or country. Such is the level of cruelty that a person kills other human beings even if they are innocent, even if they are helpless women and children. Modern technology makes this tragic violence terrifyingly devastating—perhaps worse than ever before in human history. Therefore, more than ever before, a basic change is needed today to protect humanity from these inhuman, heinous crimes arising out of negative emotions.

The world is afflicted with the malady of hatred, anxiety and fear. It needs a remedy from an extraordinary physician. The Buddha was such an extraordinary physician, a great physician of peace and happiness. His teaching of peace and harmony is as relevant today as it was 26 centuries back, when he set in motion the Wheel of Dhamma, the Wheel of Peace. Indeed, it is much more relevant today. We have gathered here this afternoon to honor the teaching of this outstanding person in human history. Let us see how his teaching eliminates the negative emotions that are at the root of cruel violence, and how these can be changed to positive compassion. Most of the time, blind belief and strong attachment to one's views cause negativity, which in turn produces such atrocities.

I came in contact with the Buddha's teaching when I took my first Vipassana course in my motherland of Myanmar. I remember that before the course started, my Teacher gave me a booklet to read. It began with a quotation from a discourse of the Buddha to the Kālāmas.

The Buddha Advises:

Don't accept something:
because you have heard it many times;
because it has been believed traditionally for generations;
because it is believed by a large number of people;
because it is in accordance with your scriptures;
because it seems logical;
because it is in line with your own beliefs;
because it is proclaimed by your teacher, who has an attractive personality and for whom you have great respect.
Accept it only after you have realized it yourself at the experiential level and have found it to be wholesome and beneficial to one and all. Then, not only accept it but also live up to it.

This message was like a magnetic pull. I was born and brought up in a different tradition, where I was taught to accept the words of the scriptures and the teacher without asking any questions. At the age of 31, these were the very first words of the Buddha that I came across. I was thrilled to read them.

This was perhaps the first charter of freedom of thought in human history. It became clear to me that there is no scope for blind belief or blind faith in the teaching of the Enlightened One. I decided to give it a fair trial with an open mind, accepting the truth as I experienced it. As I walked on the path, the experience of each day convinced me that the path is rational, pragmatic and scientific. There is no need for any blind acceptance. There were no doubts, as I was told to accept a truth only after I had experienced it. I also found that every step on the path is universal and non-sectarian. This gave me great confidence.

At the end of the 10-day course, I found the teaching to be completely results-oriented. It proved so beneficial to me physically, mentally and spiritually. Therefore, at the end of the first course I accepted it wholeheartedly and thereafter, I continued to walk on the path as taught by the Enlightened One.

After about 15 years, I was authorized by my Teacher to teach Vipassana courses in India and throughout the world. Hundreds of thousands of people from different countries, belonging to different sects and various traditions, have achieved the same good results. The teaching attracts people from all walks of life because they find that it is totally non-sectarian and results-oriented.

The Teaching: The Dhamma

The qualities of the path given by the Buddha are:

Svākkhāto—It is simple and well-defined so that anyone can practice it without any confusion in the mind.

Sandiṭṭhiko—Every step is based on the reality of this moment. There is no imagination, no speculation, no auto-suggestion or outer suggestion.

Akāliko—Every step gives wholesome results here and now in this very life. No effort on the path goes waste.

Ehi-passiko—The teaching invites you to come and see for yourself, to experience the truth yourself.

Opaneyyiko—The path is straight; every step

on it takes one nearer and nearer to the final goal of liberation from all misery.

Paccattaṃ veditabbo viññūhīti—It is for every sensible and rational person from every community to experience the truth within oneself by oneself.

As one continues to walk on the path and goes through the words of the Buddha, it becomes clearer and clearer that the teaching is not intended to convert people from one organized religion to another. The teaching itself is not an organized religion. It can be practiced by one and all.

When one reads the words of the Buddha and the commentaries and sub-commentaries, one is surprised to find that throughout the literature the words "Buddhism" and "Buddhist" are conspicuously missing. The Buddha never used these words. His followers also did not use these words for a number of centuries. He called his teaching the Dhamma—that means the Law, the Truth. He called his followers Dhammi, Dhammaṭṭho, Dhammiko, Dhammacāri, Dhammavihāri, and so on. In Indian languages, the word for "Buddhism" or "Buddhist" is Bauddha—a word without equivalent in the vast Pāli literature.

If the word "Buddhism" is used for the Buddha's teaching, it becomes limited to a particular community, but Dhamma is limitless—*appamāṇo dhammo*. It is not for one particular community or religion. It is for all. We all know that the word "Buddhism" has now gained currency and is convenient to use. Many who use the word also understand that they are using it for the universal Dhamma or Dharma.

The Noble Eightfold Path

Let us understand what is the Buddha's teaching. It is the Noble Eightfold Path. The path is noble in the sense that anyone who walks on this path diligently becomes a noble person, a saintly person, a pure-hearted person.

The Noble Eightfold Path is divided into three divisions.

1. The first is *sīla*—morality, which is summed up as:
   Sabba papassa akaraṇaṃ
   Abstain from all sinful actions—that is, all unwholesome actions, physical or vocal, which hurt other beings and disturb their peace and harmony.

2. The second part of the Path is *samādhi*—one-pointed concentration of wholesome mind, summed up as:
   Kusalassa upasampadā
   Perform wholesome actions with concentrated, wholesome mind.

3. The third part is *paññā*—wisdom or insight, summed up as:
   Sacittapariyodapanaṃ
   Purify the totality of mind by developing insight.

These three trainings are the teaching of all the Buddhas of the past and will be the teaching of all the Buddhas of the future. That is why it is said,

Etaṃ Buddhāna sāsanaṃ.
This is the teaching of all the Buddhas.

(To be concluded. Dhamma Giri edition—March 2003)

Buddha: The Super-Scientist of Peace–Part Two

S. N. Goenka

(The following address was delivered at the United Nations on Vesākha, the full moon day of May, which is celebrated each year as the day marking the birth, the enlightenment and the passing away of Gotama the Buddha. The first part was published in the March 2003 issue of the Vipassana Newsletter. This is the concluding part of the address.)

The Practical Teaching of the Buddha

To live the life of morality is the teaching of every religion. It is the quintessence, the inner core of every spiritual teaching. However, the Buddha was not interested in merely giving sermons to live a moral life. He taught us to take the next important step of *samādhi*—mastery over the mind. For this one needs an object of concentration. There are many objects by which one can train the mind. The Buddha himself gave many objects, and of these, one of the most popular was one's own respiration. He called this *Ānāpānassati* —developing the faculty of awareness of inhalation and exhalation. Respiration is common to all human beings belonging to any community. Nobody can have an objection to the practice of awareness of respiration. How can one label breath as Muslim or Hindu, Christian or Jewish, Buddhist or Jain, Sikh or Parsi, Caucasian or African or Asian, male or female?

Ānāpānassati requires us to remain aware of the breath on the area below the nostrils and above the upper lip. It is one-pointed concentration at the middle of the upper lip—*uttaroṭṭhassa vemajjhappadese.*

As the mind gets concentrated on this small area, it becomes more and more sharp, more and more sensitive. After just three days of practice, one starts feeling physical sensations on this part of the body. And then, one turns to the next training of *paññā*, that is, wisdom or insight.

One observes sensations throughout the physical structure, from the top of the head to the tips of the toes. In doing so, one notices that the sensations are closely related to what happens in the mind. It becomes clear that every time one performs an unwholesome action, one has to generate some impurity or other in the mind. Before one kills, one has to generate immense hatred. Before one steals, one generates greed. To indulge in sexual misconduct, one has to generate immense passion. One cannot do any harm to others without first harming oneself—*Pubbe hanati attānaṃ, pacchā hanati so pare.* Negativities such as anger, hatred, greed, ill will, jealousy, egotism and fear make a person unhappy, miserable and violent. One becomes agitated. When one is agitated, one doesn't keep this agitation to oneself: one starts distributing it to others, one starts harming others in society. One realizes this law of nature within the framework of one's own mind and body.

Someone may seem outwardly happy while performing unwholesome actions but their real situation is like burning charcoal covered with a thick layer of ash—*bhasmacchannova pāvako*. One is burning inside because of the mental negativities, and yet one is totally ignorant of what is happening inside.

This is *avijjā, moha*, ignorance. For the Buddha, ignorance is not lack of knowledge of some philosophical belief. It is lack of knowledge of what is happening within oneself. One doesn't understand how one becomes miserable because of this veil of ignorance. No one wants to remain miserable and yet one continues to be miserable because one continues to generate *taṇhā*—craving and aversion—all the time; one keeps on reacting to the sensations. When ignorance is removed, as one starts looking inside one realizes, "Look, I am generating misery for myself by generating *taṇhā* in response to these sensations. When they are pleasant, I generate craving and when they are unpleasant, I generate aversion. Both make me miserable. And look, I have the solution now. When I understand the impermanent nature of sensations and maintain equanimity, there is no *taṇhā*, no craving and no aversion. The old habit pattern of the mind starts changing and I start coming out of misery."

This is *vijjā* or wisdom according to the Buddha. It has nothing to do with any philosophical or sectarian belief. It is the truth about one's happiness and misery, which all people can experience within if they take steps on the path. The Four Noble Truths are not philosophical dogma. They are actual realities pertaining to myself that I start realizing within myself. They are Noble Truths only when one experiences them, and thus, starts becoming a noble person.

When one is working with sensations, one is working at the depth of the mind. Whatever arises in the mind is accompanied by sensations within the body—*Vedanā-samosaraṇā sabbe dhammā*. Even the most transient thought that arises within the mind is accompanied by a sensation within the body—*Vedanā-samosaraṇā saṅkappavitakkā*. This was a great discovery of the Buddha.

Another great discovery of the Buddha was that we generate *taṇhā* in response to the sensations. This was not known to the other teachers before the time of the Buddha, at the time of Buddha or after the Buddha. The teachers before the Buddha and at the time of the Buddha kept advising people not to react to the sensory objects that come in contact with the sense doors—eyes with visual object, nose with smell, ears with sound, and so on. They taught, "When sensory objects come in contact with your senses, don't react by judging them as good or bad; don't react with craving or aversion."

This teaching was already in existence. But the Buddha said that, actually, you are not reacting to these objects. He gave the example of a black bull and a white bull (one representing the sense doors and the other the sense objects) tied together with a rope. Neither the black nor the white bull is the bondage; the rope is the bondage. The Buddha said that the rope of *taṇhā* is the bondage, and that one generates *taṇhā* (craving or aversion) in response to *vedanā* (sensations)—*vedanā paccayā taṇhā*. This was the great discovery of the Enlightened One. He became an enlightened person because of this discovery.

There were many other people saying that one should not react to the objects of the senses. But they didn't become Buddhas. There were teachers who taught that one should not generate *lobha* (craving) and *dosa* (aversion).

The Buddha explained that *lobha* and *dosa* would last as long as there was *moha*. He, therefore, advised us to come out of *moha*. And what is *moha*? *Moha* is ignorance. *Moha* is *avijjā*. You don't know what is happening inside. You don't know the real cause of *lobha* and *dosa*. You are ignorant. How will you come out of ignorance? Strike at the root of the problem and come out of misery by working with sensations.

As long as you are not aware of sensations, you keep fighting with outside objects, thinking, "This is ugly" or "This is not ugly." You keep working on the surface. You are thinking of the black bull or the white bull as the cause of the bondage. In fact, the bondage is the craving and aversion that one generates in response to sensations. An alcoholic thinks that he is addicted to alcohol. He is actually addicted to the sensations he feels when he drinks alcohol.

When one observes sensations objectively, one starts coming out of ignorance. By understanding the impermanent nature of sensations, one generates *paññā* in response to *vedanā*. This is the law of nature. *Dhamma niyāmatā* is the law behind the natural order of phenomena. Whether there is a Buddha or no Buddha, *Dhamma niyāmatā* remains eternal.

The Buddha said:

Uppādā vā tathāgatānaṃ anuppādā vā tathāgatānaṃ, ṭhitāva sā dhātu dhammaṭṭhitatā dhammaniyāmatā idappaccayatā. Taṃ tathāgato abhisambujjhati abhisameti. Abhisambujjhitvā abhisametvā ācikkhati deseti paññāpeti paṭṭhapeti vivarati vibhajati uttānīkaroti. 'Passathā'ti cāha.'

He said, "I have experienced this law of nature, the Law of Dependent Origination, within myself; and having experienced and understood it I declare it, teach it, clarify it, establish it and show it to others. Only after having seen it for myself, I declare it."

This is the bold declaration of a supreme scientist. Just as whether there is a Newton or no Newton, the law of gravity remains true. Newton discovered it and explained it to the world. Similarly, Galileo or no Galileo, the fact that the earth revolves around the sun remains true.

The feeling of sensation is the crucial junction from where one can take two paths going in opposite directions. If one keeps on reacting blindly to pleasant and unpleasant sensations, one multiplies one's misery. If one learns to maintain equanimity in the face of pleasant and unpleasant sensations, one starts changing the habit pattern at the deepest level and starts coming out of misery. The sensations are the root. As long as one neglects the root, the poisonous tree will grow again even if the trunk is cut. The Buddha said:

Yathāpi mūle anupaddave daḷhe,
chinnopi rukkho punareva rūhati
Evampi taṇhānusaye anūhate,
nibbattati dukkhamidaṃ punappunaṃ.

Just as a tree with roots intact and secure,
though cut down, sprouts again;
even so, while latent craving is not rooted out,
misery springs up again and again.

Thus, this super-scientist discovered that to become fully liberated from mental defilements, one has to work at the root of the mind. Each individual must cut asunder the roots of *taṇhānusaya*.

When the entire forest is withered, each tree has to be nurtured, its roots cleared of disease, and then watered. Then, the entire forest will bloom again. Similarly, for the betterment of society, each individual has to improve. For society to become peaceful, each individual has to become peaceful. The individual is the key.

Attaining Peace

For the world to become peaceful, each country or society has to become peaceful. Here, I would again like to quote a very important exhortation from the Buddha to the Vajjīan republic of Licchavīs. The Buddha gave the following practical instructions, which would make the Licchavīs unassailable:

As long as they maintain their unity and meet regularly, they will remain invincible.

As long as they meet together in unity, rise in unity and perform their duties in unity, they will remain invincible.

As long as they do not transgress their ancient principles of good governance and their system of justice, they will remain invincible.

As long as they revere, respect, venerate, and honor their elders and pay regard to their words, they will remain invincible.

As long as they protect their women and children, they will remain invincible.

As long as they venerate the objects of worship inside and outside their republic, and maintain monetary support for them, they will remain invincible.

There were many sects in those days too, with their own temples and places of worship. Wisdom lies in keeping all people happy and satisfied. They should not be subjected to harassment, which compels them to become enemies of the state. Their places of worship should receive adequate protection. As long as the rulers provide protection and support to saintly people, they will remain invincible.

This wise counsel of the Buddha is also applicable today to maintain peace and harmony in the world. We cannot ignore issues related to religion if we are to be successful in bringing peace to the world.

It is the duty of every government to protect its people from external attacks, to do everything possible to make its people and territory secure. While this is done, it must be borne in mind that such measures give only short-term benefits. Goodwill and compassion alone can remove the hatred that lies at the root of all such acts performed by anyone belonging to any sect. In India, the United States and other countries where Vipassana courses are held in prisons, we already see how people change. The roots of terrorism lie in the minds of terrorists. We have seen how some hardened, violent criminals have been transformed in our prison courses. Anger, fear, vengefulness and hatred start dissolving, creating a peaceful and compassionate mind. We first ask some members of the prison staff to learn Vipassana and only then give courses for the inmates. This gives wonderful results.

In the Buddha's teaching, we will find a bridge that can connect various sects. The three fundamental divisions of the Buddha's teachings—morality, concentration of mind and purification of mind—are the essence of every religion and spiritual path. *Sīla, samādhi* and *paññā* are the common denominators of all religions. There can be no conflict over these three basic factors necessary for living a beneficial life. The whole emphasis of the Buddha's teaching is on the practice of these three in order to apply Dhamma in real life. This is the inner core of every religion. Instead of giving importance to this core, we keep on quarreling about the outer shell, which may be different in different religions.

History has proved that whenever the universal, non-sectarian teaching of the Buddha has gone to any place or community, it has never clashed with the traditional culture. Instead, like sugar dissolving in milk, the teachings have been gently assimilated to sweeten and enhance society. We all know how much the sweetness of peace and tranquillity is needed in the bitter world today. May the teaching of the Enlightened One bring peace and happiness to more and more individuals, thus making more and more societies around the world peaceful and happy.

May all beings be happy!
May all beings be peaceful!
May all beings be liberated!

(Dhamma Giri edition—April 2003)

On Pilgrimage with our Teachers

The following article is based on the yatra reflections posted on the Old Student Website by one of the pilgrims.

Words of Dhamma

Cattārimāni, Ānanda, saddhassa kulaputtassa dassanīyāni saṃvejanīyāni ṭhānāni. Katamāni cattāri?
'Idha tathāgato jāto'ti, Ānanda, saddhassa kulaputtassa dassanīyaṃ saṃvejanīyaṃ ṭhānaṃ.
'Idha tathāgato anuttaraṃ sammāsambodhiṃ abhisambuddho'ti, ...
'Idha tathāgatena anuttaraṃ dhammacakkaṃ pavattitan'ti, ...
'Idha tathāgato anupādisesāya nibbānadhātuyā parinibbuto'ti, ...
Imāni kho, Ānanda, cattāri saddhassa kulaputtassa dassanīyāni saṃvejanīyāni ṭhānāni.

There are four places, Ānanda, which a devout person of good family should visit with feelings of reverence and awe. Which four?
Where a devout person can say, "Here the Enlightened One was born." That place, Ānanda, should be visited with feelings of reverence and awe.
"Here the Enlightened One attained to the supreme and perfect insight." ...
"Here the Enlightened One set in motion the incomparable Wheel of Dhamma." ...
"Here the Enlightened One Attained to *Nibbāna* without remainder." ...
Indeed, Ānanda, these four places should be visited with feelings of reverence and awe.

—Mahāparinibbāna *Sutta* **(DN 16–5–8)**

Day 1—All aboard

On 17 February, 2001, Goenkaji, Mataji and almost 1,000 others from around the world board 17 train carriages and set off on a yatra, or pilgrimage to the historical places in India and Nepal related to Buddha's life and teachings. In addition to the 830 pilgrims, the train also carries 130 catering and security staff, water, a coal-fuelled kitchen, and all ingredients for meals. Another 100 pilgrims wait patiently in Varanasi to join the train.

The official program for the pilgrimage contains the following message from Goenkaji: "The merits acquired by this Dhamma-yatra are dedicated to the victims of the Gujarat earthquake. May all regain their mental strength and a happy, peaceful life."

Day 2—Outward bound 1-day course

A special speaker system pops magically into life along the length of the train and we hear Goenkaji's voice:

"Come let us start our meditation on

wheels, the moving wheels of the vehicle of Dhamma. This pilgrimage should not be taken as a blind rite or ritual, not by the present generation and not by future generations. There is no blind belief involved in this—a positive and wholesome meditation—while we are moving on these wheels visiting all the important places of the Enlightened One. Seeing where he was born, where he became enlightened, and where throughout his life he continued to guide people in Dhamma, we shall take advantage of the wonderful vibrations of this land, the wonderful land of India, the country of origin of pure Dhamma. May we all work seriously."

The one-day course ends with sharing of merits, and Goenkaji and Mataji walk through the length of the train chanting and giving *mettā* to all the pilgrims.

Days 3 & 4—Varanasi & Sarnath

The first stop is the ancient city of Varanasi, and here the pilgrims transfer to buses and travel to a public talk at the Deer Park in Sarnath and to nearby *Dhamma Cakka* for lunch and meditation.

We attend a convocation ceremony at the Central Institute of Higher Tibetan studies, where an honorary doctorate is awarded to Goenkaji. While there he gives an address entitled "The Buddha and His Discovery," stating that, "The discovery of the Buddha that the real cause of *taṇhā* (craving) lies in *vedanā* (body sensations) is his unparalleled gift to humanity."

Day 5—Bodh Gaya

The train travels overnight from Varanasi to Gaya where breakfast is served on the train platform. The pilgrims are bused the short distance to Bodh Gaya, where we are to stop for three days at the Bodh Gaya International Vipassana Meditation Center, *Dhamma Bodhi.* A huge colorful tent city has been erected to cater for 1,000 people. The facilities seem quite comfortable, with stretcher beds, mattresses and adequate bathrooms with running water. After settling in and lunch, a tour of the important places in Bodh Gaya is arranged.

Across the Nirañjanā River from Bodh Gaya is a cave where Prince Siddhattha practiced severe austerities for six years. Here, realizing the futility of extreme practices, he decided to resume taking food, thereby disappointing his five companions. One night, shortly before sunrise, after meditating under a banyan tree, he lay down to sleep and had five dreams which were portents of his imminent enlightenment. It became clear to him that his teaching would not be limited to his country, but would spread to many other countries for the benefit of innumerable people. The exact location of this tree is not known, but it may have been on the western bank of the river near what is now known as Sujātā's place. Sujātā was the woman who offered milk rice to the bodhisatta the morning before he became enlightened. Today many temples are there.

When Goenkaji first came from Burma (Myanmar) in 1969, the Samanvaya Ashram and Burmese monastery offered their premises for the organisation of Vipassana courses, and this is remembered with much gratitude.

Often on *Mettā* Day of the early Teacher's self-courses at the Burmese Vihara, Goenkaji and old students would go to the Maha Bodhi Temple to meditate at night under the Bodhi Tree. So also, this evening, we go there to meditate with Goenkaji and Mataji.

Day 6—1-day course at *Dhamma Bodhi*

Goenkaji tells us, "In a wonderful place like this, where an enlightened person meditated and realised this wonderful Truth, the vibrations of the entire atmosphere were charged with his love and compassion. These vibrations are still here and we benefit from them by meditating at this place. We are meditating only for short periods on this tour, but when 10-day courses are held here in Bodh Gaya people realise a great benefit. In five or 10 courses elsewhere they might not get the benefits they would get from one course in this place. This is one reason why we want a good meditation center to be developed at Bodh Gaya. But it is only if you meditate that you benefit from coming here."

Goenkaji further exhorts us to be real followers of Buddha, to practice what Buddha taught. "No Vipassana meditator should have the madness of a blind believer, a devotee who thinks that, by simply visiting the four places where the Buddha sat, one will get liberated. Liberation can only happen when one starts experiencing the Truth within oneself."

"The large number of people who died in the recent earthquake in India and many more who are still suffering from this catastrophe—we must share our merits with them."

The one-day course ends with a late-night group sitting under the Bodhi Tree and *mettā* is given by Goenkaji and Mataji. Many people around the world purposely meditate at this exact time, sharing their peace and harmony with others.

Day 7—Bodh Gaya

Today *Dhamma Bodhi* holds a *Saṅgha-dāna* (giving to monks). Early in the morning a special donation box is provided so that we also can participate. About 250 bhikkhus attend and are given a meal served by Goenkaji, Mataji and the pilgrims. The monks are also given robes and other personal items such as blankets. This is clearly a new experience for most of the pilgrims, so Goenkaji carefully explains two reasons why give to the Saṅgha.

"Firstly, the bhikkhus are people who have renounced the householder's life, and it is the duty, the responsibility, of those of us who have a household to provide for their physical requirements. The second reason is gratitude. We are certainly grateful for the Buddha's teaching when we gain so much from the practice of Vipassana. We should therefore be grateful to the Bhikkhusaṅgha, because they have preserved his teaching up to the present day so that we can receive it. In several of India's neighboring countries, the theoretical teaching, the words of Buddha, were preserved. In one country, Myanmar, they also maintained the purity of the practical teaching that we have learned, and for this we owe them great respect and gratitude."

In the evening we are fortunate to go again for a last meditation under the Bodhi Tree and to experience the wonderful atmosphere there. Goenkaji's *mettā* chanting is very long. He gives *mettā* to all the beings in the earth, the water, the trees, and the sky in all directions. He gives *mettā* to the Bodhi Tree, the temple grounds, and those who take care of it.

Day 8—Rājagaha & Nālandā

It's a long day, starting from *Dhamma Bodhi*, traveling in the morning over rough roads to Rājagaha (modern-day Rajgir), then to Nālandā in the afternoon and back another 50 miles in the evening. The crowded and bumpy bus rides are long and tiring. At times the program appears chaotic. The facilities in the tent city at the center are stretched. There are power and water failures, and blocked toilets. There are last minute changes of plan and difficulties in communication among the 900 people.

Yet the general atmosphere is bright. Someone reminds us that in times past pilgrims faced great hardship, and many died on the way. The organisers, despite complaints, remain cheerful and helpful, and on our buses we share snacks and stories.

Outside Rajgir there are several caves where the Buddha meditated with his disciples. The more energetic pilgrims hike up to them to meditate. Others choose the easier option of the cable car which deposits them at a beautiful stupa built by the Japanese. Walking down they reach the caves where the peaceful vibration is inspiring and refreshing. A highlight of the day is a lively and informal question and answer session with Goenkaji and Mataji under a tree in the carpark.

Later that afternoon we travel to Nālandā—a simple one or two-hour bus trip. Travelers in the Buddha's day used Nālandā for a one-day rest stop when going from Rājagaha to Sāvatthi. For several centuries after the Buddha, Nālandā was an important center of learning, with a university/monastery complex for up to 8,000 students, covering an area three to six miles wide. It was arranged in a symmetrical formation of huge Dhamma halls, each surrounded by large cells for group accommodation and meditation. The remains of these halls have brick walls almost six feet thick, indicating that the buildings were several stories high. These are built on the rubble of an earlier complex, which was again built on a more ancient one.

Day 9—Vesālī & *Dhamma Licchavī*

We say goodbye to *Dhamma Bodhi* early in the morning and travel by bus to Vesālī where the Licchavī clan lived at the time of the Buddha. We visit the place where the Buddha's cremated remains are enshrined, and also the nearby Ashokan pillar and stupa which have served as models for similar monuments in India and around the world.

Goenkaji and Mataji meditate here briefly and give *mettā* in the Dhamma hall as the sun sets. Unfortunately they and the pilgrims have little time together: their vehicle had gotten lost and some buses were delayed during the long trip. They depart to give a public talk at a Muzzafarpur business club, a committment which can't be broken.

Most of the pilgrims stay at the center for a meal and a group sitting in the large shamianas (marquee-type tents) erected especially for our visit. We pile back into the buses and arrive late with all our luggage at Gaya station, and leave after midnight for Gonda.

Day 10—Sāvatthi

We travel through the night, sleeping once again on our now very familiar train, with early morning chanting and breakfast before another bus trip. A few sick people stay behind, but most do not want to miss today's group sitting at the Jetavana grove.

Yesterday's frustration is relieved when

Goenkaji gives an hour's talk to the pilgrims explaining the significance of the places we have recently visited and telling us delightful stories about the ancient days.

We then have an hour or so to stroll around the area, which includes six acres of land set aside for a center, *Dhamma Suvatthi*, and we see the Ānanda Bodhi Tree which is said to be a sapling from the tree planted by Anāthapiṇḍika. We also visit the Angulimāla Stupa and the beautiful Jetavana Grove gardens. That evening from 6:00 to 7:00 we meditate under the stars in the gardens and are refreshed by the tranquil surroundings.

Another late evening return to the train; it's difficult to fall asleep until after midnight as we remember and discuss today's experiences.

Day 11—Kusinārā

An early morning start is complicated by delays, not getting to the platform, and missing breakfast. On the buses everyone gets out their supplies and shares them up and down the aisle. One of the foreigners says jokingly in Hindi, "Where's the chai?" After the bus stops briefly, he is both embarrassed and delighted to be offered a cup of tea by a very old and kindly Indian lady who got off the bus to buy it especially for him.

We arrive at another tent city erected at *Dhamma Vimutti* (Liberation of Dhamma). It was at Kusinārā that the Buddha died and passed into *Mahāparinibbāna*, and where he was cremated.

Goenkaji gives another discourse on the importance of this place and the benefits of meditating here: "When the Buddha finally passed away, it was not just the end of one life. Millions of lives, countless lives, had come to an end. And it was such a good end, after he had helped so many. At that moment there was very strong Dhamma dhātu, Nibbāna dhātu, and the effects have remained for centuries."

There are several stupas and temples in Kusinārā, and we go to the main site for our evening group meditation.

Day 12—Lumbini

That night spent in the tents at the center is cold, despite the comfortable stretcher beds and blankets provided. There is an early morning start on the long bus journey to Nepal, and some decide to forgo this part of the tour. Others who are tired or sick still come along because they do not want to miss seeing the birthplace of the Buddha, and they are cared for by their companions.

The border crossing of 16 buses takes time at both Indian and Nepalese immigration, and in the hustle and bustle of the town. Eventually we all find our respective buses and head through the soothing greenness of the Nepalese countryside.

Lumbini remains largely undeveloped, but we arrive at a pleasant new hotel in time for lunch provided by the Nepalese meditators. We proceed to Lumbini park which contains several historic places. The actual birthplace of the Buddha is a covered archaeological site. Excavations have been underway for several years and Goenkaji and the pilgrims are given admittance to see the stone marking the exact spot. Nearby is the water tank where his mother Mahāmāyā bathed after giving birth. There is a temple with a statue of her near the entrance to the park, the ruins of an ancient monastery, and an Ashokan pillar in good condition, although its capital now sits on the ground nearby.

We go to hear Goenkaji speak in a very

beautiful shamiana which has been erected just outside the park for the occasion of our visit. He explains how for centuries people have meditated in the Himalayas, so the vibrations here are charged with purity, peace and harmony. These have been of great benefit to the courses held in Nepal.

He goes on to say, "Lumbini is very important, being the location of the last birth of the Bodhisatta after such a long journey developing his *pāramīs* over so many lives. We must honor the two countries of Nepal and India, one land where he took birth and one where he passed away."

Goenkaji and Mataji then go to a ground-breaking ceremony on the land which has been purchased for a center called *Dhamma Janani*. This new center is on three acres of land allotted by the Nepali government just outside the sacred zone. The long bus journey back to our train at Gorakpur is delayed with visa problems at the border, and the breakdown of a bus. The train pulls out of the station at around 11 p.m., and a very late dinner is then served to the tired pilgrims.

Day 13—Homeward bound 1-day course

The day starts with morning chanting and later Goenkaji starts a course with the opening formalities and Ānāpāna given over the train's speakers. Vipassana follows later in the day. We catch glimpses of the Taj Mahal as the train passes through Agra. The students are invited to submit written questions about the yatra or their meditation, and Goenkaji and Mataji make themselves available for personal interviews after lunch.

Day 14—The final day

The mood in the 14 passenger carriages is buoyant as we discuss the benefits, problems and lessons of the pilgrimage. One student comments that it was actually just like the experience of a Vipassana course. She says, "For the first few days people are confused, not knowing what will happen next. Then all the *saṅkhārās* start coming up—discomfort, complaints, people claiming their own territory, physical and mental highs and lows. Then, towards the end, we all become more calm, more accepting of whatever comes; we are lighter and happier."

The mobile cell phones start to pick up signals from the Bombay network, so people begin to call to tell their families that they are almost home. Remembering the ancient days of the Buddha and his teaching, there is peace and harmony, a sharing among us, which needs no modern phones or internet to be spread around the world.

Pilgrim's Reflections

Pilgrim one—I feel so fortunate to be traveling in the land of Dhamma. I feel so happy to be with our Dhamma father, Goenkaji, and to be united with our Dhamma family. I wish to express gratitude to the Lord Buddha for rediscovering Vipassana and sharing Dhamma with us to help us come out of suffering.

Pilgrim two—Yesterday, while sitting at an *Adhiṭṭhāna* sitting, I heard the beautiful words *"Ananta pūṇyamayī, ananta guṇamayī, Buddha ki nirvāṇa-dhātu, dharma-dhātu, bodhi-dhātu!"* "A source of endless merit, of endless benefit, are the Buddha's vibrations of *nibbāna*, of Dhamma, of enlightenment!" Filled with joy, overflowing with happiness and love for all beings, with blissful gratitude for the teaching of Dhamma, I remembered sitting under the Bodhi Tree with 1,000 Vipassana meditators, and Goenkaji chanting these very words. They came across alive and strong, blessing anyone else who happened to be around the Mahābodhi Temple that evening. Then I remembered to stop reminiscing and start meditating.

What an incredible experience it was to participate in the yatra. There were definitely lots of hardships: confusion, delays, illness, rough bus rides. But now those hardships are fading away, and what remains in my mind and body are the incredible vibrations and peace of those very sacred sites.

I have to admit I was very sceptical of the "merits" of visiting a place. I thought, "What is all this hokey-pokey talk about vibrations that are 2500 years old?" I am very grateful that in spite of my stubbornness and doubt, I signed up for the yatra and experienced it for myself. It was so wonderful, filling me with so much inspiration to keep walking the path.

Walking near the forested area where the Buddha met and converted Angulimāla, sitting under a crescent moon and starry sky next to the fragrant hut where the Buddha resided in the Jetavana Park (site of a huge ancient monastery), meditating under that incredible Bodhi Tree evening after evening—these were the places that were special for me.

In ancient times pilgrims used to die trying to reach these holy sites. Although conditions and travel methods have improved, making the trip easier, it was still quite a journey. To make it all the way through, we had to come together and help each other out in times of sickness and suffering, we had to endure our own miseries and internal battles. It was truly a semi-mobile Vipassana course. I wouldn't have missed it for the world!

With gratitude to the organizers and *mettā* to all!

Pilgrim three—At each step of the yatra I imagined the Buddha and his followers, traveling the very soil I was privileged to walk as a participant of this pilgrimage. At each holy site Mr. Goenka's discourse inspired my devotion to the Buddha and heightened my gratitude for his contribution to mankind.

Pilgrim four—My Dhamma trip to the pilgrimage sites in India and Nepal was invaluable. There were substantial challenges, including sickness, a good dose of physical discomfort, and constant delays, but most people on the yatra took it all very well. There was wonderful bonding with other Dhamma friends, the kind of bonding and sharing which rarely seems to happen in such a spontaneous way with friends who have not yet experienced Dhamma for themselves.

The places we visited had very powerful vibrations: for me, Sarnath, the place of the Buddha's first teaching, and Bodh Gaya, the place of the Buddha's enlightenment, were particularly well-charged. At Sarnath, the first place we visited, I arrived at our Dhamma center there still recovering from a bronchial cough and a bad case of the runs, so my awareness of sensations was weak.

We arrived at about noon, and it was sunny, with a light breeze blowing in from across the valley. The center is located on a small hill of dusty earth, small rocks and pebbles, with some occasional weeds and grasses. Across from the center, separated by a small valley of grasses, water and possibly rice fields, is the main pilgrimage site.

When I sat down to meditate on the hill at the center, a strong awareness of arising and passing away of sensations rose immediately. Within half an hour, when I rose to queue up for lunch, both balance of mind and fitness of body were restored. It was all somewhat astonishing and I stayed quiet during the long queue for lunch.

At Bodh Gaya I had what amounted to a mini-course, all in less than half a day—from mid-afternoon to the group sitting ending at 9:00 p.m. Initially, there were two very deep and blissful meditation sessions, first at the site where the Buddha meditated during the seventh week following his enlightenment, and then under the Bodhi Tree. The first session for no more than five minutes while standing (our tour guide was a delivering brief lecture about the site at the time), and the second session was perhaps twice as long, while sitting under the Bodhi Tree.

In both cases, when I closed my eyes the meditation was immediately deep and more blissful than anything I had experienced previously, particularly since only moments before I was somewhat extroverted. There was strong arising and passing of sensations—which was not so new—but also deep peace and bliss and a strong sense of an expanded connection with the sky—which definitely was new.

Soon we were told to depart for another site, and we boarded the bus for what turned out to be the nearby Thai temple. When we arrived, I noticed that the temple was lovely, but I told myself I was not here to be a tourist. So I quickly boarded another bus to return to the Bodhi Tree.

What really made the Bodh Gaya experience a mini-course was that when I returned a little later for a second round of meditation, I was having a major storm: there were only heavy, gross sensations and my mind was craving for bliss. So, as at courses, the lesson was not to play games with sensations, and here was an opportunity to come out of these games.

Finally, the evening came to a close with a group meditation led by Goenkaji and, as at courses, my first day at the Bodhi Tree ended with *mettā*, this time live from Goenkaji. With that, my short course was complete!

Pilgrim five—The yatra has left me with a feeling of fullness and wholeness. I'm so looking forward to a return to India. I hope for all beings to feel the joy and peace that I feel because of and thanks to Goenkaji and his son and those who made this journey possible!

Kapilavatthu & Lumbini

In Ancient Times: Lumbini was the birthplace of Prince Siddhattha. His mother, Mahāmāyā, toward the end of her pregnancy wished to return to her ancestral home in nearby Devadaha to give birth. However, en route she stopped at Lumbini gardens and gave birth in the sāla grove there, standing and grasping a branch of a sāla tree.

In Modern Times: Lumbini was discovered in 1896, 11 miles from Bhairawa in Nepal. The site has an Asokan pillar, erected in the twentieth year of the emperor's reign. As well, there are the ruins of several temples, a stupa and a pond where legend says Mahāmāyā bathed.

In Ancient Times: Kapilavatthu was the capital of the Sakyans. It was a republic and the Sakyans were the royal clan who collectively ruled it. It got its name from having been founded on the site of the hermitage of the sage Kapila. The city with its 30 foot high backed onto the great forest which stretched up to the Himalayas to the north. It was close to the Rohini River which formed the border between the territory of the Sakyans and that of the Koliyans.

When Prince Siddhattha was born his father Suddhodana was the king of the Sakyans. Some of the other members of his family were Mahāpajāpati Gotami, his aunt and adoptive mother, his brother Nanda, his wife Yasodharā and his son Rāhula.The Buddha spent the first 29 years of his life at Kapilavatthu and it was here that he saw the four signs that led to his Great Renunciation and search for liberation.

The Buddha's first return to his hometown after his enlightenment was quite eventful. He shocked his father by begging in the streets, he preached to large crowds, and many of the Sakyans ordained as monks. After initial doubts large numbers Sakyans took refuge in the Buddha.

The stories say that 2,000 families decided to give up one prince each to the Order. Among these were six princes related to Buddha: Ānanda, Anuruddha, Devadatta, Bhagu, Kimbila, and Bhaddiya. They collectively requested that their barber, Upāli, be ordained before them so that they would always have to regard him as their elder, thereby helping them to disolve their egos.

The Sakyans met their demise at the hands of Vidudabha. King Pasenadi of Kosala, a large state to the south, had developed devotion to the Buddha. He thus wished to become closer to the Saṅgha and thought if he were to have a Sakyan princess to wed he would acomplish this; he therefore asked for a bride of royal Sakyan blood. The Sakyans looked down on the Kosalans and out of contempt devised a scheme to pass off a slave girl (Vasabhakhattiya) as a princess. Pasenadi was taken in and took her home, annointing her queen. Together they had a son, Vidudabha. When Vidudabha grew up he visited Kapilavatthu and came to know the insult > Dharmaṣṛiṅgad against his father and himself. When he assumed the throne on Pasenadi's death, he took his vengence, massacring the Sakyans.

In Modern Times: The location of Kapilavatthu has been a subject of contention. During Victorian times several sites were thought to be Kapilavatthu. However, in 1898 the English archeologist Peppe tunneled into a stupa at the village of Piprāwā in India about eight miles from Lumbini and found a burial casket containing bone relics. Subsequent excavations in the 1970's have proved the village of Piprāwā to be Kapilavatthu and the relics to be the Sakyan's share of the Buddha's remains.

Other things of interest at Piprāwā include the Sakyan stupa, several monestaries and what may have been the Sakyan's public hall.

Bodh Gaya

In Ancient Times: Bodh Gaya was known as Uruvelā on the banks of the Nerañjara River. It was here that Prince Siddhattha fought his great battle with Māra and gained the Supreme Enlightenment.

The Bodhisatta had tried all the different

Prince Siddhattha's parents look on as Asita examines their new-born baby (Kosetu Nosu)

spiritual practices prevailing in India at that time. He now was engaged in severe austerities and accompanied by his five companions, had chosen this spot to practice. It was a comfortable and hospitable area which attracted many ascetics who wished to practice in a serene environment.

After nearly starving himself to death and torturing his body in various other ways, he concluded that this was not the right path and decided to abandon his austerities. His companions, feeling he had returned to the life of luxury left him; but actually he had started the search for a middle way between the extremes of self-indulgence and self-torture.

A village girl named Sujātā saw him sitting under a tree near her home and, thinking him a tree deity, offered the milk pudding she had prepared. This meal was sufficient to sustain him for the ordeal he was now to undergo. He crossed the river to the tree which would become known as the Bodhi Tree. Here he sat with the strong determination that, even if his legs should dry up and his bones scatter, he would persevere until he reached his goal.

During the night he confronted Māra (the personification of the impurities within all of us) and his army. He soon prevailed, penetrating to the most profound truths of mind and matter, thus liberating himself from all ignorance. The prince had become a *Sammāsambuddha*, a Fully Awakened One. For the next seven weeks he remained in the area of the tree contemplating what he had achieved.

Bodh Gaya is one of the few ancient Buddhist sites not lost over time. Pilgrims visited it throughout the last 2,500 years. Various temples and stupas were erected and restored by different wealthy patrons, kings or simple traveling pilgrims.

In Modern Times: Bodh Gaya has become the primary pilgrimage stop for all devout Buddhists. A collection of temples and viharas both ancient and modern have arisen around the sacred site. The tree itself is not the original but is a cutting from the famous tree at Anurādhapura in Śri Laṅka which is itself a cutting from the original tree. The main attraction at Bodh Gaya, the gigantic Mahābodhi Temple, towers 170 feet over the site of the original tree. The modern tree sits just to the west of the main temple.

The central chamber of the temple encloses the place where Buddha sat on the night of enlightenment and is called the Vajirasana or "Victory Throne of all Buddhas." The present temple is one of several built over the centuries, one upon the other. Asoka may have built the original with others enlarging it later.

During British times the grounds were claimed by a local landowner and all the temples etc. had fallen into a state of neglect. The temple was restored to its present form by the British archaeologists Beglar and Cunningham using a model found in the excavations. The untiring work of Anagarika Dharmapala from Śri Laṅka and others brought ownership back into public hands.

Around the main temple we find many stupas and small shrines commemmorating different events of the seven weeks after enlightenment, erected by various pilgrims

This painting by Kosetu Nosu depicts the four auspicious signs seen by Prince Siddhattha: an old man, a sick man, a dead man and a mendicant monk

Goenkaji serves some of the 250 bhikkhus who gathered to receive alms at *Dhamma Bodhi*

A view of the Mahābodhi Temple

over the centuries. The surrounding town is a collection of viharas representing every Buddhist country and sect in Asia.

Regular 10-day courses for up to 70 students have been held at *Dhamma Bodhi* since 1994. The 18-acre center is situated adjacent to Magadh University on the Gaya-Dobha Road. One can see the spire of the Mahābodhi Temple across the rice fields. It is hoped that this center will take on global significance in the future.

Sarnath

In Ancient Times: Sarnath, near Varanasi, was known as Isipatana, so called because the isis or sages of those days used to gather there on their way to and from the Himalayas. It was here in the Migadāya or Deer Park that the Buddha gave his earth-moving first sermon, the *Dhammacakkappavattana Sutta.*

He had traveled here to find the *pañcavaggiyā*, the five men who had served as his attendants since the time he left Kapilavatthu. The eldest, Kondañña, had been present when Asita, the court chaplain of King Suddhodana, made the prediction that the newborn Prince Siddhattha would become a *Sammāsambuddha*. The others, Bhaddiya, Vappa, Mahānāma and Assaji were sons of other Brahmins who had been there as well. They had been advised by their fathers to follow the Prince's career and to join him if he renounced the world. These five had left him in Uruvelā when they felt he had given up the austerities that were so necessary to become enlightened; and now the Buddha went to them to share the Dhamma.

The *Dhammacakkappavattana Sutta* (SN V 12–2–1), the Discourse on Setting the Wheel of Dhamma in Motion outlined in brief the core of the Buddha's teaching: The Middle Way, the Eightfold Noble Path and the Four Noble Truths discernible in three ways. At the end of the sermon the Venerable Kondañña was established as a Stream-winner, thus becoming the first of thousands to achieve saintly states as students of Buddha.

The Buddha stayed for some time at Isipatana teaching the five. The second important *Sutta* taught there was the *Anattalakkhaṇa Sutta* telling that there is nothing of substance in mind and matter. At the conclusion of this sermon all five Bhikkhus attained to Arahantship.

Later Yasa, a young man from a wealthy family of Varanasi, who had become disgusted with the life of luxury, came to the park. He also was soon to become an Arahant as were 54 of his friends. It was not long before there were 60 Arahants at Isipatana. The Buddha then sent them out, no two in the same direction to spread the Truth to all.

Caratha, bhikkhave, cārikam
bahujanahitāya bahujanasukhāya
lokānukampāya atthāya hitāya
sukhāya devamanussānaṃ.

"Go forth, o Bhikkhus, for the good of many, for the happiness of many, out of compassion for the world, for the benefit and welfare of gods and men."

—Mahāvagga, Mahāpadāna *Sutta* **(D.N.)**

The Buddha gave other sermons there, as did some of his Disciples. Over the centuries the site became a place of pilgrimage and scholarship as large monasteries grew and flourished. It was a center of Buddhist activity from the third century BCE, up until the second half of the twelfth century when it met a fiery end at the hands of Muslim invaders. Much of the ruins was lost during Moghal and British days when they were demolished and used for other construction purposes.

In Modern Times: Sarnath has not only the archeological park but an extensive pilgrimage-friendly town as well. The Chinese, Thais, Burmese, Tibetans and Śri Laṅkans all have temples and rest-houses nearby.

The Archeological Museum across from the Park contains a wonderful collection with the lion capital from Asoka's pillar, immediately recognizable as India's emblem, as its masterpiece. Also there is the famous Gupta period (4th cent. CE) statue of the Buddha discovered in 1905.

Next to the park is the modern-day Mulagandhakuṭi Vihara built by the Anagarika Dharmapala in 1931. The extraordinary frescoes on the interior walls by the Japanese artist Kosetsu Nosu follow the life of Lord Buddha from birth to death. The temple also houses relics of Buddha from Taxila and Nagarjunakonda.

The park, of course, is the main focus for a pilgrim. The grounds are extensive with ruins from Asoka's time up until the late 12th cent. CE. Asoka's pillar lies beside its base which is still where it was originally erected. The inscription it bears is an admonition against splitting the Saṅgha (Order of monks). Next to the pillar is the foundation of the Mūlagandhakuṭi or Fragrant Hut, as Buddha's residences were generally called. This is actually a shrine built over the original spot. The original Gupta period structure was 200 feet tall according to 7th cent. Chinese pilgrim Huien Tsiang.

Also near the pillar is the foundation of the Dharmarajika Stupa, probably built by Asoka on the spot of the *Dhammacakkappavattana Sutta*. Sadly, the stupa was demolished in 1796 by the local Maharaja for its bricks.

The massive Dharmek Stupa stands a little off from the other main objects and it is not clear what it was meant to commemorate. Cunningham tunneled down from the top and found no relics. He did find, though, a stone slab near the top from the 6–7th cent. CE bearing a Sanskrit inscription. Lower down he found a smaller stupa of Mauryan brick.

The foundations of a number of monasteries were also unearthed. Most of them show the signs of a violent end. Cunningham noted, "It will be observed the every excavation made near Sarnath has revealed traces of fire... (Major Kittoe)...summed up his conclusions to me in a few words: 'All has been sacked and burnt; priests, temples, idols, all together. In some places, bones, iron, timber, idols, etc. are all fused into huge heaps; and this had happened more than once.'"

Archeological park with Dharmek Stupa in background

Kusinārā

In Ancient Times: Kusinārā was famous primarily for the *Parinibbāna*. It was the capital of the Mallas who were great devotees of the Buddha. In fact, once when he visited them there was a decree that anyone who didn't turn out to welcome him would be fined. The Buddha visted there several times and stayed at the Baliharaṇa.

It was a small city with no political force and Ānanda complained to the Buddha that he should have chosen a larger town than this for such an auspicious event. Actually, the Buddha had reason to go there for his *Parinibbāna*. Firstly he wanted to preach the *Mahāsudassana Sutta* about the distant past of Kusinārā, but also to meet Subhadda and Doṇa.

The events of the last weeks, before the *Parinibbāna*, unfold vividly in the *Mahāparinibbāna Sutta* of the *Dīgha* Nikāya. The final chapters concerning Kusinārā have many poignant moments: The Buddha's last meal and last drink of water, the scene of the sāla grove, his advice to the Saṅgha, the devas jostling for position to see, his gentle admonitions to Ānanda, the coming of the Mallas, the grief of the unenlightened and the steadfastness of the Arahants.

His last compassionate act as a teacher, the winning over of the wandering ascetic Subhadda, gave the Buddha one last opportunity to teach. Subhadda asked about all the other teachers of that time who claimed to be saints as well. The Lord explained to Subhadda that only in an order of discipline where the Eightfold Noble Path could be found, would one find ascetics of the four levels of saintliness and that only the Buddha's own Order fit that description. Subhadda then asked for ordination and went off to practice in the sāla grove. He was to return that very night with the announcement that he had become an Arahant, the last in the lifetime of the Buddha.

The Buddha gave the assembled Saṅgha one last chance to ask a question, but none of them spoke because they were all Ariyas. Then the Buddha spoke his last words:

Handadāni, bhikkhave, āmantayāmi vo, vayadhammā sankhārā, appamādena sampādetha.

"Now, monks, I exhort you: All conditioned things have the nature of decay. Strive on diligently".

After his final passing his body was given to the Mallas to be prepared for cremation. Then there was a week of festivities. When the Mallas tried to light the pyre it would not ignite. Finally, only after Mahākassapa arrived and paid his final respects to the Lord did flames rise from the pyre. When only bones remained a cloudburst put out the fire.

Soon requests came from all directions for shares of the relics. In fact, the clans of northern India were on the verge of fighting over them when the wise Brahmin Doṇa proposed that the relics be shared into eight portions to be given to all the different kingdoms. The clans agreed and each one took their share of relics to be enshrined; even the ashes and the urn which held the relics were given out. Great stupas to hold the relics were built at Rājagaha, Vesālī, Kapilavatthu, Allakappa, Rāmagāma, Vethadipa, Pāvā and Kusinārā.

In Modern Times: Kusinārā is found at the small town of Kasia at the junction of the Rapti and Gondak Rivers near Gorakhpur. Kasia was proposed to be the lost site in 1854 and excavations began in 1876. Not until 1904 and 1912 did positive identification of the site come to light.

The Indian government erected the *Parinibbāna* Temple in 1956. It houses an image of a reclining Buddha probably from the 5th cent. CE. Just behind is the *Parinibbāna* Stupa on the very spot that Buddha achieved *parinibbāna* between the sāla trees. It consists of several stupas, one within the other, the last shell dating from the fifth century CE. About one mile down the road the pilgrim will find the Makutabandhana or Cremation Stupa.

The town has the usual set of viharas, rest-houses, where a pilgrim can stay. There is also a tourist hotel-restaurant.

Parinibbāna Stupa and Parinibbāna Temple

Rajgir

In Ancient Times: Rajgir was known as Rājagaha, the royal abode. It is one of the oldest continually inhabited sites in India. At the time of the Buddha it was the capital of Magadha and the largest city in the Middle Land. The old part of the city was nestled amid five mountains.

The Prince Siddhattha visited Rājagaha soon after he renounced the householder life. Word of the shining ascetic reached the ears of King Bimbisāra who went to meet him. He was so taken with the prince that he offered him a high position at court. Siddhattha refused, of course, but promised to return once he had fulfilled his goal of enlightenment to teach the king what he learned.

And so, during the first year after his enlightenment he returned to Rājagaha and was received with much pomp. While there, he accepted the donation of Veluvana park from the king with a ceremonial pouring of water from a golden vessel onto the ground. He also met and ordained many important Theras there, including Sāriputta and Moggallāna. Large numbers of householders also joined the order as well the adherents of other prominent teachers.

The Buddha spent probably Six rains retreats in Rājagaha . He gave more sermons there than any other place except Sāvatthi. His favorite places were Gijjhakūṭa also known as the Vulture's Peak, Veluvana, and in later life, Jīvakambavana, the mango grove donated by the court physician, Jīvaka. Buddha also complimented many of the other parks and grottos around the city.

Later in his life his evil cousin, Devadatta, tried to split the Saṅgha at Rājagaha. He had asked the Buddha to allow him to lead the Order because the Buddha was now too old and should rest. The Buddha refused which angered Devadatta. He temporarily succeeded in taking away a large number of immature Bhikkhus, but Sāriputta and Moggallāna were sent after them and brought them back to the Buddha's fold. Next, Devadatta tried to kill the Buddha, first by casting a boulder at him and then by arranging the release of Nalagiri, a ferocious elephant. The first attempt ended with the Buddha being wounded on the foot and the second with the taming of Nalagiri. Devadatta, because of these deeds could not achieve access to the Noble stages of the Path.

Prince Ajātasattu, the son of King Bimbisāra also played a large role in the events surrounding the Buddha at Rājagaha. In the beginning, he fell in league with Devadatta who led him astray. He ended up murdering his father after the King had abdicated in his favor. He also helped Devadatta in his attempts on the Buddha's life. In the end, though, he gained faith in, and became a patron of the Buddha. In fact, he sponsored the first great council of Arahants after the Buddha's *Parinibbāna*, held at Sattapaṇṇiguhā, a cave on one of the nearby hills.

After the *Parinibbāna*, the capital of Magadha was soon moved to Pataliputta, the present-day Patna, and Rājagaha began to decline in importance. The Chinese pilgrims who visited the area 1,000 years later saw nothing but ruins.

In Modern Times: Rajgir is a ghost town. The ruins are spread over a large enough area to make walking impossible. Many of the important sites of ancient days have been identified and excavated.

There is an ancient wall which climbs up

Gijjhakūṭa or the Vulture's Peak, seen from above

and down these peaks surrounding the old city, following the crests for almost 30 miles. The walls are made of massive rough-hewn stones over four ft. long closely fitted without mortar. The finished dimensions of the original wall were about 12 ft. high by 18 ft. wide. It probably had a superstructure on top made of less durable materials. Bastions located at points along the wall measure up to 40 ft. by 60 ft. The wall was also fitted on its inside face at strategic places with stairs to the top. The Pali texts say the wall had 32 large gates and 64 smaller ones.

One can visit Veḷuvana, with its squirrel's feeding ground, bamboo groves and lotus pond. Nearby are the Tapodārāma hot springs, Ajātasattu's stupa, the Pipphaliguhā where Mahākassapa would meditate and where the Buddha visited him while sick. Just outside the walls we find Asoka's stupa, and New Rājagaha, a fortified town built just outside the mountain sanctity.

High on the hill over looking Veluvana is Sattapaṇṇiguhā. Here Ānanda, Mahākassapa and 498 other Arahants recited and compiled the Tipiṭaka. This trek is not for the faint of heart. It is an hour's walk up steep slopes, but a well beaten pathway leads you there. Although the site is supposed to have six or seven openings, only two are easily found by pilgrims and their smallness makes one wonder how all the Arahants could fit in. Most likely a grand pavilion was built near the cave entrance and such a ruined foundation does exist on a spur of the slope just below the cave.

On the other side of the valley you take a chair lift to the top of Chhatha Hill to visit the modern-day Peace Pagoda built in 1969 by the Japanese. From there you walk down to Vulture's Peak where the meditation caves of the Buddha and his chief disciples invite you. The foundations of many monastic buildings cover the site.

After descending from Vulture's Peak one soon comes to Jīvakambavana. The court physician Jīvaka donated this mango grove to the Saṅgha so he wouldn't need to travel so far to treat the Buddha. It was here that Jīvaka brought King Ajātasattu to meet the Buddha.

Sāvatthi

In Ancient Times: At the time of the Buddha, Sāvatthi was the capital of Kosala, one of the more powerful states of Northern India. It derived its name from the caravan trader's expression *sabbaṃ atthi*, everything is available, although the sage Savattha could have lent his name as well. Kosala had conquered Kāsi (with Vārānasi as its capital) and was in conflict with Magadha. Eventually Magadha prevailed in the time just following Buddha. Pasenadi was the monarch of note at Sāvatthi through most of the Buddha's time but he passed away outside the gates of Rājagaha shortly before the *Parinibbāna*. After the *Parinibbāna*, Sāvatthi began to decline in influence. By the time Huien Tsiang arrived Sāvatthi and Jetavana were in ruins.

The Buddha spent much of the latter part of his life in Sāvatthi and as a result it is considered one of the most important sites in a Pilgrimage. He spent 25 rains in Sāvatthi,19 at Jetavana and six at Pubbārāma. He gave more sermons in Sāvatthi then anywhere else, 871 by one reckoning.

The founding of Jetavana Monastery is a story of great interest. The merchant Sudatta also known as Anāthapiṇḍika, because he fed the poor, was once doing business in Rājagaha. He was surprised to find his in-laws were ignoring his arrival and were busy preparing a feast. On questioning them if the King was coming they replied, "No...The Buddha will eat here tomorrow."

Hearing this, Anāthapiṇḍika was filled with a thrilling feeling. On asking, "Can I meet him now?" his brother-in-law says, "No, it's too late now. The city gates are locked. Tomorrow you will meet him."

Sudatta, however couldn't wait, and before dawn found himself walking toward the place where Buddha was staying. The Buddha greeted him by name and taught him Dhamma. In a few days he became sotāpanna.

Anāthapiṇḍika now understood the real meaning of *dāna*, and that the highest *dāna* was the gift of Dhamma. He invited the Buddha to Sāvatthi, saying he would provide a suitable place for the Saṅgha to meditate. He then returned home proclaiming to all along the way that Buddha would soon come their way and they should prepare viharas etc. for him and the monks with him.

On arriving at Sāvatthi he began looking for a peaceful place to purchase and came upon the private park of Prince Jeta. The prince didn't want to sell, however, and told Anāthapiṇḍika that even if he spread gold coins on the land he wouldn't part with it. Anāthapiṇḍika took this as a price and forced the sale. He brought cartloads of gold coins and laid them on the ground. The prince, on seeing this, asked what was the reason that this land could be so valuable and Anāthapiṇḍika told him the Buddha would live here. Now the prince said, "Well, at least let me give some of it", and he donated the last bit near the gate and built a gateway there.

Anāthapiṇḍika built a grand monastery where 10,000 could meditate together. In fact he spent his entire fortune funding the land, the buildings, and the inaugural ceremonies. He continued to come to Jetavana for the rest of his life to meditate and to provide all the necessities of the center. He was by far the Buddha's greatest donor .

Sāvatthi was the scene of many other famous incidents in the latter part of Buddha's life. Here we find Visākhā who became a lay-disciple of Buddha at age seven while living at Sāketa. Later she married the son of a rich man of Sāvatthi and came to live there. She was also a big donor, building the Pubbārāma monastery.

Among those who came to Buddha in Sāvatthi were Angulimāla who had murdered 999 people and was about to murder his own mother before the Buddha saved him, Ciñcā who tried to fraudulently defame Buddha in public by saying he fathered her baby, Pātācārā who after losing her entire family went mad, and Kisāgotamī clutching her dead baby and asking for help to revive it. King Pasenadi and Queen Mallikā also were great devotees along with many at court.

In Modern Times: ¨Cunningham, using the accounts of Chinese pilgrims, was able to locate Sāvatthi. It lies at the present-day village of Sahet-Mahet near Balrampur in Gonda district. The Jetavana Monastery has been restored as a national monument. The foundations of the most important buildings have been identified although the exact location of the gate with its Asokan pillars is not known.

Things of interest for the pilgrim include the Gandhakuṭi, or perfumed hut, so-called because devotees would lay bouquets of flowers there. This was the principle dwelling of Buddha while at Jetavana and is a center of attraction even today. Another stop of interest is the Ānanda Bodhi Tree. This was planted as a place for meditators to pay respects to Buddha when he wasn't there. Digging has exposed many other foundations and extensive grounds.

The town itself is small and not well equipped for pilgrims although there are many modern-day viharas built by the various Buddhist countries.

The foundation of the Gandhakuṭi, or perfumed hut at Jetavana

Vesālī

In Ancient Times: Vesālī was the capital of the Vajjī federation and the home town of the Licchavīs. At the time of the Buddha, Vesālī was a very large city, rich and prosperous, crowded with people and with abundant food. The Buddha visited Vesālī many times in his life and found the shrines and temples there to be delightful and the city beautiful with its parks, ponds and fine buildings. Vesālī had three walls a league apart with gates and watchtowers in each one.

On one occasion, while the Buddha was at Vulture's Peak, King Ajātasattu of Magadha sent his chief minister Vassakāra to tell the Buddha that he was planning to invade the Licchavīs, just to see what Buddha would say. The Buddha then began questioning Ānanda about whether the Licchavīs were still following the guidelines he taught them so that they might be expected to prosper and not decline. Ānanda affirmed they were and Vassakāra returned with the knowledge that the Vajjīs were presently invincible and this was not the time to invade. (DN 16) The Buddha then went on to tell Ānanda how the Saṅgha could continue to prosper and not decline. Ajātasattu sent his chief minister Vassakāra to Vesālī to undermine the seven causes of invincibility, which he was able to do and several years after the passing of Buddha, Ajātasattu invaded and took his vengeance on the Licchavīs.

One notable visit to Vesālī was the occasion of teaching the *Ratana Sutta*. Vesālī had been suffering from drought, famine, and pestilence, people were dying of dysentery and corpses were gathering in the street faster than they could be removed. The people asked that the Buddha be invited to teach there so that this shroud of disaster could be lifted. As soon as the Buddha set foot on Vajjīan territory a great rain washed the corpses away. He then taught the *Ratana Sutta* which deals with the virtues of the Triple Gem, i.e., Buddha, Dhamma and Saṅgha. Buddha then told Ānanda to walk around inside the walls of the city reciting it as well. Before long the pestilence abated and things returned to normal.

Mahāpajāpatī Gotami was the aunt and adoptive mother of the Buddha. When her husband, King Suddhodana died she decided to renounce the world. When the Buddha returned to Kapilavatthu to settle the dispute between the Sakyans and the Koliyans, each clan gave 250 young men to the Order. Their 500 wives with Mahāpajāpatī Gotami at the head then asked for ordination also. The Buddha refused and departed for Vesālī. The women, however cut their hair, donned orange robes and followed barefoot all the way to Vesālī. Again they begged for ordination and again the Buddha refused. On the third try, however, Ānanda intervened on their behalf and this time the Buddha agreed provided the new Order of Bhikkhunis accept eight additional rules.

The Buddha made an important visit to Vesālī in the last year of his life. He stayed at the mango grove of Ambapāli, a famous courtesan. After inspiring her with a discourse she invited him and all the monks with him to take their meal at her residence the following day. When the Licchavī Princes heard this, they tried to buy the privilege for themselves but she refused saying that even if they offered her all of Vesālī she would not trade away this opportunity.

This incident provides an interesting insight into the culture of Vesālī. When the Licchavī princes were approaching the Buddha and his monks he told the monks that if they had not seen the devas of the realm of the 33 gods, they should cast their eyes on these Licchavī princes. The princes were very colorful in appearance with some wearing blue clothes, blue ornaments , blue makeup and driving blue chariots; others were entirely in yellow or red or white. They also invited the Buddha to a meal and when he told them he would eat at Ambapāli's they snapped their fingers in frustration saying, "We have been beaten by the mango-woman" (making a pun on her name and the words for mango, amba).

That year the Buddha spent his last rains at Beluva, a village near Vesālī. During this stay he fell quite ill but managed to keep going by force of mind. Here he told Ānanda that he had held nothing back; that he had not been closed-fisted with the teaching; there had not been an inner teaching and an outer teaching. He explained that after him there should be no successor, but that the Dhamma was there to guide the Saṅgha. He said that the monks should practice self reliance; that they should live as islands unto themselves, having no refuge except themselves and the Dhamma. It was then that he gave Ānanda the hints whereby he could request the Buddha live longer but Ānanda did not understand. So the Buddha purposely gave up the life sustaining force causing the earth to shake and announced that he would live only three months more.

Vesālī comes into Buddhist history once more 100 years later when it was the venue for the second great council. The so-called "Ten points" regarding deviation from the Vinaya or monk's code of discipline was the main focus. It was held at Vālikārāma.

In Modern Times: Vesālī has almost disappeared due to flooding over the centuries.

The ruins there have only been excavated this century although the location was known to Cunningham.

The most important find was the Licchavī Stupa. According to Huien Tsiang, this stupa originally housed their 1/8 share of the Buddha's relics. Asoka opened the stupa and removed 9/10 of the relics, then closed it up and built a larger stupa around it. A future king tried to open it as well but was dissuaded by an earthquake just then. The stupa was discovered in 1958 and excavations then proved the old stories to be true. In fact within was found a small soapstone casket containing burnt bones and various other objects. All evidence points to this being the Licchavī stupa and the contents to being Buddha's relics; yet, like the discovery of the relics at Piprahwa, this discovery made hardly a ripple on the Buddhist world and the relics languish in the dusty storerooms of the Patna Museum.

Another interesting monument at Vesālī is a 45 ft. high pillar with a lion capital. It is often attributed to Asoka but it differs enough from the Asokan style to be from another source, perhaps pre-Mauryan. Next to the pillar is an Asokan stupa excavated in 1976.

Please note that Vipassana centres in this tradition have been established in locations close to many of these pilgrimage sites and courses are regularly held. For the latest information, please visit ***www.dhamma.org/os***

"Along the Path" by Kory Goldberg and Michelle Décary (Pariyatti Press 2009) provides in-depth background for Dhamma travellers in these parts.

Books used in writing articles on holy sites:

Malalasekera, G.P., Dictionary of Pali Proper Names, London, 1938.

Dhammika, S., Middle Land Middle Way: A Pilgrim's Guide to the Buddha's India, Kandy, 1992.

Maurice Walshe, Thus have I Heard, London, 1987.

Archaeological Survey of India, Sarnath, Calcutta, 1956; Sravasti, Calcutta, 1956; Rajgir, Calcutta,1956.

T. W. Rhys Davids, Buddhist *Sutta*s, (Sacred Books of the East), First published Oxford,1881.

(International edition—April 2001)

Pilgrimage to the Land of Dhamma

The following article by S. N. Goenka was specially written for the Vipassana Newsletter. Goenkaji recently visited Myanmar with over 750 foreign meditators.

Words of Dhamma

Patirūpadesavāso ca,	A suitable abode,
pubbe ca katapuññatā,	the merit of past good deeds,
atta-sammāpaṇidhi ca—	right aspirations for oneself—
etaṃ maṅgalamuttamaṃ.	this is the highest welfare.

— **Maṅgala** *Sutta*

My revered Teacher Sayagyi U Ba Khin ardently wished that Myanmar repay its debt to India by returning the invaluable jewel of Vipassana to the land where it had originated more than two millennia before. He was confident that there were many in India with immense *pāramīs* who would wholeheartedly accept Vipassana and would join in the effort to spread it around the world. He was also confident that there were many in other countries with *pāramīs* who were waiting for this jewel, who would feel blessed to obtain it and would contribute in different ways to help its spread. This is exactly what happened. Sayagyi's Dhamma wish is being fulfilled.

With the coming of the Sayagyi Centenary Year at the beginning of the new millennium, a similar Dhamma wish arose in my mind: that meditators from India express their gratitude to Myanmar, the country that returned Vipassana to their homeland, and that they be joined by the hundreds of thousands of meditators around the world who have benefited from Vipassana. In fulfillment of this wish, a pilgrimage was planned to the Dhamma country of Myanmar. Despite short notice, it was hoped that 200 to 250 meditators from India and abroad might take part. Instead, it was a pleasant surprise to see 750 meditators from 32 countries and all five continents come to Yangon. After participating in an International Conference at the *Dhamma Joti* center in that city, many then set out on the pilgrimage.

In spite of all the efforts made to provide proper facilities, the pilgrims had to face hard traveling. Still, these Dhamma sons and daughters always had smiles on their faces and a reverential attitude toward my motherland, Myanmar, in their hearts. I was deeply touched to see this.

Since ancient times, people have gone on pilgrimage to India from Myanmar and other countries where the Teaching of the Buddha has been preserved. But this was the first time in history that hundreds from India and around the world went on a pilgrimage to Myanmar.

The pilgrims meditated together with large numbers of their local Dhamma brothers and sisters at *Dhamma Joti.* The big Vipassana family gathered as well to meditate at Shwedagon, the largest and most revered pagoda in Myanmar, which enshrines hair relics of the Buddha. With the kind permission of the management and trustees, entry was permitted in the early morning and late evening, when the Pagoda gates are normally closed. Meditators sat at the International Meditation Center in northern Yangon, where I learned Vipassana at the feet of Sayagyi. For the welcome they received, we are grateful to the teacher there, my Dhamma brother U Tin Yi, and to Mother Sayama.

Another destination for the pilgrims was the village of Dalla across the Yangon River, where a center still exists established by Saya Thetgyi, the first lay teacher of Vipassana. Further from Yangon is the famous Kyaiktiyo Hill, where a pagoda stands atop a balancing rock on the edge of a cliff. After the exertion of climbing the hill, all tiredness was removed by meditating in an atmosphere charged with the pure vibrations of Dhamma.

The pilgrims proceeded northward to Mandalay. There they meditated at the *Dhamma Mandapa* center and the Mahāmuni Pagoda, and visited the Sagaing Hills where for centuries Vipassana has been practiced. At the monastery of their Dhamma brother, Sithagu Sayadaw Nyanissara, they were received with great kindness and hospitality.

The pilgrims visited sites associated with Ledi Sayadaw, who was responsible for the rebirth and spread of Vipassana in modern times. They went to Monywa and the nearby Ledi village, where he was born and taught Dhamma, and they also saw the hillside cave where he used to meditate. In addition, in Kyaukse they visited the monastery of Webu Sayadaw, a revered monk of recent years who gave so much encouragement and inspiration to Sayagyi.

A few of the pilgrims went to Mogok to meditate at the two Vipassana centers there, *Dhamma Ratana* and *Dhamma Makuta.* In this city famed for its gems of ruby, they experienced the gem of Dhamma in all its splendor. The return journey southward led through the historic city of Pagan, ancient capital and city of pagodas, which left an indelible impression.

All arrived back in Yangon feeling joyful though tired by the journey. Since then I have been receiving letters from pilgrims telling about their happy experiences. I am pleased to see so many enchanted by my motherland. Their words recall to mind an important incident in my life.

When I came to India in 1969 to begin teaching Vipassana, the Government of Myanmar kindly issued me a passport, something almost impossible to obtain then. This allowed me to hold the first Vipassana course in India, with my parents participating. The Ganges of Dhamma started flowing all over the country after that.

From the very first year, many foreigners participated in Vipassana courses alongside Indians. After their courses they entreated me to come help their families, friends and others who could not visit India to benefit from the munificent Dhamma. In doing so they were simply voicing Sayagyi's wishes. But I was unable to accede to them: the passport I had received in Myanmar was valid for travel only to India, not to any other country. I sought

Goenkaji and Mataji lead a group sitting at the magnificent Shwedagon Pagoda

endorsements for other countries but government policy made it impossible to grant my request.

Finally I made a Dhamma resolution: if the policy did not change even after I had spent 10 years serving in India, I would apply for Indian citizenship and travel to teach Vipassana in other countries on an Indian passport. 10 years passed; I obtained Indian citizenship and an Indian passport, and was able to set forth on a Dhamma journey abroad.

At this point I learned that the Myanmar government would not give an entry visa to any former citizen who had changed his nationality after leaving Myanmar on a Myanmar passport. This news was extremely painful for me. I did not want to be prevented from entering my motherland. On the other hand, the momentous duty of *Dhamma Dūta*—Dhamma envoy—beckoned. Therefore I had given up citizenship of the country of my birth, dear to my heart. I consoled myself with the thought that perhaps this was the working of Dhamma, so that both the countries of origin of Vipassana—India and the protector country of Myanmar—should receive credit for the spread of Vipassana around the world. This is what is happening.

Nevertheless, the longing repeatedly arose in my mind to return somehow to my motherland. I wanted to meet my Dhamma brothers and senior monks to gain further strength and knowledge of Dhamma. I was also confident that sooner or later the Myanmar government would grant me entry since it knew that I had changed my nationality only to serve the Dhamma, not for any personal, political or commercial gain. This Dhamma service was increasing the prestige not only of India but also of Myanmar. Sooner or later I would certainly get the opportunity to go back to my motherland.

Dhamma is truly powerful. The opportunity indeed came when the Myanmar government invited me to Myanmar to talk to senior monks about my Dhamma work. I returned with great joy. With humility I spoke at the monks' Pariyatti Universities in Mandalay and Yangon. The bhikkhus were fully satisfied that what I was teaching was nothing but pure Dhamma. For my part, this visit to Myanmar gave me incomparable joy. It was natural that I was delighted to return to my motherland after 22 years. And this motherland gave me birth not once but twice—first when I emerged from my mother's womb, and second when I broke the shell of ignorance by learning Vipassana at the feet of my revered Teacher.

The moment I stepped on that land I felt that I had come back to my mother's lap. The entire atmosphere was charged with the vibrations of Dhamma, and I received immense Dhamma strength. I was so delighted to meet my Dhamma brothers U Tin Yi, U Ba Pho and U Ko Lay. I was very fortunate to be able to pay respects to the Venerable Mingun Sayadaw, and receive blessings and guidance from him. Later, when I would remember my experience of Dhamma vibrations in Myanmar and the strength I derived there, I would attribute these to my natural attraction toward my motherland and my delight in returning there after so long. But now on this pilgrimage, my Dhamma children had the same experience; they strengthened my conviction that my motherland is charged with Dhamma vibrations, giving boundless joy to any meditator who goes there.

I find the people of my motherland amiable and virtuous. Is it because I am biased in their favor? I think not. On the pilgrimage all the participants felt the same. People in the cities and villages of the Dhamma country of Myanmar are peaceful and simple, contented in every situation. A Dhamma daughter from the U.K. writes, "The January trip to Burma was so special for me.... I think that the Burmese are among the nicest, kindest and most humble people in the world."

Meditation hall at Saya Thetgyi's center

Pagoda at Sayagyi U Ba Khin's International Meditation Center in Yangon

An Indian pilgrim writes, "This tour was no less than a tour of the celestial realm.… The influence of Dhamma is evident all over Myanmar. People there are so innocent and serene. We in India cannot even imagine that people could be like this." Who would not be elated to read and hear such comments about one's motherland and its inhabitants! When I hear the comments of the pilgrims about the people of Myanmar, my mind is filled with delight.

Blessed is the land of Myanmar, which preserved in its pure form the technique of Vipassana for more than 2,000 years. We are grateful to Thailand, Śri Laṅka, Cambodia and Laos along with Myanmar, as these five countries preserved the words of the Buddha. But Myanmar alone preserved the beneficent practice of Vipassana. If the Bhikkhu *Saṅgha* of this country had not kept the practice of Vipassana alive, today the entire world would have been in darkness for want of this technique.

Hail to the land of India, where this pure meditation originated. Hail to the land of Myanmar, which again made available the pure Dhamma, which gave the path of pure Dhamma to the world and showed the way leading to welfare for the suffering people of the world.

Two Pilgrims' Impressions of Northern Myanmar

We were very excited about going back to Myanmar; we had not been there since 1979. The purpose of this visit was to join other foreigners in celebrating the birth centenary of Sayagyi U Ba Khin, the renowned modern-day meditation master who was our teacher's teacher.

We fell in love with Myanmar and its wonderful people. This is a land that is magical. Being there is like entering a river with a gentle swirling current; all you have to do is surrender to it and it will carry you to places you never imagined. At times it appears that the entire landmass is decorated with thousands and thousands of golden pagodas and stupas providing brilliance and radiance to an otherwise arid landscape. But what really makes this country so special are the gracious and generous people who inhabit it. Everywhere we went we were greeted with a generosity that is almost incomprehensible given the relative poverty of these unaffected and hospitable people. The Buddha taught that generosity is the first step on the path of Dhamma; it is abundantly clear that the Burmese people have understood this noble teaching.

We travelled to Mandalay and, with the unsparing assistance of Ven. Nyanissara and his monastery, we visited sites in the area associated with Vipassana. Our journey to the town of Monywa was a bumpy three-hour trip, punctuated by photo stops and a mechanical breakdown. The purpose was to visit the

Goenkaji shares the stage with U Ko Lay, listening to a student of Saya Thetgyi speak at the Sayagyi U Ba Khin Centenary Seminar held in January, 2000 at *Dhamma Joti*, Yangon

birthplace, monastery and forest mediation cave of the great scholar and monk Ledi Sayadaw, who lived there over 100 years ago and to whom this tradition of meditation is traced. As we embarked on our journey we were well aware that we owed a great debt of gratitude to the foresight of Ledi Sayadaw, since it was he who foresaw that Dhamma would spread around the world. He realized that, for this to happen, the technique of Vipassana meditation would have to be taught to and by lay people. Until his time meditation practice was almost wholly limited to monks. Few Westerners visit Monywa, so we were definitely a curiosity. However, it was clear that we were welcomed. The hospitality of a local family meant that we were well fed and guided further on our pilgrimage.

One of the highlights for us was crossing the Chindwin River to Ledi Sayadaw's cave. We squatted in a sleek shallow wooden boat that was silently thrust along with a long bamboo pole by our boatman. The atmosphere felt strangely romantic, only in the sense that it was so remote, timeless and almost dreamlike; the vibration akin to a thin mist, unseen to the eye yet tangible to the senses in an uncanny way. As is so often the case in Myanmar one is naturally drawn inward. Upon reaching the far sandy shore we walked to a cave where the great Sayadaw spent much of his time in deep meditation. We encountered a couple of monks at this cave and joined them for meditation and a limited conversation in a few words of

English on the purpose of our visit and our meditation technique. Our life's experiences were so vastly different, yet in this droplet of time, we shared together a common quest and path.

Long after the dust of Myanmar has worn from the soles of our feet and the clarity of these memories has inevitably faded with the passing of time, this Dhamma land and its great sages will, no doubt, continue to have a deep impact on us for the rest of our lives ... and maybe many more to come.

(International edition—March 2000)

Meditation Now—Goenkaji's Tour of Europe and North America

Words of Dhamma

Nidhīnaṃva pavattāraṃ,
yaṃ passe vajjadassinaṃ.
Niggayhavādiṃ medhāviṃ,
tādisaṃ paṇḍitaṃ bhaje.
Tādisaṃ bhajamānassa,
seyyo hoti na pāpiyo.

The disciple should associate with a wise friend, who detects and censures one's faults, and who points out virtues as a guide tells of buried treasures. There is happiness, not woe, to one who associates with such an intelligent friend.

—Dhammapada, 76

Sace labhetha nipakaṃ sahāyaṃ, saddhiṃ caraṃ sādhuvihāridhīraṃ.
Abhibhuyya sabbāni parissayāni, careyya tenattamano satīmā.

If you find a wise companion to associate with, one who leads a virtuous life and is diligent, you should lead a life with this person joyfully and mindfully, conquering all obstacles.

—Dhammapada, 328

United Kingdom

This year Goenkaji and Mataji made an unprecedented whistlestop tour of Europe and North America, stopping at over 40 destinations to encourage old students and to expose millions more to Vipassana. They began their four and a half months of travel with a nine-day visit to England starting April 10. There, over 1,700 people attended his public talks and 750 students came to one-day courses. Goenkaji was interviewed live on the *Jimmy Young Show*, a BBC radio program with a listenership of 5.5 million.

The Teachers paid their respects and gave *dāna* at a *Saṅghadāna* for 21 monks. As well, Goenkaji spent time with old students, advising them on the growth of Dhamma in the British Isles.

United States and Canada

In North America the tour really started many months before Goenkaji and Mataji left India. It was then that the Logistics Committee began planning the enormous task of moving our Teachers in comfort across the continent in a caravan of motorhomes. This task was met head on, most often tirelessly. Detailed plans developed as all aspects of the tour were assessed—what was needed to look after Goenkaji, Mataji, sometimes family members, and 18 or so tour crew members; how to create a system to provide prepared food and provisions across the whole of America for a caravan that had little time between stops; how to prepare in advance to facilitate crossing the US-Canada border four times in the middle of the tourist season with eight motorhomes and 20 people from three countries; how to organize media coverage both nationally and locally in two countries; and how to assist local communities to prepare for the caravan, the one-day courses, the public talks, the local media events and business meetings. The lists seemed endless, but the results of the hard work paid off and the tour ran very smoothly.

Goenkaji, Mataji, three of their family members and two assistants arrived in New York on April 19. After a brief stay in New York and Massachusetts they began a journey of more than 13,000 miles by road through the United States and Canada—through the lush green of the eastern spring; through the sweet smelling early summer bloom of the South; through deserts; past towering mountains; over gently rolling plains that stretched to the horizon in all directions; into towns, villages and cities that seemed to go on forever. He joyfully spread the gift of Dhamma over all the land. The pace was often tiring, but he always bounced back quickly with another burst of energy for the job he loves.

Public talks were held in schools, churches, temples, city halls, theaters, and hotels. In the United States, Goenkaji gave more than 40 public talks to over 25,000 people. In Canada over 8,000 people attended 10 public talks. Goenkaji's ability to convey the essence of the Dhamma with great *mettā* produced an avalanche of calls to centers and local contacts across the continent. Many noncenter courses are being hurriedly assembled to handle the numbers of people wanting to try Vipassana.

Goenkaji and Mataji participated in more than 20 one-day courses in addition to many group sittings and sessions in six 10-day courses. It is estimated that more than 5,000 of his students were able to meditate with him, most for the first time. At courses, Goenkaji gave *Ānāpāna, Vipassana* or *Mettā* and often held an open question and answer session in the hall before leaving.

Goenkaji and Mataji participated in four *Saṅghadānas* attended by a total of more than 200 venerable monks and nuns. This celebration of the giving of food and requisites was a time for the lay people of many communities to come together and express their gratitude to the *Saṅgha;* for it was they who maintained the accurate transmission of the teachings of the Buddha from teacher to pupil. It was also a time for the lay people to pay respects to those who have renounced everything to dedicate their lives to practicing the Buddha's teachings. At the end of each *Saṅghadāna* Goenkaji addressed the venerable *Saṅgha* and the lay people to tell them about the practical aspect of the teaching Vipassana meditation.

Goenkaji and Mataji share a light moment with the trust in Edmonton, Alberta

At stops across the country hundreds of people spent months preparing: arranging venues, handling publicity, organizing talks and one-day courses. When the caravan arrived, they prepared the tour's meals, providing both Indian and Western food and assisted the crew with laundry, transportation and the other necessities of a traveling caravan.

Meeting People Along the Way

Goenkaji met with local Vipassana trusts across the continent, addressing their concerns and encouraging them in many cases to begin looking for centers. He looked at potential properties for several trusts.

At one meeting he explained to trust members, "All of you are representatives of Dhamma. People will look at your lives to judge Vipassana. Two qualities are rare in human beings: selfless service and gratitude. Selfless service means helping others without expecting anything in return, without expecting money or name or fame. You are here to serve others. Sometimes, you may not expect money or name or fame but you wish for respect, or you develop arrogance. This is very harmful for you. A branch of a tree that bears fruit bows down due to the weight of the fruit. Similarly a person who develops wisdom becomes more humble."

A meeting between Goenkaji and Jean Chrétien, the Prime Minister of Canada, was described as a meeting between a master of the art of politics and a master of the art of living a happy life. Goenkaji, who has been practicing Vipassana for more than 40 years, told Mr. Chrétien, who has been a Member of Parliament for about 40 years, about Emperor Ashoka. Throughout his vast empire that spread from present day Afghanistan to the Bay of Bengal, Ashoka promoted the Dhamma with the practice of meditation (Vipassana). The many different sects present in his empire lived peacefully together then, just as the multicultural population in Canada does today.

Interview for a PBS series

Goenkaji met many business and public leaders throughout his tour—in personal meetings, at conferences, and at the executive course held in Lenox, Massachusetts in April.

He told one group, "At one time kings had the most power and were the biggest influence on society. Now, politicians, administrators, and businesspeople have that position. Good and bad qualities percolate down from the top. Therefore it is very important that business people live a moral and righteous life, for their own good and for the good of others."

"The Buddha taught us how to develop the four sublime qualities of *karunā, muditā, upekkhā* and *mettā.* When we see a miserable person, instead of thinking that it's his or her own doing or his or her own karma, we generate compassion, *karunā.* When we see a successful person, instead of developing jealousy we develop sympathetic joy, *muditā.* Or when we face an adverse situation, instead of losing the balance of the mind, we remain calm and equanimous, *upekkhā.* And we feel selfless love for all beings everywhere, *mettā.* These are the qualities of a spiritual person. All businesspeople should try to develop these qualities for their own good as well as for the good of others."

Two prisons invited Goenkaji to come and give *mettā* at the end of courses being held there. Goenkaji expressed appreciation for the initiative taken by these institutions' corrections officers in organizing Vipassana courses.

He advised, "Criminals are sent to prison with the aim of correcting their behavior, but after spending time in the punitive and crime-infested prison environment, they often turn into hardened criminals. For a prison to become a truly correctional facility, the inmates should be given tools to reform themselves in order to become honorable members of society."

Meeting with bhikkhunīs near Seattle, Washington

Goenkaji visited the Museum of Tolerance in San Diego; not only because its theme is an issue for which he has worked tirelessly for over 30 years, but also because he wanted to see for himself how museums use modern technology for educational purposes. (The exhibition gallery in the Global Pagoda in Mumbai, India, will be a powerful tool to educate millions of visitors every year, bringing alive the truth about the Buddha and his teachings.) Although Goenkaji and those accompanying him knew the gruesome details of the Holocaust, when they toured the museum they were again deeply touched by the immensity of this man-made tragedy.

He said, "Tolerance is one of the *pāramī* necessary to attain the final goal of full liberation. Tolerance is important to keep peace in human society—tolerance of different cultures, languages, faiths and ethnic backgrounds, as well as tolerance for the actions of others that one finds disturbing, and above all tolerance of views that are different from one's own. Such tolerance comes naturally when there is love and compassion in the mind."

Before a public talk, Madison, WI

United Nations

On May 29, Goenkaji gave the keynote speech at the United Nations for the Celebration of International Recognition of Vesākha (full moon of May) honoring the birth, enlightenment and final passing away of the Buddha.

The talk was extremely well received by the entire audience. Later, at a reception at the United Nations, many of the diplomats came to meet Goenkaji and enthusiastically expressed their appreciation for his address.

Goenkaji and Mataji in Europe

Goenkaji and Mataji arrived at *Dhamma Pajjota*, Belgium, on August 8. In preparation for their visit, large dormitory tents, dining tents and a huge meditation tent were erected at the center to accommodate students from all over Europe and beyond: in all, over 800 students from 20 countries.

Goenkaji's first engagement was a press conference at the center. That evening he gave a well received public talk in the nearby city of Hasselt. The talk, entitled *Inner Peace for a Better World*, with a simultaneous translation into Dutch, attracted over 800, filling the hall.

Next day a one-day course took place at *Dhamma Pajjota*. Meditation cushions had been borrowed from two neighboring centers to seat the many students. On the night before, however, a severe rainstorm flooded parts of the meditation hall tent, soaking carpets and cushions. A small crew of Dhamma servers worked all night to dry the hall and replace the carpets. At 5:00 a.m. the hall was finally ready for the 750 students and 75 servers. This was the biggest course ever held outside Asia.

A film crew from Reuters news agency arrived to film the day's events, producing a five-minute news article that was sent to over potentially 900 TV stations around the world. Subsequent local news coverage showed *Dhamma Pajjota* and extracts of the interview with Goenkaji.

Goenkaji met with students for an open session of questions and answers. For many newer students, this was their first chance to meet with Goenkaji and to meditate in his presence. The international flavor of the event was clear from the variety of languages spoken and the food provided.

August 11 was reserved for various trusts and groups representing the spread of Dhamma in Europe to meet with Goenkaji and Mataji. This provided an opportunity for countries with centers and those holding noncenter courses, like Serbia, Hungary and Scandinavia, to discuss their problems and responsibilities with Goenkaji and to clear up many local issues.

Over 700 meditators gathered for a one-day course at *Dhamma Pajjota*

On August 12 Goenkaji gave the keynote speech to 100 participants at the *Spirit in Business Conference* near Den Bosch, Holland. After his talk Goenkaji took questions from the audience and a panel discussion followed. As well, following on the success of the Executive Course in Massachusetts in April 2002, a decision was made to schedule an Executive Course at *Dhamma Pajjota* from May 7 to 18, 2003.

Next day, Goenkaji met with reporters from Belgium, Holland and Germany at *Dhamma Pajjota*, and that evening he gave a public talk in Cologne, Germany, for over 1,000 people who filled the hall.

On the last day of his tour Goenkaji met the European Commissioner of International Trade, Mr. Pascal Lamy. Mr. Lamy congratulated Goenkaji on the success of his tour and told him how appropriate it was that this method of mental culture (Vipassana) was finding wider acceptance in the West.

He asked Goenkaji various questions on spirituality in general and Vipassana meditation in particular. Goenkaji explained the universal and practical nature of the technique. and said he hoped that today's leaders would accept Vipassana, which in turn would help society in general.

Caravan Personnel

Whenever the caravan rolled into a town, there would be as many as 20 people with it, each one fulfilling some duty or the other. Of course, Goenkaji and Mataji were central, but around them circled their attendants, the drivers, the logistics people, the food people, the media people and the support crew.

Goenkaji's family and attendants provided him and Mataji with a little bit of home on a long journey. At first, one of their sons and other members of the family traveled with them, and in June his sister joined for the rest of the tour. Always present were Goenkaji's personal secretary and cook, who were up first in the morning and saw to his every need throughout the day.

A travel day for the caravan

The drivers were a crew of five or six, trained to drive the leviathan motorhomes. Sometimes two shifts were needed in a day as the morning hours continued into evening. These stalwarts also substituted as dishwashers and maintenance people when needed, or spent countless hours working on computers. They hooked up the hoses and cables wherever we stopped for the night, and unhooked them when we left.

The logistics team, continuing the work of the tour planners, needed to be on top of every detail as the trip unfolded. They were in continuous contact by e-mail and phone with the many local planners in towns and cities down the road as they coordinated the events of the day.

Every morning the food person was up at dawn laying out breakfast, encouraging everyone to finish so that things could be packed up before we all had to rush away. This ritual was repeated twice more each day before the sun set. She also made up unending shopping lists and met the local food providers, accepting all they brought us.

There were two groups of media people. The job of one was to archive all the speeches, trust meetings and interviews. They arrived at the events an hour or two early to set up their cameras, mikes and the rest of their equipment; and in the moments after the talk, break it all down and pack it up again for the next event.

The other technical crew followed the tour with the intention of creating a documentary film about Goenkaji. The videographer, who had previously won an Emmy award for his first feature-length video documentary was, with his two helpers, an ever-present part of the tour team.

There were as well one or two people on the tour who covered many other details: shopping at each stop, cleaning, organizing, and helping out whenever and wherever needed—setting up, breaking down, scouting ahead for lunch stops, and in a myriad of other ways.

A Day in the Life of the Tour

The days began early, especially in mid-summer. We would rise just about 5:00 a.m. and begin our morning meditation. Those in tents would sometimes be driven out early by the sun beating down. Those who liked to jog would take advantage of what was left of the cool morning air. Breakfast was usually set out by 7:00 when we gathered around the picnic tables to eat.

There were travel days and event days. After breakfast we would prepare for one or the other. If traveling, we tried to gas up and be on the road by 10:00. The planners usually gave us about six to eight hours to get where we were going. This included stops along the way for lunch, tea, dinner and a chance for Goenkaji and Mataji to take a walk.

At some point after 1:00 someone would speed ahead and try to find a good place to park for lunch. Often it would be a shady grove in a state or provincial park, but just as often we would end up in a truck-stop parking lot, amidst the rumbling compressors of the 18-wheelers. As Goenkaji's cooks began their routine of preparing and serving the Teachers' food, the rest of us would haul out tables, the kettle, the snacks and all the meticulously stored lunch that our last hosts had given us. In about an hour and a half, after the dishes were washed and everything tucked away, we would line up our vehicles and head out to the highway. On the longest travel days we would do this twice more before arriving at our destination.

At the end of a travel day we rolled into an RV campsite, organized for us by local meditators. As we approached town, the walkie-talkie crackle increased as the local guide met us to lead us in and team leaders allotted prearranged campsite numbers. We arrived in a bustle, connecting the motorhomes, setting up the tents, meditating, and maybe having one last meal if not too late. Sometimes we would awake to do it all over again the next day.

The event days were a little more relaxed for the crew, but these were the days that Goenkaji worked harder. There was a steady stream of personal interviews and trust meetings in the early part of the day, and then we would prepare for a public talk in the evening. Many of the crew tried to get to the event site a couple of hours early to attend the group sitting that was always held there and to set up whatever equipment was necessary. If the venue was close to the RV park someone would drive the Teachers in a car but if the distance was a little longer, the two largest motorhomes would go. This allowed Goenkaji time and space to rest prior to the talk and to eat afterwards. The crew were always served a meal at these talks by the local organizers. Sometimes the RVs would not return to the campsite until very late, the latest being 3:00 a.m. after one especially long day.

(International edition—September 2002)

SECTION FOUR

APPLIED DHAMMA

Applied Dhamma—Introduction

The main purpose of learning Vipassana meditation is to apply the technique in everyday life situations. Taking the training from a course and one's daily sittings and transferring it from the cushion to relationships with family and friends, the workplace, social and leisure activities. Changing oneself progressively, developing more awareness and equanimity, more kindness and compassion towards others, reducing self-centredness, agitation and reactive thoughts and actions. The articles in this section show examples of how the practice of Dhamma, a personal internal process, can be productively applied in the outside world.

The brief opening article written by Goenkaji for the first International edition of the *Vipassana Newsletter* in 1974 offers an inspirational personal message to old students: the work of applying Dhamma starts inside ourselves with a committed, thoughtful and evolving meditation practice. By one's personal example, living a Dhamma life, others will be attracted to a Path out of suffering.

In 2000 Goenkaji took part in the Millenium World Peace Summit of religious and spiritual leaders hosted at the United Nations. His message was that the inner peace of individuals is the key to world peace and that spiritual traditions should unite to promote this common human goal rather than quarrelling over superficial differences. This presentation can be viewed via the internet at ***www.dhamma.org/os*** and at ***www.vridhamma.org***

The December 2001 International edition took its lead from the tragic events of 9/11, when terrorists shocked the world by simultaneously attacking a number of targets in the USA with the loss of many lives. Goenkaji wrote a personal message on this subject and some other short pieces about the power of equanimity and love to overcome hatred were included with the article.

An unusual news item follows about Benazir Bhutto, former Prime Minister of Pakistan, and her interest in this technique. Fortunately she was able to learn the initial exercises in Vipassana before being deposed. After years in exile, she bravely returned to Pakistan as a leadership contender against security advice and was assassinated by extremists.

The following two articles also relate to tragic circumstances—the earthquakes in Gujarat, those still suffering from the Khmer Rouge abuses in Cambodia—and the practical role of Vipassana in helping to assist the survivors.

Goenkaji spoke at a seminar at *Dhamma Giri* "On Addiction", presenting a Vipassana perspective on how to combat the root cause of mental impurities, not just their symptoms. "Keeping Our Minds Healthy" is based on a talk to social workers in the USA in which he encouraged the professional audience to take steps to purify themselves in order to help make a change in others.

Newsletters have carried various reports of the Vipassana Prison course programme from time to time. This edited article takes stock of developments worldwide as of 2003.

With his own background, Goenkaji has always taken a keen interest in bringing leaders in the fields of business, administration and the professions into contact with Vipassana, sometimes through arranging 10-day courses specifically for this target group or else through presentations to interested executives. The following two articles reflect some of his input when invited to participate at the World Economic Forum at Davos, Switzerland in 2000.

Issues specific to young people and students who wish to practise Vipassana are dealt with in the next two articles.

In "Why I Sit" we encounter one meditator's personal rationale for regular Vipassana practice, 'to know myself'. ('simply education, learning to modulate turmoil through insight into equipoise,' he has written elsewhere.)

The section concludes with "Apply Dhamma In Life", an exhortation by the Teacher to make use of this technique of liberation for one's entire life, for one's own benefit and for the benefit of many others.

Message from Goenkaji

The following message was written for the first issue of the International edition of the Vipassana Newsletter in 1974

Dear Travelers on the Path of Dhamma,

Be happy!

Keep the torch of Dhamma alight! Let it shine brightly in your daily life. Always remember, Dhamma is not an escape. It is an art of living: living in peace and harmony with oneself and also with all others. Hence, try to live a Dhamma life.

Don't miss your daily sittings each morning and evening.

Whenever possible, attend weekly joint sittings with other Vipassana meditators.

Do a 10-day course as an annual retreat. This is essential to keep you going strong.

With all confidence, face the spikes around you bravely and smilingly.

Renounce hatred and aversion, ill will and animosity.

Generate love and compassion, especially for those who do
not understand Dhamma and are living an unhappy life.

May your Dhamma behavior show them the path of peace and harmony. May the glow of Dhamma on your faces attract more and more suffering people to this path of real happiness.

May all beings be happy, peaceful, liberated.

With all my *mettā*,
S.N. Goenka.

Inner Peace for World Peace

Address by S.N. Goenka to the Millennium World Peace Summit, UN General Assembly Hall, United Nations, N. Y., August 29, 2000. In late August of this year, Goenkaji participated in the Millennium World Peace Summit, a gathering of 1,000 of the world's religious and spiritual leaders, held at the United Nations under the auspices of Secretary-General Kofi Annan. The purpose of the meeting was to promote tolerance, foster peace and encourage inter-religious dialogue. Many different viewpoints were represented and the potential for disagreement was strong. Goenkaji, in his presentation to the delegates, tried to highlight what they and all spiritual paths have in common: the universal Dhamma. His remarks were received with repeated ovations.

Words of Dhamma

Vivādaṃ bhayato disvā	Seeing danger in dispute,
avivādaṃ ca khemato.	Security in concord,
Samaggā sakhilā hotha,	Dwell together in amity.
esā buddhānusāsanī.	This is the teaching of the Buddhas.

—Khuddāka-nikaya, Apadāna 1–79

Na hi verena verāni,	Hatred never ceases,
samantīdha kudācanaṃ;	by hatred in this world;
averena ca sammanti,	by love alone it ceases.
sa dhammo sanantano.	This is an eternal law.

—Dhammapada – 5

Friends, leaders of the spiritual and religious world, this is a wonderful occasion, when we can all unite and serve humanity. Religion is religion only when it unites; when it divides us, it is nothing.

Much has been said here about conversion, both for and against. Far from being opposed to conversion, I am very much in favor of it—but not conversion from one organized religion to another. No, the conversion must be from misery to happiness. It must be from bondage to liberation. It must be from cruelty to compassion. That is the conversion needed today, and that is what this meeting should seek to bring about.

The ancient land of India gave a message of peace and harmony to the world, to all humanity, but it did more: It gave a method, a technique, for achieving peace and harmony. To me it seems that if we want peace in human society, we cannot ignore individuals. If there is no peace in the mind of the individual, I do not understand how there can be real peace in the world. If I have an agitated mind, always full of anger, hatred, ill will and animosity, how can I give peace to the world? I cannot, because I have no peace myself. Enlightened persons have therefore said, "First find peace within yourself." One has to examine whether there is really peace within oneself. All the sages, saints and seers of the world have advised, "Know thyself." This means not merely knowing at the intellectual level, or accepting at the emotional or devotional level, but realizing by experience at the actual level. When you experience the truth about yourself, within yourself, at the experiential level, the problems of life find their own solutions.

You start understanding the universal law, the law of nature—or, if you prefer, the law of God Almighty. This law is applicable to one and all: When I generate anger, hatred, ill will or animosity, I am the first victim of my anger. I am the first victim of the hatred or animosity that I have generated within. First I harm myself, and only afterwards do I start harming others. This is the law of nature. If I observe within myself, I find that as soon as any negativity arises in the mind, there is a physical reaction: My body becomes hot and starts burning; there are palpitations and tension; I am miserable. And when I generate negativity within me and become miserable, I do not keep this misery limited to myself; instead I throw it onto others. I make the entire atmosphere around me so tense that anyone who comes in contact with me also becomes miserable. Although I talk of peace and happiness, more important than words is what is happening within me. And if my mind is free of negativity, again the same law starts working. The moment there is no negativity in the mind, nature—or God Almighty—starts rewarding me: I feel peaceful. This too I can observe within myself.

Whatever one's religion or tradition or country, when one breaks the law of nature and generates negativity in the mind, one is bound to suffer. Nature itself provides the punishment. Those who break nature's laws start feeling the misery of hellfire within, here and now. The seed they sow now is a seed of hellfire, and what awaits them after death is nothing but hellfire. Similarly, by the law of nature, if I keep my mind pure, full of love and compassion, I enjoy the kingdom of heaven within here and now. And the seed that I sow will have as its fruit the kingdom of heaven after death. It makes no difference whether I call myself a Hindu, a Muslim, a Christian or a Jain: A human being is a human being; the human mind is the human mind.

The conversion that is needed is from impurity of mind to purity of mind, and this conversion changes people in wonderful ways. There is no magic or miracle; this is the pure science of observing the interaction of mind and matter within. One examines how the mind influences the material body, and how the body influences the mind. Through patient observation the law of nature becomes so clear: Whenever one generates mental negativity, one starts suffering; and whenever one is free from negativity, one enjoys peace and harmony. This technique of self-observation can be practiced by one and all.

Taught in ancient times by the Enlightened One in India, the technique spread around the world. And still today, people from different communities, traditions and religions come and learn this technique, to obtain the same benefit. They may continue to call themselves Hindu, Buddhist, Muslim or Christian. These labels make no difference; a human being is a human being. The difference is that through their practice they become truly spiritual people, full of love and compassion. What they are doing is good for themselves and for all others. When someone generates peace in the mind, the entire atmosphere around that person is permeated with the vibration of peace, and anyone who encounters that person also starts enjoying peace. This mental change is the real conversion that is required. No other conversion has meaning

Permit me to read a benevolent message from India to the world. Inscribed in stone 2300 years ago, these are the words of the Emperor Ashoka the Great, an ideal ruler, explaining how to govern. He tells us, "One should not honor only one's own religion and condemn other faiths." This is an important message for our time. By condemning others and insisting that one's own tradition is the best, one creates difficulties for humanity. Ashoka continues, "Instead, one should honor other religions for various reasons." Every religion worthy of the name has a wholesome essence of love, compassion and good will—every religion. We should give honor to religions because of this essence. The outer form always differs; there will be so many variations in rites, rituals, ceremonies or beliefs. Let us not quarrel about all that, but instead give importance to the inner essence. As Ashoka says, "By so doing one helps one's own religion to grow, and also renders service to the religions of others. In acting otherwise, one digs the grave of one's own religion and harms other religions as well."

This is a serious warning for us all. Ashoka says, "Someone who honors his own religion, and condemns other religions, may do so out of devotion to his religion thinking, 'I will glorify my religion,' but his actions injure his own religion most gravely."

Finally, Ashoka presents the message of the Universal Law, the message of Dharma: "Let all listen: Concord is good, not quarrelling. Let all be willing to listen to the doctrine professed by others." Instead of disagreeing and condemning, let us give importance to the essence of the teaching of every religion. And then there will be real peace, real harmony.

(International edition—November 2000)

Hatred Never Ceases Through Hatred

Words of Dhamma

Paradukkhūpadhānena, attano sukhamicchati.
Verasaṃsaggasaṃsaṭṭho, verā so na parimuccati.

Those who seek happiness for themselves by inflicting injury on others are not freed from hatred, being themselves entangled in its bonds.

—Dhammapada, 291, Narada translation.

A Message from Goenkaji

September's tragic events have shaken us all. Our hearts go out to those who lost their lives or were injured; to their families, friends and colleagues; and to the millions who watched in helpless horror.

This was an attack on the right of men and women to live in peace and safety, and to work toward a better future for themselves and their children. The tragedy occurred in a country that has opened its doors to the people of the world, that has championed the ideal that all human beings are equal, and that gives hope for a better future.

We must not allow that hope to be dimmed. In a time of darkness, we must bring light—the light of the Dhamma. Deep wounds caused by the darkness of ignorance can be healed by the wisdom that the light of Vipassana brings.

On September 11, within a few moments, ordinary superficial reality was stripped away and we saw the harsh truth: that suffering is inescapable, that everything we cling to is bound to pass away, that we have no real control over what happens.

This vision may seem unbearable, but Vipassana teaches us how to bear it. By learning to observe *dukkha, anicca, and anattā* within ourselves we can develop balance of mind—the balance that will enable us to face any situation and not be overwhelmed.

It is the duty of every government to protect its citizens from external attack, and to do everything possible to make its people and territory secure. At the same time, it must also be borne in mind that such measures give only short-term benefits. Goodwill and compassion alone can remove the roots of all such acts of hatred, no matter who performs them nor what justification they claim.

Certainly now is the time to have a balanced mind, the time to generate goodwill and compassion for others. We have seen how great some people's hatred is, and how dangerous and corrosive. If we can do anything to reduce the sum total of hatred in the world, we shall have achieved a significant victory.

The Buddha said, "Never in this world is hatred quenched by hatred. By love alone is it quenched; this is an eternal law." (Dhp, 5) This law has nothing to do with Christianity,

Islam, Hinduism, Buddhism, Jainism, Judaism, Sikhism, or any other "ism." It is a universal law of nature.

Therefore we must develop *mettā* toward all who share in this tragedy. And our *mettā* must extend even to those very deluded beings who perpetrated such attacks. They have thrown away their precious lives for a mistaken conception of religion, and in harming others they have much more seriously harmed themselves.

It would compound the tragedy to regard their distorted views as being representative of Islam. The Holy Quran proclaims unequivocally that there can be no violence or compulsion in the name of religion. Those who truly follow the teachings of Islam are peace-loving, like all genuinely religious people. Now is the time for us to demonstrate solidarity with innumerable peace-loving Muslims and Arabs. Let not the cowardly acts of a few cloud our perception of one of the world's great faiths.

Good is bound to triumph over evil and all acts, good and evil, originate in the mind. The greatest good is to have a pure mind free of taints. With such a mind we can weather even the greatest vicissitudes of life. We can return goodwill for hatred. We can forestall hateful acts without provoking more hatred. We can live without fear, and in peace with all others.

The Quran tells us, "Virtue and vice can never be the same; therefore repel vice with virtue. In the end this will prove better, for enemies will then become friends, and hatred forever will disappear." (Surah Ha-Min, 34–35)

The Dhamma gives us a way to repel evil within ourselves, which in turn will help to dispel hatred in the world. Let us be diligent in practicing the Dhamma, and let us bring the light of Dhamma to all those who are suffering or in sorrow.

May all the wretched people of the world be free of suffering.
May all who fear be rid of their fear.
May all people forsake enmity and live in peace.
May the Dhamma arise in the minds of all.
May all beings be happy, be peaceful, be liberated!

Love and Hatred

Akkocchi maṃ avadhi maṃ,
ajini maṃ ahāsi me."
Ye ca tam upanayhanti,
veraṃ tesaṃ na sammati.

"He abused me, he beat me,
he defeated me, he robbed me,"
In those who harbor such thoughts,
hatred is never appeased.

—Dhammapada, 3

Nowadays there is dissatisfaction
almost everywhere.
Dissatisfaction creates ill feeling.
Ill feeling creates hatred.
Hatred creates enmity.
Enmity creates war. War creates enemies.
Enemies create war. War creates enemies,
and so on—it's now a vicious circle. Why?
Certainly because there is lack of control
over the mind.

—Sayagyi U Ba Khin

Susukhaṃ vata jīvāma,
verinesu averino.
Verinesu manussesu,
viharāma averino.

Blessed indeed are we who live
among those who hate, hating no one;
amidst those who hate,
let us dwell without hatred.

—Dhammapada, 197

Mettāvihāri yo bhikkhu
pasanno buddhasāsane
adhigacche padaṃ santaṃ
sankhārūpasamaṃ sukhaṃ.

The meditator who abides in loving-kindness,
who is devoted to the Buddha's Teaching,
attains the peace of Nibbāna,
the bliss of cessation of all conditioned things.

—Dhammapada, 368

Hindi Dohas by S.N. Goenka

Dveshha aura durbhāva kā,
rahe na nāma nishāna.
Sneha aura sadbhāva se,
bhara leṅ tana mana prāna.

Of hatred and ill will
may not a trace remain.
May love and goodwill
fill body, mind, and life.

Jage pyāra hi sarvadā,
roma roma laharāya.
Dharama Gaṅga aisī bahe,
dveshha droha dhula jāya.

May love forever arise
and reverberate through your being.
May the Dhamma flow like the Ganges,
washing away hatred and ill will.

Jale holikā dveshha kī,
bhasmibhūta ho jāya.
Umade Gangā pyāra ki,
jana jana mana laharāya.

May the bonfire of hatred burn down
to nothing but ashes.
May the Ganges of love spill over
and flow through the hearts of all.

From The Art of Living by William Hart

The absence of craving or aversion does not imply an attitude of callous indifference, in which one enjoys one's own liberation but gives no thought to the suffering of others. On the contrary, real equanimity is properly called "holy indifference." It is a dynamic quality, an expression of purity of mind. When freed of the habit of blind reaction the mind for the first time can take positive action, which is creative, productive, and beneficial for oneself and for all others. Along with equanimity will arise the other qualities of a pure mind: goodwill, love that seeks the benefit of others without expecting anything in return; compassion for others in their failings and sufferings; sympathetic joy in their success and good fortune. These four qualities are the inevitable outcome of the practice of Vipassana.

Previously one always tried to keep whatever was good for oneself and pass anything unwanted on to others. Now one understands that one's own happiness cannot be achieved at the expense of others, that giving happiness to others brings happiness to oneself. Therefore one seeks to share whatever good one has with others. Having emerged from suffering and experienced the peace of liberation, one realizes that this is the greatest good. Thus one wishes that others may also experience this good and find the way out of their suffering.

This is the logical conclusion of Vipassana meditation: *mettābhāvanā*, the development of goodwill toward others. Previously one may have paid lip service to such sentiments, but deep within the mind the old process of craving and aversion continued. Now, to some extent the process of reaction has stopped, the old habit of egoism is gone, and goodwill naturally flows from the depths of the mind. With the entire force of a pure mind behind it, this goodwill can be very powerful in creating a peaceful and harmonious atmosphere for the benefit of all.

There are those who imagine that always remaining balanced means that one can no longer enjoy life in all its variety, as if a painter had a palette full of colours and chose to use nothing but gray, or as if one had a piano and chose to play nothing but middle C. This is a wrong understanding of equanimity. The fact is that the piano is out of tune and we do not know how to play it. Simply pounding the keys in the name of self-expression will only create discord. But if we learn how to tune the instrument and to play it properly, then we can make music. From the lowest to the highest note we use the full range of the keyboard, and every note that we play creates nothing but harmony, beauty.

Questioner: *What is true compassion?*

Goenkaji: It is the wish to serve people, to help them out of suffering. But it must be without attachment. If you start crying over the suffering of others, you only make yourself unhappy. This is not the path of Dhamma. If you have true compassion, then with all possible love you try to help others to the best of your ability. If you fail, you smile and try another way to help. You serve without worrying about the results of your service. This is real compassion, proceeding from a balanced mind.

(International edition—December 2001)

Benazir Bhutto and Vipassana

Dr. Roop Jyoti, Kathmandu

In the summer of 1994, I got a call from the Home Ministry in Kathmandu. Prime Minister Benazir Bhutto, who was on an official visit to Nepal, wanted to visit *Dharmashringa* Vipassana Center in Kathmandu. Arrangements were made to show her around and explain the Vipassana meditation technique in the tradition of Sayagyi U Ba Khin as taught by S. N. Goenka. Unfortunately, the visit was cancelled. Two years later, the Foreign Ministry contacted us again. Prime Minister Sher Bahadur Deuba was going to Pakistan and there was a specific request from Benazir Bhutto to bring along a Vipassana teacher.

Our Principal Teacher, Acharya Goenkaji asked me and Nani Maiya Manandhar, both senior teachers, to go with the delegation. Benazir Bhutto was busy with the state visit and sent word that she would meet us as soon as she was free. On the last day of the state visit, the Nepali delegates were returning to Karachi in the afternoon to fly back to Kathmandu. Nani Maiyaji and I were finally summoned at 3pm, after the rest of the delegation had flown off. Benazir Bhutto had heard much about Vipassana and wanted to learn the technique there and then. We told her it required a 10-day retreat. She did not have such time, and insisted to be taught right away. Acharya Goenkaji had foreseen such a response and had given permission to teach her the *Ānāpāna* technique. So, Nani Maiyaji taught her *Ānāpāna*. Benazir Bhutto started practising right away and found it very calming. She said that she had not slept for days and after the session of *Ānāpāna*, she wanted to take a nap because she felt so tranquil.

We waited while she had a restful sleep. After a few hours, she emerged looking refreshed and happy. We explained to her the salient aspects of Vipassana: a means out of human suffering and misery; not a ritual of an organized religion but an art of living. Vipassana involves no conversion from one religion to another and is open to all without any barrier of caste, creed or gender. The technique helps people control unruly minds and cleanse them of impurities like fear, anger, hatred, ill will, animosity, greed, passion and restlessness. Vipassana teaches how to diminish the ego and to find truth about oneself and to achieve inner peace.

We talked a bit more about Vipassana and where she could possibly sit through a full 10-day course. We also gave her books, tapes and videos. By this time, it was late in the evening and the last flight from Islamabad to Karachi was about to leave. We rushed to the airport. Upon the prime minister's order, two seats had been kept for us and the plane took off as soon as we boarded it. When we landed at Karachi that night, we learnt that there had been a military coup and Benazir Bhutto had been deposed. We were the last visitors she met as prime minister.

Last week, as news of her assassination

came in, I was filled with sadness, but took solace in the fact that she had learned *Ānāpāna*, an important part of the Vipassana technique. May she be happy and peaceful in her heavenly abode.

(Dhamma Giri edition—January 2008)

Relief for the Earthquake-Affected

S. N. Goenka

The following has been translated and adapted from an article by Goenkaji published in the March 2001 issue of the Vipaśyanā Patrikā)

Words of Dhamma

Sabbadānaṃ dhammadānaṃ jināti,
sabbaṃ rasaṃ dhammaraso jināti;
sabbaṃ ratiṃ dhammarati jināti,
taṇhakkhayo sabbadukkhaṃ jināti.

The gift of Dhamma excels all other gifts, The flavour of Dhamma excels all other flavours; The pleasure of Dhamma excels all other pleasures, One who has eradicated craving overcomes all sorrow.

—Dhammapada, 354

How catastrophic was the wrath of nature! The earth trembled and shook violently. Such a massive earthquake! Such a terrible earthquake! Such a destructive earthquake! Such a devastating earthquake! It seemed as if the whole region has been affected by the frenzied dance of death.

The breast of the earth was torn open and developed wide cracks in it. As a result, cracks were also produced in the walls of houses. Small huts as well as big buildings began to shake uncontrollably. Many of them collapsed like castles of sand, like houses of cards.

Those who were outside by chance or had left their homes earlier survived. But the remaining thousands of people fell victim to this cruel misfortune. Many were killed, many were crippled, many were injured. A great disaster had befallen the people leaving them sorely distressed. The sound of crying, the sound of weeping, the sound of lamentation, the sound of wailing could be heard all around. Wherever one looked, there was ruin and desolation. Such great devastation was wrought within just a few minutes. It was a heart-rending sight, a terrifying spectacle of death and destruction.

A beloved husband was buried in the ground. A loved child was buried forever. A mother had died, leaving her weeping child behind. A father had departed leaving his loved ones without protection. The only child of a family had died, extinguishing the family line. The support of elderly parents was snatched away. Life was shrouded by darkness. The cries of those wounded and trapped beneath the rubble of the fallen buildings were heart-rending. What was the condition of those trapped beneath the rubble? Were they alive or dead or near death?

This great disaster took place so swiftly that it was not possible for anyone to help others. At some places, whole villages were buried; whole localities were destroyed. Who was left to save others, to help others, to console others, to comfort others? The entire family as well as the shops and godowns (warehouses) of a wealthy person were completely wiped out. He was the only one to survive—weak and helpless. A poor person who lived in a hut with his family and eked his livelihood by running a small tea-shop in front of his hut had also lost everything. He was also the only one to survive—weak and helpless. Rich or poor, nature did not spare anyone. Hindu or Muslim, Buddhist or Jain, all of them fell victim to this earthquake. This catastrophe affected all of them equally. Thousands were suddenly rendered homeless and destitute. There was no food, no water, no clothes, no bedding, no shelter, and no protection. The groans from their battered hearts, the painful sighs from their distressed minds were unbearable. There was no limit to their suffering; it was so intense that it was beyond imagination.

Many people from India and other countries as well as organisations and governments came forward to help them as much as possible. Food, water, tents, blankets, medicines and other material began to arrive there. Though this was very little in comparison to the amount needed, at least the relief work had started.

The Buddha said that *kālikadāna* (timely aid) is most beneficial, most meritorious. If whatever is essential to save someone's life is given immediately, that is called *kālikadāna.* The people affected by this natural calamity are in dire need of this kind of assistance. Such aid should definitely be given. But this material aid only is not sufficient.

The wounds of the body will heal but what about the deep wounds on the mind? One whose house has been buried in the ground can build a new house but what about the one whose mind is mired in a bottomless pit of despair? There used to be an invaluable technique in ancient India for this purpose that fortunately has again arisen in this country. The Buddha said that the *dhammadāna* (of Vipassana) is the greatest of all gifts. But he also said that it is necessary to give *kālikadāna* first.

An incident from his life:

Once an extremely distressed person came to him. People beseeched the Buddha to teach Dhamma to this person so that he could gain liberation from his misery. The Buddha looked at him and asked,

"Have you had food?"

"No." was the reply.

"Did you have food yesterday?"

"No."

"Oh, he has been hungry for two days! First, give him food. Only then, I will teach him Dhamma."
Therefore, even though the *dāna* of Dhamma is supreme, it is extremely important to give *kālikadāna* first. After the people get relief by this *kālikadāna*, they should be given the gift of spiritual peace and happiness.

The greatest destruction by this cataclysmic earthquake was caused in Kutch, Kathiawad and Ahmedabad. There are Vipassana meditation centres already at these three places: *Dhamma Sindhu* at Bada near Bhuj, *Dhamma Koṭa* at Rajkot, and *Dhamma Pīṭha* near Ahmedabad. People join 10-day courses at these centres to strengthen and purify their minds and gain much benefit.

It is good that many Vipassana meditators have already undertaken the meritorious work of giving *kālikadāna*, individually and in groups. Now continuous courses will be organised at these three meditation centres as soon as possible so that those who have been afflicted by the earthquake can join these courses in large numbers and gain mental strength to rebuild their lives. So far, about 100 to 150 people have been taking part in these courses here because there were facilities only for this number. But now, with the use of tents, courses for 500 to 1,000 meditators will be organised here so that the quake-afflicted can gain relief from their mental trauma. Vipassana works as a healing balm on the wounds of the mind; it does the work of healing broken hearts.

In such great adversity, the practice of Vipassana enables one to live an equanimous life. The unbalanced mind becomes balanced; the agitated mind becomes calm; the suffering mind becomes free from suffering. This has been confirmed by the experience of thousands of Vipassana meditators.

Just now, I have received a message that a meditator, Meena Asher, from Kutch passed away peacefully and equanimously in this earthquake. She had done her first Vipassana course in 1978 and had been meditating regularly for the past 23 years. She benefited greatly from it and inspired her brothers, sisters and other members of her family to take part in Vipassana courses. Today, five of them are serving as assistant teachers of Vipassana and conducting courses at various places.

Like everyone else, this Dhamma daughter also had to face many ups and downs in her life. Because of her practice of Vipassana she always maintained the balance of her mind. She lived an exemplary life: accepting all situations with composure without ever complaining about anyone. Her life was exemplary. When the earthquake struck at 8:50 a.m. on 26th January 2001, she was working in the kitchen and was trapped under the rubble of the collapsed building. The bones of her neck and back were broken. The others—her only daughter and her elder sister-in-law with her son and daughter—were also crushed near her and passed away. We cannot imagine the mental state of a woman trapped under the debris of stone and brick, who is alive but cannot make the slightest movement. How must she have passed each moment! One cannot imagine how painful each moment must have been waiting and hoping that someone would remove the pile of rubble or at least hoping to hear someone's voice or to see a ray of light from outside.

She was trapped under the rubble in this unbearable condition not merely for one or two hours but for 10 hours. She was finally rescued from the rubble at about 7:00 p.m. that day. People saw that there was not the slightest sign of agitation on her face. The pain in her back and neck must certainly have been unbearable. But, let alone crying or lamenting, she did not even sigh in pain. Nor did she have any tears in her eyes. She was lying peacefully with her head on the lap of her nephew, who had survived because he had been outside at the time of the earthquake. It was not that she was unconscious; she was fully conscious. She asked for water to drink. But there was no sign of misery on her face or in her voice. Lying in this condition and practising Vipassana, she passed away peacefully after an hour and a quarter. Truly, she had learned the art of dying. She used to say repeatedly that Vipassana had taught her the art of living. The technique that taught her the art of living happily and equanimously in every situation had also taught her the art of dying peacefully even in the presence of excruciating pain. In the present history of Vipassana, there have been many meditators who have peacefully embraced a painful death in this way. Among them, there have been some who refused to take narcotic painkillers even while suffering from the extreme agony of the terminal stage of cancer, choosing instead to observe the pain dispassionately, and passed away peacefully. This meditator also has left an ideal example of an inspiring Dhamma death.

The technique of Vipassana teaches one to live a life of peace and harmony even in the face of the greatest adversity. May it benefit all those affected by the earthquake. May their broken hearts be healed. May they get the strength to start their lives anew. May they become peaceful! May they become contented!

(Dhamma Giri edition—March 2001)

Course for Cambodians

The following letter was received from a student in the U.K.

Not long ago, a course organized by and for Cambodian people was held in France, near Paris. The students were all between the ages of 60 and 80 years old. Some had physical handicaps, or had to take drugs such as valium. The majority were women, most of them widows. They are "boat people"—refugees from Cambodia, having lost some or all of their families, having gone through the war, the refugee camps, with much pain and sorrow. They live in a country foreign to them in every respect.

The discovery of Vipassana brought them all so much happiness that, at the end of the course, they couldn't stop expressing it in any way they could. It was quite incredible, and a balm to the heart to see such a quick, real, tangible result. Never had I seen so much joy at the end of a course—joy at being able to do away slowly with heavy medication and to make physical handicaps gradually better. And such a joy to know how to carry on with their lives in peace, in love, beyond their deep pain and sorrow. A 75-year old woman seemed to just melt with happiness as she told the teacher that, at last she'd found what she had been looking for all of her life.

A few days later, I visited an old people's home. What a difference! So much misery and bitterness; so much helplessness on their faces and bodies. And all the more sad, because we know that it could, it can, be otherwise.

This Cambodian course was such a strong example of what Vipassana meditation can do for old people (and others). I wanted to let you know about the course, since I understand that steps are being taken to bring Dhamma to other sectors of society.

Thanking you, I wish all beings will get a chance to know peace, harmony and happiness.

(International edition—June 1998)

On Addiction

The following is excerpted from an address by S.N. Goenka to the Seminar on Vipassana, Addictions, and Better Health, held at V.I.A., Dhamma Giri in November, 1989.

Words of Dhamma

Phassa paccayā vedanā; *Vedanā paccayā taṅhā;* *Taṅhā paccayā upādānaṃ;* *Upādāna paccayā bhavo.*	With the base of contact, sensation arises. With the base of sensation, craving and aversion arise. With the base of craving and aversion, attachment arises. With the base of attachment, the process of becoming arises.
Phassa nirodhā vedanā nirodho; *Vedanā nirodhā taṅhā nirodho;* *Taṅhā nirodhā upādāna nirodho;* *Upādāna nirodhā bhava nirodho.*	With the cessation of contact, sensation ceases. With the cessation of sensation, craving and aversion cease. With the cessation of craving and aversion, attachment ceases. With the cessation of attachment, the process of becoming ceases.

—From Paṭiccasamuppāda *Sutta*, Saṃyutta Nikāya, XII (I.), 1.

The Buddha proclaimed that one who understands Dhamma understands the law of cause and effect. You must realize this truth yourselves. Here is a process by which you can do so. You take steps on the path and whatever you have realized, you accept it; and step by step, with an open mind you keep experiencing deeper truths.

It is not for the sake of curiosity that you investigate the truth pertaining to matter, mind and mental contents. Instead you are seeking to change mental habit patterns at the deepest level. As you proceed, you will realize how mind influences matter, and how matter influences mind.

Every moment within the framework of the body, masses of subatomic particles—*kalāpas*—arise and pass away. How do they arise? The cause becomes clear as you investigate the reality as it is, free from the influence of past conditionings or philosophical beliefs. The material input, the food that you have eaten, is one cause for the arising of these *kalāpas*. Another is the atmosphere around you. You also begin to understand how mind helps matter to arise and dissolve. At times matter arises from the mental conditioning of the past—that is, the accumulated *saṅkhārās* of the past. By the practice of Vipassana, all of this starts to become clear. At this moment, what type of mind has arisen and what is the content of this mind? The quality of the mind is according to its content. For example, when a mind full of anger, passion or fear has arisen, you will notice that different subatomic particles are generated.

When the mind is full of passion, then within this material structure, subatomic particles of a particular type arise, and there is a biochemical flow which starts throughout the body. This type of biochemical flow, which starts because a mind full of passion has arisen, is called in Pali *kāmāsava*—the flow of passion.

As a scientist you proceed further, observing truth as it is, examining the law of nature. When this biochemical flow produced by passion starts, it influences the next moment of the mind with more passion. Thus the *kāmāsava* turns into *kāma-taṅhā*, a craving of passion at the mental level, which again stimulates a flow of passion at the physical level. One starts influencing and stimulating the other, and the passion keeps on multiplying for minutes, even hours together. The tendency of the mind to generate passion is strengthened because of this repeated generation of passion.

Not only passion but also fear, anger, hatred and craving—in fact, every type of impurity that comes into the mind—simultaneously generates an *āsava*, a biochemical flow. And this *āsava* keeps on stimulating that particular negativity, or impurity. The result is a vicious circle of suffering. You may call yourself a Hindu, a Muslim, a Jain or a Christian; it makes no difference. The process, the law is applicable to one and all. There is no discrimination. Mere understanding at a superficial, intellectual level will not help break this cycle, and may even create more difficulties. Your beliefs from a particular tradition may look quite logical, yet those beliefs will create obstacles for you. The intellect has its own limitations. You cannot realize the ultimate truth merely by intellect because intellect is finite, while ultimate truth is limitless, infinite. Only through experience can you realize that which is limitless and infinite. If you accept this law of nature intellectually but still are unable to change the behavior pattern of your mind, you remain far away from the realization of the ultimate truth.

Your acceptance is only superficial, while your behavior pattern continues at the depth of the mind. What is called the unconscious mind is actually not unconscious. At all times it remains in contact with this body. And with this contact a sensation keeps arising. You feel a sensation that you label as pleasant, and you keep reacting. At the depth of your mind you keep reacting with craving or aversion. You keep on generating different types of *saṅkhāras*, negativities, impurities, and the process of multiplying your misery continues. You can't stop it because there is such a big barrier between the conscious and the unconscious mind. Without the practice of Vipassana, this barrier remains.

At the conscious, intellectual level of the mind, one may accept the entire theory of Dhamma, truth, law, nature. But still one keeps rolling in misery because one does not realize what is happening at the depth of the mind. But with Vipassana your mind becomes very sharp and sensitive so that you can feel sensations throughout the body. Sensations occur every moment. Every contact results in a sensation: in Pali, *phassa paccayā vedanā*. This is not a philosophy; it is the scientific truth which can be verified by one and all.

The moment there is a contact, there is bound to be a sensation; and every moment, the mind is in contact with matter throughout the physical structure. The deeper level of the mind keeps feeling these sensations, and it keeps reacting to them. But on the surface the mind keeps itself busy with outside objects, or it remains involved in games of intellectualization, imagination, or emotion. Therefore you do not feel what is happening at the deeper level of the mind.

By Vipassana, when that barrier is broken, one starts feeling sensations throughout the body, not merely at the surface level but also deep inside. By observing these sensations, you start realizing their characteristic of arising and passing, *udayavyaya*. By this understanding, you start to change the habit pattern of the mind.

Say, for example, you are feeling a particular sensation that may be caused by the food you have eaten, the atmosphere around you, your present mental actions, or old reactions that are now giving their fruit. Whatever the cause may be, a sensation has occurred. With your training in Vipassana, you observe it with equanimity, without reacting to it. In those few wonderful moments, you have started changing the habit pattern of your mind by observing sensation and understanding its nature of impermanence. You have stopped the blind habit pattern of reacting to the sensation and multiplying your misery. Initially you may be able to do this only for a few seconds or minutes. But by practice, you gradually develop your strength. As the habit pattern becomes weaker, your behavior pattern changes. You are coming out of your misery.

When we talk of addiction, it is not merely to alcohol or to drugs, but also to passion, anger, fear or egotism. All these are addictions to your impurities. At the intellectual level you may understand very well, "Anger is not good for me. It is dangerous. It is harmful." Yet you are addicted to anger, and keep generating it. And when the anger is over, you keep repeating, "Oh, I should not have generated anger. I should not have generated anger." Yet the next time a stimulus comes, you again become angry. You are not coming out of anger, because you have not been working at the depth of your mind.

By practicing this technique, you start observing the sensation that arises because of the biochemical flow when you are angry. You observe but do not react to it. That means you do not generate anger at that particular moment. This one moment turns into a few minutes, and you find that you are not as easily influenced by this flow as you were in the past. You have slowly started coming out of your anger.

Those who regularly practice this technique try to observe how they are dealing with different situations. Are they reacting or remaining equanimous? The first thing a meditator will try to do in any difficult situation is to observe sensations. Because of the situation, maybe part of the mind has started reacting, but by observing the sensations one becomes equanimous. Then whatever action is taken is real action, not reaction. And action is always positive. It is only when one reacts that one generates negativity and becomes miserable. A few moments of observing sensations makes the mind equanimous and able to act. Life is then full of action instead of reaction.

With regular, daily practice and application of the technique, the behavior pattern starts to change. Those who used to roll in anger for a long time find their anger diminishing in intensity or duration. Similarly, those who are addicted to passion find that it becomes weaker and weaker, and so do those who are addicted to fear. The amount of time that is needed to rid oneself of a certain impurity may vary, but sooner or later the technique will work, provided it is used properly.

Whether you are addicted to craving, aversion, hatred, passion or fear, the addiction is actually to particular sensations that have arisen because of the biochemical flow.

The *āsava*, or flow, of ignorance is the strongest *āsava*. Of course, there is ignorance even when you are reacting with anger, passion or fear; but when you become intoxicated with alcohol or drugs this intoxication multiplies your ignorance. Therefore it takes time to feel sensations, to go to the root of the problem. When you become addicted to liquor or drugs, you cannot know the reality of what is happening within the framework of the body. There is darkness in your mind. You cannot understand what is happening inside, what keeps on multiplying inside. We have found that in cases of alcohol addiction people generally start benefiting more quickly than people who are addicted to drugs. But the way is there for everyone to come out of misery, however much addicted or ignorant they may be. If you keep working patiently and persistently, sooner or later you are bound to reach the stage where you start feeling sensations throughout the body and can observe them objectively. It may take time. In 10 days you may only make a slight change in the habit pattern of your mind. It doesn't matter: a beginning is made. If you keep on practicing morning and evening and take a few more courses, the habit pattern will change at the deepest level of the mind and you will come out of your ignorance, out of your reaction—out of your suffering.

We keep advising people who are addicted even to tobacco: If an urge arises, do not take a cigarette. Instead wait a little. Accept the fact that an urge to smoke has arisen in the mind. When this urge arises, along with it there is a sensation in the body. Start observing that sensation, whatever it may be. Do not look for a particular sensation. Anything you feel at that time is related to the urge to smoke. And by observing the sensation as impermanent, *anicca*, you will find that this urge passes away. This is not a philosophy, but experiential truth.

The same advice applies to those who are addicted to alcohol or drugs: When an urge arises, do not succumb immediately. Instead wait 10 or 15 minutes. Accept the fact that an urge has arisen and observe whatever sensation is present at that time.

Those who follow this advice find that they are coming out of their addictions. They may be successful only one time out of 10 at first, but they have made a very good beginning. They are striking at the root of their problem.

It is a long path, a lifetime job. But even a journey of 10,000 miles must start with the first step. One who has taken the first step can take the second and third; and step by step, one will reach the final goal of liberation.

May you all come out of all your addictions—and not only to drugs or alcohol. The addiction to mental impurities is stronger than these. May you change this strong behavior pattern, to come out of your misery—for your own good, your own benefit, your own liberation. And the process is such that when you start to benefit from the technique, you cannot resist helping others. Your goal becomes the good and benefit of many. So many people are suffering all around: may they all come in contact with pure Dhamma and come out of their misery. May they start enjoying peace and harmony, the peace and harmony of a mind liberated from all defilements.

(International edition—June 1991)

Keeping Our Own Minds Healthy: An Address by S.N. Goenka to Health Care Professionals

The following was condensed from an address presented at Smith College School of Social Work, Northampton, Mass., July 1991.

Friends, fellow social workers: Let us try to understand the problems faced by health care workers and the solutions to these problems. The profession of social service is a very noble profession. If one gives social service selflessly, without making it a means of livelihood, there is nothing that can surpass it. Even if one makes it a means of livelihood, this profession is a very wholesome profession, a very wholesome means of livelihood. The job of a social worker is to help others. People come to you with melancholy on their faces and anguish and pain in their hearts. You help them to come out of their pain and to enjoy real peace and joy within. What better profession can there be?

Such a noble profession; and yet, it is full of hazards. This noble effort to serve others may result in misery for you if you are not taking proper care of yourself.

Suppose a person comes to you suffering from insecurity and fear of the future. This person is generating a vibration full of agitation and unhappiness; he or she is stuck in a whirlpool of misery. After counseling this person for a period of time you may notice that you also are being sucked into this same whirlpool.

At a very deep level of the mind lie seeds of different kinds of mental tendencies, which can bring various kinds of suffering. Your client's vibrations contact the seeds of fear for the future that lie latent in the depths of your mind. The vibrations of these seeds in you are exactly the same as those generated by your client. Your vibrations get tuned up with your client's vibrations, stimulating your own fear and insecurity, your own seeds of misery. You may not even know that this is happening because it may not immediately show an effect. Slowly, over time, you will continue to be in contact with patients who are experiencing fear and gradually you will find that your problem is becoming magnified. Unless you remove these seeds of misery from your mind, your job as a clinician will be harmful to your own mental and physical health. A lame person cannot support another lame person. A blind person cannot show the path to another blind person. How can you help others and protect yourself as well? The practice of Vipassana meditation provides an answer to this question.

Vipassana is the science of mind and matter: Whatever arises in the mind, be it fear, insecurity, passion or ego, does so in a very solidified, intensified way that tends to overpowers us. For example, somebody says something you do not like; someone has insulted you perhaps. You react with anger and become miserable. Whether you have harmed the other person or not by this anger you may not know, but you have certainly harmed yourself. The first victim of your anger is yourself: Although you were insulted only once, you continue to repeat this drama on the stage of your mind for long periods of time, thus strengthening the deep reaction patterns of anger.

When we react with anger at the mental level, immediately something starts happening at the physical level. There is a biochemical secretion that starts flowing in the bloodstream. This particular secretion, generated because of anger, is very unpleasant and because we feel unpleasant sensations we become even angrier. And as we become angrier we generate more biochemical secretions: A vicious circle has started. Similarly passion and fear are each associated with its own particular type of secretion. We ourselves are responsible for this flow, no one else. We multiply our own suffering every moment by reacting to these biochemicals—this flow within us. However, if we do not react, but rather observe, this vicious circle will lose its strength, become weaker and pass away. We have to understand this process in order to come out of it.

The entire psychophysical structure which we keep referring to as "I, mine" is nothing but constantly changing vibrations. We cannot control it or make it non-changing. It is bound to change and does change. It is just currents, vibrations of different frequencies, different wavelengths. This is the deeper truth of our physical structure. The direct experience of this reality has a profound effect.

We can smile at the reality of insecurity: "Look, it keeps changing—so what? Worry, anxiety——so what? This situation will change." We observe vibrations as they change, or particular emotions as they arise and pass away. If we do not observe them objectively they overpower us and multiply, making us a bundle of misery. It is not enough that this truth be accepted at the intellectual or devotional level. It has to be realized at the experiential level, and this is what Vipassana teaches.

When a student comes to a 10-day Vipassana course he or she is asked to explore what is happening within the framework of the body: What truth is manifesting itself? What is happening now?

One starts with something gross, but nevertheless real. The first thing one experiences is the flow of respiration—the breath coming in, the breath going out, naturally, effortlessly. We don't make an effort to breathe in or breathe out. We don't try to control the breath. The whole technique is to develop the faculty of observing reality from moment to moment, as it is, not as we would like it to be. So we try to observe the breath as it is. If it is deep, it is deep; we don't try to make it shallow. If it is shallow, it is shallow; we don't try to make it deep. If it is passing through one nostril, we accept this; we don't try to direct it to the other. If it is passing through both nostrils, then we accept, both nostrils. The flow of respiration is there, coming in, going out. We are observing; we do nothing.

It should be easy, and yet one finds it so difficult. One observes just one or two breaths and the mind wanders away. Only after a few minutes does one realize, "Oh, I am here to observe my breath. What happened?" Again one starts-one or two breaths and again the mind wanders away. One feels irritated; "It should be such an easy task to just observe the breath. What kind of mind do I have? It can't even observe the natural flow of the breath without running here and there."

Then your guide will say, "No, no, don't react. Just accept reality as it is. This is the truth of this moment: The mind has wandered away. Accept it smilingly."

The old habit pattern of the mind is to react when something unwanted happens. And now you don't want your mind to wander away; but it has wandered, and you react with aversion, anger. Whether you generate anger toward others or toward yourself there is no difference. Anger is anger and it will make you very miserable. We come out of this suffering by accepting the truth as it is: "My mind at this moment has wandered away." The breath is still there, and your attention easily returns to it the moment that you accept that the mind has wandered away. You may observe a few breaths and again the mind wanders away. You realize, "Oh, look—it has wandered away." And again you bring it back. One works like this for a few days and the mind starts settling down because one is learning to accept the truth as it is without reacting.

Respiration has a lot to do with the mind and the mental contents. As you observe the breath a thought may arise, maybe a thought of the past or the future, and you react with craving or aversion. Perhaps anger arises and you notice, "Look, anger has arisen." As a result of this anger the breath loses its normalcy and becomes slightly hard, slightly fast. When this particular anger subsides you notice that the breath becomes normal again. So this breath is strongly connected to your mind and your mental impurities.

After the mind calms down a little, one starts experiencing something else: Every moment throughout the body, in every particle of the body, some electromagnetic reaction, some biochemical reaction is taking place. Usually the mind at the surface level is so gross that it can't feel what is happening at deeper levels of the physical structure. But now with a concentrated mind one can feel these very subtle sensations, biochemical reactions, currents, vibrations, etc.

Because one starts with the attention at the entrance of the nostrils, one starts feeling sensations on this area first. They can manifest in a variety of ways; for example, as heat, perspiration, throbbing, pulsing, vibrating, tingling, tension, strain or many other things. You feel something or the other on this spot, and then you are also trained to observe this objectively. "Now there is heat—so what? It is heat. Throbbing, itching,"—various things—"Let me see how long they last." You just observe objectively. On the fourth or fifth day you may reach a stage where you feel sensations such as these throughout the body. You continue to move your attention from head to feet and from feet to head, observing these sensations on the body.

Just as it was with respiration, so it is with sensation. All the sensations on the body—the heat, the tension, the pressure and the vibration—all are connected with one's mental impurities, the defilements, which are the source of our suffering. When anger arises there is a reaction throughout the body. There is heat, perspiration, tension and palpitation. All these are related to our anger; similarly to our fear, our passion and our anxiety. Whatever arises in the mind manifests itself as a sensation on the body. It is this sensation on the body to which the mind reacts.

At the deepest level of the mind are many hidden reaction patterns, which are accumulations of misery from the past. They lie latent, and at any moment, due to some stimulation or the other, they can arise as unpleasant thoughts or sensations and overpower us, making us suffer again. In fact, every moment our minds generate some vibration or the other. This vibration may be positive or negative, but usually it is unwholesome because we remain ignorant of what is happening deep inside. Even though we do not want to, we harm ourselves because we react to the sensation on the body. We thus multiply our suffering. Because the entire atmosphere becomes influenced by these vibrations of negativity, we harm others as well. Every person is generating vibrations and influencing the atmosphere around, and in turn is getting influenced by the vibrations of other people.

So if you are dealing with a client who has a vibration in harmony with reaction patterns deep within you, this will trigger something at the depths of your mind, often overwhelming you. If you can free your mind of these patterns then the service you give will be wonderful, because your mind will be sound and healthy. You will smilingly face the vibrations being generated by others.

Even if this triggers something in you, you will observe your reaction, float over it, but you will not sink. It will not overpower you. This means you are free from this particular misery. All this has to be realized at the experiential level. Merely talking or discussing will not help. Discussions and talks can give us inspiration, some guidelines perhaps. They can show us a path but we must walk on the path. We have to make a journey inside to realize the truth, the truth of the interaction of mind and matter. But this has to be practiced. It requires a lot of practice.

There are many students of Vipassana who have the job of serving others. They may be counselors, social workers, massage therapists—those practicing different ways of helping people. I advise these students to take a short break between one patient and the next. I advise them; wait a little—ten minutes or so-and relax. One can easily do this at the physical level, easing the tension accumulated by counseling someone. However, unknowingly you have absorbed the vibrations of that person deep inside you, and they make you a bundle of tension. Unless you first calm that reaction, you should not work with another person. By practicing Vipassana, and feeling sensations throughout the body, within 10 minutes or so you will feel refreshed. Your battery will be charged again, and you will be ready to work with another patient.

A pure mind is a powerful mind. A pure mind is always full of infinite love; full of compassion, without a trace of passion. You expect nothing in return; you just feel like giving. This is the quality of a pure mind—full of love, full of compassion, full of sympathetic joy, full of equanimity. If you speak even two words with this kind of mind they will be very effective, because your mind has such a pure vibration. The patient will feel healed just by these few words spoken by you. However, if at the surface level you speak very healing, counseling words, and deep inside you are agitated, then the vibration that goes with your words will not have that positive effect.

So be a good healer; and to be a good healer first heal yourself. Go deep inside; calm your mind, purify your mind. See that it is full of pure love, expecting nothing in return, full of compassion, full of sympathetic joy, and full of equanimity. You will find that all the hazards of your work disappear; all the pitfalls are gone. You will become strong, not a lame person helping another lame person, not a blind person showing a path to another blind person. Vipassana will help you to become a good human being, a healthy human being, full of harmony, full of peace, full of tranquility, with a sound mind and sound body. With a sound mind you can help others better and become a really effective social servant. May all of you become good social servants.

May you all be peaceful, be happy, be liberated.

A question and answer session after Goenkaji's address included the following two questions:

Question: ***I feel that our emotions can be teachers, that we can learn from our anger or our sadness. What is the view of Vipassana on this?***

Goenkaji: Emotions by themselves do not make us miserable. If we can learn how to observe our emotions, we come out of misery and therefore learn something from them. But if we allow ourselves to be overpowered by these emotions then we suffer. One thing Vipassana teaches us is this: Emotion will arise; let me observe it objectively. "Look, this is an emotion: anger or sadness," or this or that. "Along with this let me observe what sensation is on the body. Ah, this sensation is impermanent. Let me see how long it lasts." This is how we come out of our suffering.

Question: ***Vipassana focuses on the internal reality. That's fine, but what about the external reality that really causes a great deal of suffering? What use is Vipassana in dealing with the real pain of the world?***

Goenkaji: Understand, Vipassana is not an escape from the problems of day-to-day life. One comes to a course for 10 days to learn the technique of Vipassana and gain strength to face the problems of the outside world—just as you might go to a hospital to become physically healthy, and then leave to live healthily in the world. Similarly, when you learn to use this technique of observing the reality inside, you can face the problems outside more easily. It is not that by the practice of Vipassana all the problems will disappear; but rather, your ability to face them will improve.

The problems of the outside world are created by individuals living in the darkness of ignorance. Just as lighting one lamp will dispel the darkness around it, similarly, one person practicing Vipassana will affect the society. If more people practice Vipassana, slowly this will start having a positive influence in thc world. Even if only this one person is practicing Vipassana at least he or she will be able to face the problems and find solutions. And those solutions will be healthy solutions.
(International edition—April 2005)

Vipassana: Self-observation & Self-correction

In the summer of 2002, as part of his North American Meditation Now tour, S. N. Goenka came to the North Rehabilitation Facility in Seattle, Washington. He met with course students and others on Mettā Day and later addressed an assembly gathered on Day 11 of the last men's course to be held there. His address has been edited and adapted for the Newsletter.

Words of Dhamma

One day, 30 bhikkhus came into Sāvatthī for alms-food. While they were on their alms-round, they saw some prisoners being brought out with their hands and legs in chains. Back at the Jetavana monastery, after relating what they had seen in the morning, they asked the Buddha whether there were any other bonds stronger than these. To them the Buddha answered, "Bhikkhus! These bonds are nothing compared to those of craving for food and clothing, for riches and for family. Craving is 1,000 times, 100,000 times stronger than those chains, handcuffs and cages. That is the reason why the wise cut off craving and renounce the world." Then the Buddha spoke in verse as follows:

Na taṃ daḷhaṃ bandhanamāhu dhīrā,
yadāyasaṃ dārujapabbajañca.
Sārattarattā maṇikuṇḍalesu,
puttesu dāresu ca yā apekkhā.
Etaṃ daḷhaṃ bandhanamāhudhīrā,
ohārinaṃ sithilaṃ duppamuñcaṃ.
Etampi chetvāna paribbajanti,
anapekkhino kāmasukhaṃ pahāya.

The wise do not call strong that fetter which is made of iron, wood or hemp. Rather do they call attachment to jewels, ornaments, and family a far stronger fetter. That fetter is strong, say the wise, which drags one down; which, although slack, is difficult to escape from. Severing even this, they set forth, desiring nothing and abandoning all sensuous pleasures.

—Dhammapada 345, 346

Friends, I am so glad to be here with all of you this morning. You have given this technique a fair trial and you have received good results. Now, you must maintain the practice and apply it in day-to-day life. It is important to learn the technique under an experienced guide, but merely taking a course of 10 days is not sufficient. Now, applying it in life—this is also very important. Nobody else can correct you. You have to correct yourself; you have to develop self-awareness. Keep examining yourself, keep correcting yourself.

And you have two great friends to help you. One friend is your own respiration and the other is sensations on your body. More and more, as you become established in this technique, these two friends will be there to help you throughout life. Whenever the mind becomes unbalanced with some negativity, you will notice that your breath loses its normality. It will be slightly hard, slightly fast, giving you a warning, Look, something is wrong in your mind, something is wrong in your mind! And you will try to make your mind more balanced.

The second guide and friend with you is your sensations, the physical sensations that you have learned to observe in these 10 days. Whenever you find you are generating any negativity it will become clear that you are the first victim of your negativity. Being a good Vipassana meditator, as soon as you generate anger, hatred, ill-will, or animosity, you will notice there is a burning sensation throughout the body. The heart beat increases, tensions build up. Misery! Look, I am making myself miserable!

Immediately, you start to observe the sensations, or you observe the breath, with equanimity. You try to maintain a perfect balance of the mind, a perfect equilibrium of the mind, and you find that your negativity is becoming less. Your mind becomes more and more pure, and the law of nature is such that when the mind is pure it becomes full of love, compassion, goodwill, tolerance. These qualities will arise, provided the purity of mind is maintained.

Not that in 10 days you will become so perfect that there will be no more defilements. Oh, no! The old habit patterns are still there; they continue to arise, but now you have a technique that will help you to eradicate them. Don't allow them to multiply and overpower you. When you are unaware of what is happening deep inside, you will only see things happening outside: Someone has insulted me! This thought becomes predominant in your mind, and you keep thinking, So and so has insulted me; that's why I am generating anger. You generate anger and want to retaliate, to have revenge, to harm this person, but you don't understand that you are harming yourself.

You can't harm anybody else without first harming yourself. You have to generate some defilement or another in your mind in order to harm somebody; and when you do, then you are a miserable person. You don't want to harm yourself. And yet, out of ignorance, without knowing what is happening at the depth of the mind, you keep generating impurity after impurity, defilement after defilement, more and more anger, hatred, jealousy, ego. And the sensations that arise at that time make you feel very miserable.

Before learning Vipassana, you used to react in a certain way in a situation. Now, a similar situation has arisen. Ask yourself, am I reacting in the same way or has some positive change developed in my behavior? Now self-awareness, self-examination you are your own master. Nobody else can correct you; you have to correct yourself. It is not necessary for anybody else to warn you. You have to warn yourself: Oh, look, what I am doing is so harmful. I am harming myself. I can't harm anybody else without doing harm to myself. When I generate negativity, I become so miserable and I keep throwing this misery on others. Anyone who comes in contact with me at this time becomes miserable. The entire atmosphere becomes so tense, so full of misery! And when I am free of this negativity my mind is pure, full of love, compassion, goodwill. I feel so much peace and harmony. The entire atmosphere around me becomes permeated with the vibrations of peace and harmony. Anybody who comes in contact with me starts to experience peace and harmony. This is the correct way of life. My whole life I have continued harming myself and harming others. This was not the proper way of life.

Now, morning and evening you must practice every day. Just as when you learn to do some kind of physical exercise but don't practice, it won't be of any help to you, so also, this technique, this mental exercise will not be of help to you unless you practice it.

The technique you have learned during this course is an invaluable jewel that will help you throughout your life. Maintain it and keep progressing on the path. And to those of you who have never experienced this technique, I recommend you spare 10 days of your life. Don't assume that those who are in prison are the only prisoners. Those who are outside the walls of the prison are also prisoners. Everyone is a prisoner of the unwholesome habit patterns of their minds at the deepest level. Come out of this prison! Come out of the defilements and enjoy life! You will find such a big change in your life. With my experience, I found I gained so much peace. It was a total change of life. I wanted to share my peace and harmony with others, and now thousands upon thousands of people around the world are sharing it. They are practicing, they are getting the same results. This technique helps you to become very peaceful—good for you, good for others.

Staff and inmates, even those who had never taken a course, appreciated the extraordinary nature of this event (the Day 11 reception at NRF) and found a shared sense of gratitude and optimism. Many former inmates who had taken their first Vipassana course at NRF returned to see Goenkaji and to thank him. After the reception, Goenkaji met with staff members, old students and their families in the jail library. People took the opportunity to meet him, ask questions, or express their gratitude, while others watched quietly, staying until Goenkaji left. That day, no one expressed any regrets or concerns about NRF's imminent closure, only gratitude for benefits received and hopefulness for the future.

Several former NRF residents took the opportunity to express how Vipassana has impacted their lives: One male student said: I took the course here at NRF, and through the course I've learned the Vipassana meditation technique and it puts my mind at peace. When I left NRF, I was transferred to another prison. I was put in confinement where it was pretty isolating. I contacted *Dhamma Kuñja* and they sent me many pamphlets and information. I sat and meditated in the morning and evening, pretty much a lot of time all day, and I read my journal and books. I noticed I was being treated differently by the guards from anyone else. Other inmates were coming up to me and asking, What do you have? So I talked about Vipassana with them and told them that this is an ancient teaching that has been handed down through the ages in its purest form. I have not been in one bit of trouble since I've been out (of prison). I've followed the path of right speech, right action, right thought. I've taken care of business and made the practice of Vipassana my Dhamma.

Another old male student: I'd been drunk all my life before taking the first Vipassana course at NRF in 1997. Since then, I've not had a fight, not a drink. I have a family life. My family appreciates you so much.

Wisdom and Rehabilitation around the World

Even before there were established Vipassana meditation centers in our tradition, trail-blazing 10-day courses were being conducted in correctional facilities. While meditation centers provide a consistent atmosphere for the development of Dhamma, the environment of prisons and jails is much more challenging and unstable with their changing administrators and transient inmate populations.

Politics, government funding and meditators working in correctional settings often determine whether a particular facility will be able to sustain a Vipassana program. Often there is initial resistance, then further obstacles, and many attempts before a course gets organized in a prison. Because of our tradition's requirement that correctional personnel attend a Vipassana course prior to implementing it at their facility, and the requirement that Dhamma workers be able to stay overnight inside a facility for the 10 days, it is a small miracle that courses have been allowed in jails and prisons at all. Nonetheless, since 1975, thousands of incarcerated meditators all around the world have participated and benefited from Vipassana. More often than not, the presence of Vipassana has transformed not just the individuals in these institutions, but the institutions themselves.

India

The story began nearly 30 years ago in India. The first Vipassana courses in jails were conducted by Goenkaji in 1975 and 1977 for 120 inmates at the maximum-security Central Jail in Jaipur at the invitation of Mr. Ram Singh, then Home Secretary to the Government of Rajasthan. A third course for senior police officers and jail officials was also held at the Police Academy in Jaipur. Despite these first successful courses, no further prison courses were taught for nearly 15 years. Then in 1990 and 1991, seven more prison courses were held in the states of Rajasthan and Gujarat. These courses were the subject of several sociological studies conducted by the Gujarat State Department of Education and the University of Rajasthan. The research indicated definite positive changes of attitude and behavior in the participants, demonstrating that Vipassana can help criminals become wholesome members of society.

In November 1993, a 10-day course was conducted for 96 inmates and 23 jail staff at Tihar Jail in New Delhi, one of the largest jails in Asia, housing approximately 10,000 inmates. The following January, a second course for 300 inmates was conducted by six assistant teachers. Three months later in April 1994, the largest Vipassana course held up to then was conducted by Goenkaji and 10 assistant teachers for over 1,000 inmates. After its successful completion a permanent center for Vipassana was established inside the jail itself. Since then, 10-day Vipassana courses have been conducted twice monthly at Tihar Jail and less regularly at more than 15 other jails in India.

In 1997, 75 Vipassana courses were conducted in Indian jails. At one point there were two permanent Vipassana centers in Indian jails—one at Tihar and the other at Nasik Jail in Maharashtra where Mohandas Gandhi had once been imprisoned. Because of administrative changes, the Vipassana program at Nasik Jail has been cancelled. However, in Delhi, *Dhamma Tihar* thrives and 20-day courses are being held there on a regular basis. In 2001, there were a total of 39 jail courses in India with 1,420 inmates attending: 978 new and 442 old.

A research study entitled Psychological Effects of Vipassana on Tihar Inmates was conducted at the All India Institute of Medical Sciences in New Delhi in 1997. This study determined that Vipassana meditation helps increase inmates control of their emotions resulting in a reduction of feelings of anger, tension, hostility, revenge and helplessness. Drug addiction, neurotic and psycho-pathological symptoms also diminished. (Chandiramani, Verma, Dhar & Agarwal, 1995; Kumar, 1995; Vora, 1995) In addition, inmates practicing Vipassana have shown an increased willingness to work, to participate in other treatment programs, to abide by prison rules and to cooperate with prison authorities. (Vora, 1995)

The sheer number of inmates who have benefited from Vipassana is nearly matched by the number of police cadets who have attended courses at the Police Training Academy in New Delhi. By 2001, 17 courses, some of them for as many as 1,265 police cadets at a time, had been conducted.

With India as the exemplary leader in bringing Dhamma to prisoners, meditators began the work of spreading Vipassana into prisons around the world. Sometimes the efforts brought only one course, but the seed was sown. At other times programs continue with great success.

Taiwan

In 1996, Goenkaji met with the Taiwanese Minister of Justice in Taiwan. As a result of this very brief meeting, a 10-day course was held at the Ming Te Branch Prison near Tainan on the southwestern coast of Taiwan. Ming Te Prison is an experimental drug rehabilitation institution situated in lush, wooded mountains, housing inmates convicted of narcotics use. It implements religious programs to help substance abusers in their recovery. In a move unprecedented in Taiwan penal history, Goenkaji was invited to give the closing address to the group of 24 prisoners attending the course. Since then, nothing further has developed in Taiwan.

Europe

Until 2003, the only Vipassana course to be held in a European prison was conducted at the HMP Lancaster Castle Prison in the U.K., November 1998. The course took place after two officers learned Vipassana and, encouraged by their own experience and the knowledge of prison courses being held in other countries, decided to explore the possibility of running a course in Lancaster. Eight inmates started and completed the program.

The Prison Journal Service, issue 127 reported that Lancaster's Education Department had noted: There was a marked change for the better in personal discipline, willingness to learn and quality of output from the incarcerated students.

Now, four years later, a second course has

taken place in Europe. The Spanish government gave approval for the first prison course in mainland Europe which took place in April 2003 at Can Brians high-security facility near Barcelona. The story behind the approval for this course and its preparation is insightful.

About two years ago a retired man came to sit his first course at Spain's Vipassana Center, *Dhamma Neru*, near Barcelona. He was so enthusiastic about the technique that he decided to take up voluntary work in Can Brians with the intention of having Vipassana introduced into the jail. He chose this jail because it is charged by the government to experiment with new ways of transforming prisoners, and is at the cutting edge of the Spanish prison service. There are 600 staff to 1,400 inmates.

Last summer the director of the prison invited some trustees to make a presentation to prison staff and visiting professionals. About 30 attended, including a senior judge whose wife had previously sat a course. The response was positive. Some trustees and the area teacher met with the director, staff and prisoners on several occasions, and in October four staff members and one male inmate, out on a 10-day release, sat a course at *Dhamma Neru*. Then, a detailed report in Spanish, showing all the guidelines and requirements, was prepared and submitted to the government.

During the eight weeks prior to the course, there were many preparations. Five orientation classes with interested inmates were held over a period of about a month. The separate facility within the prison that would be used for the course had a capacity for about 25 students; this was checked and approved. Special permission from the government was required for the teacher and servers to stay at the prison for the duration of the course. As well, a system was needed for preparing course food in the prisons main kitchen.

Interest has also been expressed by prisons in Madrid and Granada, but the trust decided not to move forward with presentations until the course was completed at Can Brians. The Director indicated that if the April course was successful, he would give support to these other initiatives.

With well-thought-out plans in place and only a few last minute hitches that made the start of the course look dubious, it started on time and was a great success. Eighteen smiling students completed the course. They shared their experience with other prisoners, family and guests at a Day 11 reception. One student requested the teacher of the course to write an article about Vipassana for a prison magazine that is distributed to 7,000 inmates throughout Catalunya. The director was clearly struck by the change in the inmates. He arranged for daily sittings for them and asked for another course of 30 students in autumn 2003.

New Zealand

Since 1999, Vipassana courses have been held in New Zealand at Te Ihi Tu, a rehabilitation center run by Maoris (the indigenous people of New Zealand), for Maori pre-release prisoners and parolees. Although a private initiative, it is funded by the Department of Corrections. The center is Maori Kaupapa, i.e., based on Maori values and culture. This three-month pre-release program starts with a 10-day Vipassana Meditation course. The staff at Te Ihi Tu are 100% supportive of Vipassana for they have seen that it helps prisoners participation in other programs.

Vipassana Meditation was incorporated into the Te Ihi Tu program in September 1999 after two staff members sat a 10-day course at the Vipassana Meditation Centre, *Dhamma Medini*, near Auckland. The other staff members became quickly convinced that Vipassana Meditation would be beneficial and decided to give it a trial at Te Ihi Tu. There have now been nine courses at Te Ihi Tu and it has become an integral part of their program.

The Department of Corrections only permits a maximum of 10 prisoners to participate in each Te Ihi Tu Vipassana program. It is difficult to get even 10 prisoners, as the Department is cautious about releasing the prisoners to the Te Ihi Tu rehabilitation center. There has been an average of four to seven prisoners finishing each course. Male and female students from the community who have an association with Te Ihi Tu also attend these courses. Since Vipassana has been introduced to the Te Ihi Tu program, the recidivism rate among prisoners has decreased.

Thailand

After an Inspector General from the Thai Department of Corrections read about the film, Doing Time, Doing Vipassana, she arranged for local assistant teachers to make a presentation to her staff. But after learning that the Vipassana volunteers would need to reside at the prison with the inmates, her staff tabled the matter.

Then, five years later, an old student involved with one of Thailand's television stations arranged to have the film dubbed in Thai. The Director General for the Department of Corrections watched the video on television, and afterwards felt enthusiastic about giving Vipassana a try in a Thai prison.

In May 2002, a Vipassana course was conducted by a Bhikkhu Acharya (a member of the centuries-old order of monks established by the Buddha, who also teaches Vipassana in this tradition). Forty-nine male drug offenders and two prison staff attended this course at the Kolong Pai Prison in Sikhiu District, northeast of Bangkok. A second course for 50 women at a separate women's facility was held two months later. The Inspector General who had originally proposed having prison courses, attended this course as a student, choosing to occupy a prison cell with basic toilet facilities just like the other students. At the end of this course the Director General announced that both of these course sites would be turned into permanent Vipassana centers.

On the eves of both the third men's course and the third women's course, many inmates from another prison unexpectedly arrived. They were sent by an administrator who thought Vipassana Meditation would magically turn unruly inmates into angels! Unfortunately many of them were not processed in time and were sent back.

All in all, six courses for 377 men and women were conducted in 2002, and six more are planned for 2003. Last August, the Bangkok Post reported that the Corrections Department planned to turn three prisons into meditation centers for inmates after the retreats at Klong Pai proved such a success. In the North, a center would open at Phitsanulok prison; in the South, at Koh Taew prison in Songkhla and in the Central region, at Rayong prison. Klong Pai prison would be the center for the Northeast. However, since then the Department of Corrections has undergone recent changes and it is uncertain whether current reform policies will remain in place.

Mexico

Events leading to a course in Mexico began when an employee from the correctional system took a Vipassana course and told her boss about it. Her boss, the General Director, runs 20 facilities in the State of Mexico; and after seeing Doing Time, Doing Vipassana, she became very inspired and eager to organize a course. This was followed by three meetings with her, and a conference given by a Vipassana teacher. Eventually, 12 people from different penal system departments joined Vipassana courses. This was the critical prerequisite for holding a prison course. After two more meetings with the authorities, a date and site were decided for the course.

The course was held in March 2003 at Penal de Santiaguito, Mexico States facility in Almoloya de Juarez. This facility, housing about 1,500 inmates, has been a model for Latin American prisons; and now once again has shown itself a pioneer by implementing a Vipassana course. The course actually took place in a small separate facility just in front of the main one. It was a totally independent space where each inmate had his own room and there was a large open walking area. After interviews with more than 30 inmates (all within weeks of release), 18 were chosen for the course. The group which included murderers, kidnappers, robbers, and drug and arms dealers, were all highly motivated and worked seriously. There were few disturbances and none of the students asked to leave the course at any time. During and after the course all expressed their gratitude and their determination to change their lives.

TV and press attended a reception on Day 11 and the next day at least five newspapers reported the successful end of the course. The authorities are very happy that everything went smoothly and want to establish a more continuous and permanent Vipassana program in the Almoloya facility as early as this year. Mexicos Vipassana Association will soon have a meeting with the authorities to decide how to implement the program.

United States of America

Public opinion and policies about incarceration in the United States are varied and contentious. Advocates of rehabilitation are perceived as naive and indulgent while proponents of more punitive measures are accused of being cynical and vindictive. Even those facilities that do view rehabilitation as a viable alternative or adjunct to punishment are often hesitant to try programming that falls outside of the kinds of interventions typically used in the West. However, there is almost universal agreement that the system, as it is, does not serve us well. At this time, nearly 2,000,000 prisoners are held in Federal or State prisons or in local jails. In all, nearly 6,600,000 people in the United States are on probation, in jail or prison, or on parole—about one in every 32 adults. Although prison sentences have become increasingly severe, recidivism rates are alarmingly high—about 67.5% within three years of release according to a study of almost 300,000 prisoners released in 1994. (U.S. Department of Justice)

Vipassana has brought to the American correctional system a way out of the debate about how to administer change from the outside, by directly giving to the inmate, the responsibility and means to change from within. As of this issue of Vipassana Newsletter (May 2003), only a few correctional facilities in the US have opened their doors to Vipassana, but these have created a strong foundation for the future. Following is an overview of the history of Vipassana courses in correctional facilities in the United States.

King County North Rehabilitation Facility, Seattle, Washington

The King County North Rehabilitation Facility (NRF) was the first correctional facility in North America to hold Vipassana courses in this tradition and the only facility to hold ongoing courses. Already committed to rehabilitation as a form of enlightened self-interest, NRF was a receptive site. Nonetheless, there were many concerns on the eve of NRF's first course in November 1997. Recidivism rates are typically very high in jail populations, and cynicism among inmates and staff alike can be pervasive. Many in the institution lacked confidence that the inmates would be able to sustain silence, long hours in a sitting posture and the rigorous course schedule. Moreover, the course would bring them into a different cultural milieu that some might find difficult and alienating. For those inmates with limited reading skills, even the routine course signs presented a barrier.

One can only imagine what it was like for this first group of inmates as they gathered up their bedding and walked down the long hallway into the course area. At the end of the course, prison staff, other inmates, and family and friends of the 11 men who had completed the course gathered in the gymnasium to greet them. As the men filed in, the assembled inmates and staff stood and cheered. One felt that they cheered not just for the men who had completed the course, but for the possibility for change and hope that they represented.

From November 1997 to August 2002, a total of 20 courses were held at NRF at intervals of every three to four months. Courses were served by Dhamma workers from all over North America, including several NRF staff members who had taken courses. In all, 130 men and 61 women completed at least one course at NRF.

Over time, pre-course orientation classes were introduced to familiarize interested inmates with course requirements and protocols. This greatly reduced barriers associated with illiteracy and learning disabilities, cultural and religious identification, and general feelings of distrust and doubt. Vipassana courses and daily meditation at NRF became a part of the institutional routine and an ongoing exercise in teamwork across all staff disciplines. The receptions on Day 11 were often attended by staff on their day off, including the head of security who always just happened to be in the neighborhood.

Knowing the limitations of anecdotal accounts, NRF personnel began to collect objective data on the effects of these courses. In 2002, the NRF Programs Manager completed a Vipassana Recidivism Study which included data collected from courses one through eight. Final outcome results from this study revealed that approximately half (56%) of the inmates completing a Vipassana course at NRF returned to the King County Jail (KCJ) after two years, compared with 75% in an NRF General Population Study of 437 inmates. In other words, three out of four NRF inmates were re-incarcerated within two years, while only two out of four Vipassana inmates were re-incarcerated. Moreover, the average number of bookings declined from 2.9 pre-Vipassana to 1.5 post-Vipasssana/post-NRF release.

Using the encouraging indicators from the early stages of this study, and their experience studying meditation, alcohol problems and criminal conduct, a team of researchers at the University of Washington received funding in October 1998 from the National Institute on Alcohol Abuse and Alcoholism to conduct a two-year study of the effects of the NRF Vipassana courses on relapse, recidivism, psychosocial functioning and spirituality. The preliminary results of this study indicate that all study participants improved from their baseline measures but that Vipassana course completers had a significantly better outcome than the comparison group. For example: reductions in drug use, anxiety, depression, and hostility. Additional information from this study will be released in the near future.

No further courses will be held at NRF. On November 1, 2002, the King County North Rehabilitation Facility closed its doors after 21 years as an alternate detention site.

San Francisco Jail #7, San Bruno, California

The first 10-day course at the San Francisco County Jail was held in January and February 2001. This was the second corrections facility and the first medium-security jail in the U.S. to undertake a Vipassana course.

The course started with 14 students, four full-time Dhamma workers, plus Sheriffs staff of one deputy and one sergeant, who had each sat one 10-day course. The course was held in a small building next to the main jail, normally used as a computer-learning lab for prisoners and staff offices. Staff moved out of their offices to create a Dhamma center with three dormitories, servers and teacher's quarters, and separate dining and walking areas. A Deputy Sheriff was assigned to a locked control room 24 hours a day to open and close doors and provide general security. Both sworn and civilian staff worked closely together in the planning and implementation of the course. The Sheriff's staff stopped at nothing to make the course a success. They realized that these inmates were doing very hard work and felt the more support they got the better they could work.

The Dhamma community provided critical support by providing daily hot lunches to augment the jail food that was quite limited. They also provided much support in setting up the course site, bringing in things needed during the course, arranging for *Mettā*-Day, the Day 11 reception, and the clean up.

When silence was broken, the 13 students who completed the course expressed their gratitude to Goenkaji, to the Buddha and to Dhamma. During Day 10 and at the Day 11 reception they described the technique and how they found it helped with their problems and with their ability to make good choices in their lives. Short interviews with students and the Day 11 reception were videotaped for future use within the facility.

The jail arranged for weekly post-course sittings and allowed established meditators from the community to come and meditate with the inmates once a week. As well, the inmates were accommodated so that they could maintain their daily meditation practice.

The first week, all 13 meditators came to sit and discuss their experiences. They all felt that now they have a tool to help them in their lives. Most had used their new wisdom to handle difficult situations in a positive way and to avoid problems. One or two had slipped but were happy to learn that they could start again.

This first course was a very strong beginning and the Sheriff's staff was clearly impressed with the ability of inmates to learn and benefit from Vipassana. The staff seemed particularly impressed with the fact that the Dhamma community had no agenda other than to help inmates learn Vipassana Meditation. Although by all accounts the course was a great success, no further courses have been planned at this time. The facility has faced some extraordinary challenges since that first course, but there is confidence that they will have additional courses in the future.

W.E. Donaldson Correctional Facility, Bessemer, Alabama

The first 10-day Vipassana course to be held in a U.S. state prison and a U.S. maximum-security facility was held in January 2002 for 20 inmates at the W.E. Donaldson Correctional Facility in Bessemer, Alabama, just southeast of Birmingham.

There are approximately 1,500 inmates at Donaldson, which also houses a death row. The W.E. Donaldson state prison is the highest security-level prison in Alabama and has a history of being Alabama's most violent and brutal prison. Once known as the West Jefferson State Prison, it is now named after a correctional officer who was stabbed to death a number of years back. Approximately half of the 20 inmates taking the course were under a life sentence, some with the possibility of parole, others without hope of parole. Most of them had been incarcerated for violent crimes while a number were in there for non-violent crimes such as robbery and drug trafficking. Among the students were two Imams (prayer leaders) of the Shiite and Sunni Muslim traditions as well as two devoted Gospel and Baptist followers. For an inspiring account of this course, see the May 2002 issue of Vipassana Newsletter.

The second 10-day course at the Donaldson facility was held in May 2002. Eighteen men started and 17 completed the course, one of them a returning student from the first course. At the conclusion of the course, Goenkaji visited the correctional facility as part of his North American Meditation Now Tour and concluded a group sitting attended by students from both the prison courses. Goenkaji spoke to the men expressing how happy he was that they had taken the 10-day course, telling them that they now had a big responsibility to be examples of Dhamma to others in the prison and to help them purify their minds. After meeting with prison managers, Goenkaji gave a longer talk about Vipassana Meditation to both groups of inmate students, Department of Corrections officials and Donaldsons administration as well as a group of 20 inmates interested in attending the next course. At the end of the question and answer session, one inmate asked about the singing that he and his wife do at the end of the morning chanting. After a brief explanation, Goenkaji concluded his talk and immediately began chanting *Sabbakā maṅgala, sabbakā maṅgala* (May all be happy) as he walked out of the gym.

At this time, no further courses are planned at Donaldson, but many of the inmates continue to maintain the practice.

A North Rehabilitation Facility old student addresses Goenkaji:
"When I came out of my course less than a year ago, I had no idea of what I had done. I had no idea of the impact that it would have on my life in the future. Every day I see changes in myself in how I relate to people, in my own peace of mind, in how I handle situations. I admit I do not practice every day. I try to, and even if I can't sit for an hour, I'll sit a little while, and it helps!

While here at NRF, I was not happy and did not want to be here, obviously. But now I can look back on it with nothing but gratitude for the experience I've had and for being here while the Vipassana course was offered. It has totally changed my life. I especially want to thank you and your wife for your great part in this, but also the NRF staff and the local Vipassana community. All I can say is, I'm full of gratitude today."

In one letter, a student inmate quotes from the Dhammapada:

"Let it now be known that Dhamma warriors of Donaldson now offer this declaration: Blessed are we who live among those who hate, hating no one; amidst those who hate, let us dwell without hatred."

A Donaldson inmate-student writes:
"There has been a very definite impact, even with the correctional officers, and it's something that certainly needs to be continued. I firmly believe the visit from Goenkaji had a profound effect on many people here and I'm not talking about only inmates. Speaking from personal experience, I must say that Vipassana had the most profound effect I have ever witnessed on a group of inmates. The changes I've noticed within myself have made a remarkable difference in the way I view things with equanimity. I'm able to deal with situations more calmly than before because now I can see everything in a better perspective. I have given myself a substantial period of time to assure myself that everything I experienced during the Vipassana was real and not a passing fancy. Now I can testify that the experiences were indeed real. I continue to practice daily. It has brought about tremendous changes in my life.

I find such peace in sitting daily. Occasionally I sit for two hours in the morning and, as difficult as it may be to believe, the second hour is always better than the first. With this in mind, I have decided to sit through the night this Saturday and Sunday. I plan to begin at 10:00 PM and finish up at 6:00 AM. Vipassana can make such a difference in the collective minds of the men here, which in turn could let society as a whole acknowledge that people can and do change."

Tips for Introducing Vipassana to Correctional Facilities

The introduction of Vipassana to correctional facilities works best by the grass roots effort of personal contact. Old students who have contacts, or who are willing to identify and contact decision-makers in correctional facilities, can be of help in this outreach effort.

Steps to take:

Identify someone in the prison system who may have interest in the benefits of Vipassana. Professionals in prison treatment programs are a good place to start, and correctional officials also should be contacted. It is better not to approach prisoners initially with presentations, but wait until you have the support of the administration and a plan for actually having a course.

Use materials from the presentation package. These include: Guidelines for Vipassana Meditation Courses within Correctional Facilities, the American jails article, the Fact sheet, the NRF in-house recidivism report, the Associated Press article about NRF courses, and the two San Francisco Weekly articles about NRF and San Bruno and the old Doing Time, Doing Vipassana (DTDV) poster. These are available on the prison website ***www.prison.dhamma.org.***

Often a showing of *DTDV* and/or *Changing from Inside* to officials is a very powerful way to convey the benefits of Vipassana. A critical step is for prison staff, both line officers and administrators, to attend a full 10-day course before a course be given in any facility. This is the only way they can understand what it is they are undertaking and how to support a Vipassana course appropriately. This fact should be introduced fairly early in the process to facilitate planning.

Keep the area prison contact informed of your activities, and once there is serious interest by a facility, contact them for support in taking the next steps.

Serving a Prison/Jail Course

Serving a course in a correctional facility can be very rewarding, and quite challenging. All servers have frequent contact with students and may be required to function as managers do on courses at established centres. Old students should be well established both in their practice and in service of several courses before offering to serve a prison or jail course. There are many ways that less seasoned students can serve also, such as planning, set-up and food preparation. If you would like to serve a course in a correctional facility in any way, inform the prison contact in your area.

Please note that updates on Vipassana prison courses worldwide are available on the dedicated website: *www.prison.dhamma.org*

(International edition—May 2003)

Vipassana at the World Economic Forum

The annual meeting of the World Economic Forum is the pre-eminent gathering of business, industrial and government leaders in the world today. Each January it draws more than 1,000 heads of major multinational corporations, top academics and government leaders (including heads of government and heads of state) to the small Alpine ski resort of Davos, Switzerland. Meeting in private, they discuss with their counterparts current issues related to global economics, environment, health and culture. The aim is to promote shared views on how to implement solutions to the common problems of our time.

This year's meeting, the first of the new millennium, had as its theme "New Beginnings: Making a Difference." In the past, spiritual leaders have been invited to attend the WEF, and in 2,000 Goenkaji was asked to be a Forum Fellow. He spoke at several panel discussions and gave a featured address.

On the first day of the meeting Goenkaji was interviewed by CNBC, the U.S. all-news television channel, which provided internal video coverage for the Forum. Goenkaji pointed out the importance of non-sectarian spirituality in implementing business strategies. Without the base of Dhamma, he noted, all the money and all the success achieved in business would be an empty accomplishment.

Goenkaji also participated in a panel discussion entitled "The future of religion: beyond beliefs?" Along with him on the panel were a Jewish rabbi, a Muslim leader, a professor of Chinese philosophy from Harvard and a professor of religion from Oxford. Goenkaji emphasized that there are two aspects of religion. One is the outer shell, which often features rites, rituals and religious ceremonies, mythology, philosophical beliefs and dogma; these characterize most religious sects. Followers of these sects may not have a trace of morality, love, compassion or goodwill, and yet they assume that they are religious persons because they have performed certain ceremonies or profess certain beliefs. Such persons delude themselves and miss the inner essence of religion, which is living a moral life full of love, compassion, goodwill and tolerance. The inner essence is the common denominator of all religions. If people practice it, they will find real peace, and religion would never be the cause for conflict or confrontation.

Goenkaji participated as well in a dinner program on the topic "Death: exploring the taboo." In modern society, he noted, death is considered a taboo because people fear it and don't want to face even the thought of death. If, however, one becomes fearless, there is no need for the taboo. In fact the fear complex, including the fear of death, can be totally eradicated by practicing a scientific technique: a mental exercise, discovered by the Buddha, which removes all complexes, including fear. This technique is called Vipassana meditation.

The subject of another dinner program was "What to do when you are angry." Goenkaji described anger as a reaction to unpleasant physical sensations experienced with the unconscious mind. He explained how Vipassana breaks the barrier between conscious and unconscious, and how it trains the mind not to react to sensations, whether pleasant or unpleasant. In a situation that might ordinarily trigger anger, one simply observes bodily sensations with the understanding that they are impermanent. Doing so prevents anger from arising. At the same time, it gradually eliminates unhealthy habit patterns, removing the tendency to become angry.

The principal address by Goenkaji at the Forum was entitled "Is this as good as it gets? The meaning of happiness." Goenkaji explained that unhappiness occurs because of defilements in the mind, and he described how a life of true happiness is attainable through the practice of Vipassana meditation.

For many leaders of world business, professional organizations and government institutions, this was the first opportunity to come in contact with true Dhamma. Goenkaji's participation in the Forum may thus have far-reaching consequences, for the good and happiness of many.

(International edition—March 2000)

The Meaning of Happiness

S. N. Goenka

The following is adapted from Goenkaji's address "Is This All There Is? The Meaning of Happiness" at the World Economic Forum, Davos on 31 January 2000.

Words of Dhamma

Jayaṃ veraṃ pasavati,
dukkhaṃ seti parājito;
upasanto sukhaṃ seti,
hitvā jayaparājayaṃ

Victory breeds hatred,
the defeated live in pain;
happily the peaceful live,
giving up victory and defeat.

—Dhammapada – 201

Every person who is attending this Forum is among a unique group of people on our planet. They are generally among the wealthiest, most powerful most accomplished individuals in the world. Even being invited to attend the World Economic Forum is recognition of the eminent status that each participant has reached among his or her peers. When someone has all the wealth, power and status that anyone could ever want, are they necessarily happy? Are all these accomplishments and the self-satisfaction they bring 'all there is'? Or is there some greater degree of happiness, which it is possible to achieve?

Happiness is an ephemeral condition. It is rapidly fleeting; here one moment and gone the next. One day when all is going well with your business, your bank account and your family, there is happiness. But what happens when something unwanted happens? When something entirely out of your control happens to disturb your happiness and harmony?

Every person in the world, regardless of their power and position, will experience periods during which circumstances arise that are out of their control and not to their liking. It may be the discovery that you have a fatal disease; it may be the illness or death of a near and dear one; it may be a divorce or the discovery that a spouse is cheating on you. For people addicted to success in life, it may simply be a failure at something: a bad business decision, your company being acquired and the resultant loss of your job, losing a political election, someone else getting the promotion that you wanted, or your child running away from home or rebelling and rejecting all the values that you hold dear. Regardless of how much wealth, prestige and power you may have, such unwanted events and failures generally create great misery.

Next comes the question: how to deal with these periods of unhappiness, which spoil an otherwise ideal life? Such periods are bound to come in even the most charmed life. Do you behave in a balanced and equanimous manner or do you react with aversion towards the miscry that you are experiencing? Do you crave for the return of your happiness? Moreover, when you becomes addicted to happiness and to everything always going the way you want, the misery when things do not go your way becomes even greater. In fact, it becomes unbearable. It often makes us resort to alcohol to cope with these situations of disappointment and depression, and to take sleeping pills in order to obtain the rest we need to keep going. All the while we tell the outside world and ourselves that we are sublimely happy because of our wealth, power and position.

I come from a business family and was an entrepreneur and businessman from a very early age. I built sugar mills, weaving mills and blanket factories and established import-export firms with offices all over the world. In the process, I made a lot of money. However, I also vividly remember how I reacted to events in my business and my personal life during those years. Every night, if I had failed to be successful in a business transaction during the day, I would lic awake for hours and try to figure out what had gone wrong and what I should do the next time. Even if I had accomplished a great success that day I would lie awake and relish my accomplishment. While I experienced success, this was neither happiness nor peace of mind. I found that peace was very closely related to happiness and I frequently had neither, regardless of my money and status as a leader in the community.

I remember a favourite poem of mine related to this subject.

It is easy enough to be pleasant;
When life flows like a sweet song.
But the man worthwhile,
Is the one who can smile,
When things go dead wrong.

How each one of us copes with these periods of things going 'dead wrong' is a major component of the 'meaning of happiness', regardless of our money, power and prestige.

It is a basic human need that everyone wants to live a happy life. For this, one has to experience real happiness. The so-called happiness that one experiences by having money, power, and indulging in sensual pleasures is not real happiness. It is very fragile, unstable and fleeting. For real happiness, for lasting stable happiness, one has to make a journey deep within oneself and get rid of all the unhappiness stored in the deeper levels of the mind. As long as there is misery at the depth of the mind all attempts to feel happy at the surface level of the mind prove futile.

This stock of unhappiness at the depth of the mind keeps on multiplying as long as one keeps generating negativities such as anger, hatred, ill-will, and animosity. The law of nature is such that as soon as one generates negativity, unhappiness arises simultaneously. It is impossible to feel happy and peaceful when one is generating negativity in the mind. Peace and negativity cannot coexist just as light and darkness cannot coexist. There is a systematic scientific exercise developed by a great super-scientist of my ancient country by which one can explore the truth pertaining to the mind-body phenomenon at the experiential level. This technique is called Vipassana, which means observing the reality objectively, as it is.

The technique helps one to develop the faculty of feeling and understanding the interaction of mind and matter within one's own physical structure. The technique of Vipassana involves the basic law of nature that whenever any defilement arises in the mind, simultaneously, two things start happening at the physical level. One is that the breath loses its normal rhythm. I start breathing hard whenever a negativity arises in the mind. This is a very gross and apparent reality that everyone can experience. At the same time, at a subtler level, a biochemical reaction starts within the body: I experience a physical sensation on the body. Every defilement generates some sensation or the other in some part of the body.

This is a practical solution. An ordinary person cannot observe abstract defilements of the mind: abstract fear, anger or passion. But with proper training and practice, it is very easy to observe the respiration and the sensations, both of which are directly related to the mental defilements.

The respiration and the sensations will help in two ways. First, as soon as a defilement starts in the mind, the breath loses its normal rhythm. It will start shouting: 'Look, something has gone wrong!' Similarly, the sensations tell me: 'Something has gone wrong.' I must accept this. Then, having been warned, I start observing the respiration, the sensations, and I find that the defilement soon passes away.

This mental-physical phenomenon is like a coin with two sides. On the one side are the thoughts or emotions that arise in the mind. On the other side are the respiration and sensations in the body. Every thought or emotion, conscious or unconscious, every mental defilement manifests in the breath and sensation of that moment. Thus by observing the respiration or sensation, one is indirectly observing the mental defilement. Instead of running away from the problem, you are facing reality as it is. Then you find that the defilement loses its strength; it can no longer overpower you as it did in the past. If you persist, the defilement eventually disappears altogether and you remain peaceful and happy.

In this way, the technique of self-observation shows us reality in its two aspects: outside and inside. Previously, one always looked outside with open eyes, missing the inner truth. Human beings have always looked outside for the cause of their unhappiness. They have always blamed and tried to change the reality outside. Being ignorant of the inner reality, they never understood that the cause of suffering lies within, in their own blind reactions.

The more one practices this technique, the quicker one can come out of negativities. Gradually the mind becomes freed of defilements; it becomes pure. A pure mind is always full of love, detached love for all others; full of compassion for the failings and sufferings of others; full of joy at their success and happiness; full of equanimity in the face of any situation.

When one reaches this stage, then the entire pattern of one's life starts changing. It is no longer possible for one to do anything vocally or physically that will disturb the peace and happiness of others. Instead, the balanced mind not only becomes peaceful, it helps others to become peaceful also. The atmosphere surrounding such a person will become permeated with peace, harmony and real happiness, which also starts affecting others.

This direct experience of reality within oneself, this technique of self-observation, is called Vipassana and it is a simple direct way to leading a truly happy life.

There are different components of living a happy life. Several of these are relevant to the group of people attending the Forum. When you have all the money and possessions you could ever want, how can you really enjoy those blessings when millions of people in the world are unsure of their next meal. While there is absolutely nothing wrong with earning money to provide for yourself, your family and all those that depend upon you, you must also give back to society. You are obtaining your wealth from society, so you must give something back. The attitude must be: 'I am earning for myself but I am also earning for others.'

Another aspect of happiness in business is to be sure that whatever you do to earn your money does not hurt or harm others. This is a big responsibility. Money earned at the expense of the peace and happiness of other fellow human beings will never bring happiness to you. Real happiness is not possessions or accomplishments or wealth or power. It is a state of inner being that comes from a pure and peaceful mind. Vipassana is a tool that helps everyone achieve that state.

(Dhamma Giri edition—August 2000)

How to Apply Vipassana in Student Life

S. N. Goenka

The following is a talk by Goenkaji to Indian students from Symbiosis Centre of Management and HRD (SCMHRD) and Symbiosis Centre of Information Technology (SCIT) on Mettā day of their 10-day course at Dhamma Giri from 18 to 29 September 2002. It has been adapted for the Newsletter.

Here are a few words to help you understand how to apply the wonderful technique that you have learnt here in your day-to-day life. If you can't apply it in your day-to-day life, it is futile to spend 10 days in a course like this. This is not a rite or a ritual; it is an art of living. One learns how to live peacefully and harmoniously within and how to help others to live in peace and harmony. How can we use this technique for this purpose?

As students, you are very fortunate that the leaders of your institute have understood the efficacy of this wonderful technique and have given you an opportunity to learn it. This technique will help you not only in your student life but also after completing your studies. You may become an executive or a chief executive officer or the owner of a particular business.

Now, as a student, it is possible that some of you may get very nervous. You have studied your text and have understood your lessons well. But during examinations, you become nervous and forget everything and can't give the right answers. You may get very low marks or even fail the exam. With this technique, the nervousness will be reduced. Whenever you find that you are getting nervous, be aware of your respiration for just a few seconds with open eyes. Just for a few seconds, maybe for a few minutes, be aware of respiration. Your mind will calm down and the nervousness will go away. If you are taking an examination, you will give the right answers and get good results.

Again, one often becomes nervous in stressful situations such as meetings with seniors. You are unable to face the situation properly because you are so nervous. This technique will help you to calm the mind. You will be able to face all such situations successfully because a calm and tranquil mind is a very strong mind.

When your mind is agitated and confused, the capacity to understand the subject decreases. The teacher is teaching a particular subject or you are reading a book but your mind is so confused and clouded that you can't understand it properly. You keep reading it again and again but you are still not able to understand.

Whenever you find that the mind is very agitated, practise Ānāpāna for a few minutes or observe sensations for a few minutes. This will calm the agitated mind and you will find that your capacity to understand the subject will increase.

In the same way, when you are dealing with any situation and if the mind is very wild, very agitated, you can't take proper decisions. By practising this technique, you will find that you are able to take proper decisions because you know how to calm the mind.

There is another problem that arises quite naturally at this age. Passion arises, lust arises. This lust may overpower you and you may become a slave of this particular impurity. You may try to suppress it but the more you suppress it, the more agitated the mind becomes. Or you may express it by taking a wrong action and then you feel guilty, "Oh, I should not have done that, that was wrong." Again, you become miserable.

When you practise Vipassana regularly, you will find that everything that arises in the mind is accompanied by a sensation on the body. This was a great discovery of this great super-scientist. People wrongly think of the Buddha as the founder of a religion. He had nothing to do with conventional religion. He was a super-scientist who studied the interaction of mind and matter. He discovered how the mind is influencing matter and how matter is influencing the mind and how, out of ignorance, because one does not know what is happening at the depth of the mind, one starts generating some impurity or the other and becomes miserable.

The Buddha discovered a technique by which, as soon as an impurity arises, you observe it, and you are out of it. Now how to observe it? He found a way. Nothing can arise in the mind without a sensation on the body. This is the law of nature; it was not created by the Buddha. So, whenever passion or fear or depression arises, there must be a sensation in the body. This sensation is related to whatever has arisen in the mind. You just accept the fact, "This has arisen in the mind." Say, fear or passion or ego or any other impurity has arisen in the mind. You feel any sensation on the body and you start observing that sensation.

If you practise Vipassana properly and continue to practise it morning and evening, you understand, "Every sensation, pleasant or unpleasant, gross or subtle, has the same characteristic, arising, passing away; arising, passing away. So very impermanent, so ephemeral! So this particular defilement that has arisen is also impermanent. This is not eternal. Let me see how long it lasts!"

It cannot overpower you because you are observing it objectively. It becomes weaker and weaker and passes away. You can make use of this wonderful technique, which was discovered by this wonderful super-scientist in your day-to-day life as a student.

Later on, you will have bigger responsibilities in your career. As I know from my own experience, without Vipassana, negative emotions arise all the time. When you generate negative emotions, you make everyone agitated. The whole atmosphere around you becomes agitated. How can the staff under you work properly in such a negative emotional atmosphere?

By the practice of Vipassana, your whole attitude starts changing. You start generating positive emotions. Somebody has made a mistake, so what? Very lovingly, kindly, have compassion on this person: "Oh, he is ignorant or he has not understood the problem, so he has made a mistake." Explain calmly and compassionately and you will find that the result is so good. Everybody who works under you or with you will get better results because the whole atmosphere has become so peaceful and harmonious.

I know this from my own experience. After coming to Vipassana, my business turnover and profit increased many times, because the people under me also started practising Vipassana. So, the whole atmosphere was filled with positive creativity. Everyone works to get better results. This will happen. This technique will help you. Your relationship with your colleagues, with the workers under you, with your seniors will become so cordial. Life will become so peaceful and harmonious.

Here is a technique which is not a rite or a ritual. You do yoga or physical exercises to keep your body healthy, and strong, which is very important. Similarly, Vipassana is a mental exercise. If you practice it daily, morning and evening, you will find that your mind becomes stronger and stronger, more and more healthy, and it gives positive results.

Make the best use of this technique. Don't take these 10 days just as a rite or ritual or ceremony. You have come here to learn a technique in a very scientific way and to use it for your own good and for the good of others. When you generate a mental defilement, you are the first victim of your defilement. As soon as you generate any negativity, you become the first victim, you become miserable and then you start making others miserable.

By practising this technique, you will learn how to live peacefully and harmoniously within and how to generate nothing but peace and harmony for the atmosphere around you.

Students of SCMHRD, Pune have been attending Vipassana courses since December 1996. A 10-day Vipassana course and daily meditation is an integral part of their curriculum. Since 2002, students of SCMHRD, Nashik and SCIT, Pune have also been attending 10-day Vipassana courses at Dhamma Giri.

(Dhamma Giri edition—May 2004)

Questions and Answers with Young People

The following questions were asked during the first course for adolescents held at Dhamma Giri from April 12 to 19, 2004. They have been translated and adapted for the Newsletter.

Student: ***Many sensations are neither pleasant nor unpleasant, and so one does not generate craving or aversion toward them. Why should we observe such sensations?***

Goenkaji: There are three kinds of sensations: pleasant, unpleasant and neutral. One usually generates craving toward the pleasant sensations and aversion toward the unpleasant sensations. Then what about the neutral sensations? You have to observe the neutral sensations attentively so that you can understand their impermanent nature, *anicca*. If you understand their nature of impermanence, you are with the truth. Your mind will become so sharp that you will not generate craving, aversion or ignorance. Therefore make use of these neutral sensations also and understand that the nature of these sensations is also impermanent.

Student: ***While practicing Vipassana, sometimes my mind wanders a lot. Can I practice Ānāpāna in this situation?***

Goenkaji: Yes, you should practice Ānāpāna. When the mind wanders a lot, it is difficult to practice Vipassana. Whenever your mind is very agitated or very sluggish and does not want to work at all, in all such situations, you must start practicing Ānāpāna. After practicing Ānāpāna for some time, when the mind becomes calm, you can start Vipassana again. If your mind is very restless, you may do Ānāpāna for some time and then combine Vipassana with Ānāpāna. With one breath, observe sensations on one part of the body; with the next breath, observe sensations on the next part. Observe sensations along with respiration. Then the mind will wander less because you have given it two objects of meditation.

As far as possible, practice Vipassana to eradicate the mental defilements at the depth. But if the mind is so unstable that you cannot observe sensations, practice Ānāpāna. We have to use Vipassana to fight our enemies. Ānāpāna will help us to sharpen our weapons so that we can fight these enemies more effectively.

Student: ***Why do we get different sensations in different parts of the body?***

Goenkaji: There are many causes for sensations, not just a single cause. Sensations may be caused by the climate, by any injury or disease, by sitting for a long time, by the food that we have eaten or by past *saṅkhāras*. It does not matter what the cause is. Whatever the type of sensation, we observe it and remain equanimous to it. Even if the sensation is caused by mental defilements, there are so many kinds of defilements that it is not possible to know which defilement has caused this sensation. So, you should not go into these details.

For example, if we have to clean a dirty cloth, we take soap and water and scrub the cloth with the soap. There is no need to know where, how and when the cloth became dirty. The cloth is dirty, we have the soap and we have to clean the cloth. Similarly, we have learned the technique of Vipassana. Whatever the reason for the sensation and whatever the type of sensation, we have to observe it and understand its nature of impermanence.

(International edition—April 2009)

Why I Sit

Paul Fleischman

The following was taken from "Why I Sit", which was published in 1993 by the Buddhist Publication Society, Śri Laṅka. Dr. Fleischman is an assistant teacher of S. N. Goenka and a practising psychiatrist.

This morning, the first thing I did was to sit for an hour. I have done that regularly for 20 years, and have spent many evenings, days and weeks doing the same.

I would like to know myself. It is remarkable that while ordinarily we spend most of our lives studying, contemplating, observing and manipulating the world around us, the structured gaze of the thoughtful mind is so rarely turned inwards. This avoidance must measure some anxiety, reluctance or fear.

Most of our lives are spent in externally oriented functions that distract from self-observation. This relentless, obsessive drive persists independently of survival needs such as food and warmth, and even of pleasure. Second to second, we couple ourselves to sights , tastes, words, motions or electronic stimuli, until we fall dead. It is striking how many ordinary activities, from smoking a pipe to watching sunsets, veer towards, but ultimately avoid, sustained attention to the reality of our own life.

This motivated me on a search that led through intense intellectual exploration in college, medical school and psychiatric training, and finally to the art of "sitting", as taught by S. N. Goenka, a Vipassana meditation teacher with whom my wife and I first took a course near New Delhi, India, in 1974. Those 10 days of nothing but focusing on the moment by moment reality of body and mind, with awareness and equanimity, gave me the opportunity ironically both to be more absolutely alone and isolated than I had ever been before, and at the same time to cast my lot with a tradition, a way, as upheld, manifested, explained and transmitted by a living person. I am continuously grateful to S. N. Goenka for giving me this technique.

Vipassana meditation was preserved in Asia for 2500 years since its discovery by Gotama, the historical Buddha. His technique of living was labelled by western scholars, "Buddhism", but it is not an "ism", a system of thought. It is a practice, a method, a tool for living persons. It does not end its practitioner's search. For me, it provides a compass, a spy glass, a map for further journeys. With daily practice and intensive retreats mixed into the years, I find the marriage of autonomy and heritage, membership and lonely continuity. Vipassana is the binoculars now I can search for the elusive bird.

Before I received instructions on how to sit, my journey through life was predominantly intellectual. I had found lectures and books to be inspiring, suggestive, artful, but evasive.

One could advise, one could talk, one could write. But sitting is a way for me to stand for something, to sit as something, not just with words, but with my mind, body and life. Here is a way to descend the stages, protected by teacher, teaching, technique and practice into the light and darkness in me.

I want to know, to simply observe, this living person as he is, not just as he appears while careening from event to event. Of course, this will undoubtedly be helpful to me as a psychiatrist but my motives are more fundamental, personal and existential.

I am interested in my mind, and in my body. Previous to my having cultivated the habit of sitting, I had thought about myself and had used my body as a tool in the world, to grip a pen or to chop firewood, but I had never systematically, rigorously, observed my body-what it feels like; not just with a shy, fleeting glance, but moment after moment for hours and days at a time; nor had I committed myself to observe the reciprocal influence of mind and body in states of exhaustion and rest, hunger, pain, relaxation, arousal, lethargy, or concentration. My quest for knowing is not merely objective and scientific. This mind-body is the vessel of my life. I want to know it with the same organic immersion that sets a snow goose flying 10,000 miles every winter and spring.

Because the harmony in me is at once so awesome and sweet and overwhelming that I love its taste yet can barely compel myself to glimpse it, I want to sit with the great determination that I need to brush aside the fuzz or distraction, the lint of petty concerns. To sit is to know myself as an unfolding manifestation of the universals of life a gripping, unending project. Hopefully one I can use even when I look into death's funnel. For me, this knowing is a great force, and a great pleasure.

I sit because of, for, and with an appreciation of daily life. The great poets sing of the omnipresent ordinary pregnant with revelation but I know how easily and recurrently my own life yields to distraction, irritation, tunnel vision. I do not want to miss my life the way I once missed a plane at a New York airport. It may be ironic that simply to wriggle free of daydreams and worries I need a technique, a practice, a discipline, but I do; and I bow to that irony by doing what I must do to pry my mind off ephemeral worries, to wake to more dawns, to see my child unravel through his eddying transformations.

I sit to open my pores, skin and mind both to the life that surrounds me, inside and outside, at least more often if not all the time, as it arrives at my doorstep. I sit to exercise the appreciative, receptive, peaceful mode of being filled up by the ordinary and inevitable; for example, the floorboards sagging in the crooked bedroom where I sleep, or my two year old son, tugging one splinter at a time, to help me stack firewood in new January snow.

I feel a need for a rudder, a keel, a technique, a method, a way to continue on course. I need increasing moments of self-control (though not constricting, deadening inhibition). While sitting one does not get up, or move, or make that dollar, or pass that test, or receive reassurance from that phone call. But military training, or violin lessons, or medical school, are also routes to self-control in this ordering and restrictive sense. Sitting is self-control around specific values. Observation replaces all action. What is the point of committing one's life to this practice, only to spend the time with daydreams or anxious yearnings for promotion and recognition? Of course, those will happen anyway. They are part of the human make-up. Cultures would not have proliferated the ubiquitous moral codes, the 10 commandments, the five precepts, if we were not so replete with 10 million urges.

There is little I have heard from others and it is my daily business to listen that I have not seen in myself as I sit. But I also know the necessity of work, training and restraint. Dependence, loneliness, sensuality, exhaustion, hunger, petulance, perversion, miserliness, yearning and inflation are my old friends. I can greet them openly and warmly in people close to me, because I know them from the inside and therefore cannot condemn them without condemning myself. I also have been learning to harness and ride their energy.

Sitting pushes me to the limit of my self-directed effort; it mobilises my willed, committed direction, yet it also shatters my self-protective, self-defining manoeuvres and my simple self-definition. It both builds and dismantles "me." Every memory, every hope, every yearning, every fear floods in. I no longer can pretend to be one selected set of my memories or traits.

If observed, but not reacted upon, all these psychic contents become acceptable, obviously part of myself (for there they are, in my own mind, right in front of me); yet also impersonal, causally-linked, objective phenomena-in-the-world that move ceaselessly, relentlessly, across the screen of my existence, without my effort, without my control, without me. I can see more, tolerate more, in my inner life, at the same time that I am less driven by these forces. Like storms and doves, they are the persona of nature, crossing one's inner sky. Psychic complexity swirls up from the dust of cosmetic self-definition. At the same time, the determination and endurance I have to muster to just observe, grow like muscles with exercise. Naturally the repetition of this mixture of tolerance and firmness extrapolates beyond its source in sitting, out to relationships.

I sit because knowing that I will die enriches and excoriates my life, so I have to go out of my way to seek the discipline and stability that is necessary for me to really face it. Sitting rivets me on the psychological fact that death is life's door. No power can save me. Because I am aware of death, and afraid, I lean my shoulder into living; not reactively, but with conscious choice and decision of what will constitute each fleeting moment of my life. To embrace life I must shake hands with death. For this, I need practice. Each act of sitting is a dying to outward activity, a relinquishment of distraction, a cessation of anticipatory gratification. It is life now, as it is. Some day this austere focus will come in very, very handy. It already has.

I sit to be myself, independent of my own or others' judgements. Many years of my life were spent being rated, primarily in school, but, as an extension of that, among friends and in social life. As often happens, out of their concern for me, my parents combed and brushed me with the rules of comparison: I was good at this, or not good, or as good, or better, or worse, or the best, or no good at all.

Today I find that sitting reveals the absurdity of comparative achievement. My life consists of what I actually live, not the evaluations that float above it. Sitting enables me to slip beyond that second, commenting, editor's mind, and to burrow in deep with immediate reality.

I am relieved to be more at home in myself, with myself. I complain less. I can lose discussions, hopes, or self-expectations more easily and much less often because the talking, hoping, and doing is victory enough already. Without props or toys or comfort, without control of the environment, I have sat and observed who I am when there was no one and nothing to give me clues. It has happened that I have sat, asked for nothing, needed nothing, and felt full. Now my spine and hands have a different turgor. When I am thrown off balance, I can fall somewhat more like a cat than like a two-by-four. When I sit, no one beloved or enemy can give me what I lack, or take away what I am.

So as I live all day, I can orient myself into becoming the person I will have to live with when I next sit. No one else's commentary of praise or blame can mediate my own confrontation with the observed facts of who I am.

I sit in solitude to lose my isolation. What is least noble in me rises up to the surface of my mind, and this drives me on to be more than I was. When I am most shut into my dark self I find the real source of my belonging.

The two greatest difficulties I have faced while sitting for extended hours or days are physical pain, and the loss of the social position that I had previously seemed headed for and entitled to in the community. Pain that starts in the knees or back can flood the whole body and burn on and on. The self-protection of calculated membership and its comfortable rewards are lost to me in those aching, endless hours. I imagine my other options: a better house, winter vacations in the tropics, the respect of colleagues listening to me speak as I climb the career ladder. I imagine the financial crises I am less prepared to withstand. I imagine the humiliating rejection that crushes the refugee from poverty or racism or any form of powerlessness, all of which are in my heritage and possibly in my future (and in anyone's heritage or future if you look far enough). Why do I sit here? A thrush hops onto a low limb at the edge of a wooded clearing with triumphant song. Knowing yet staying, I am an inheritor and transmitter, flooded with gifts from those who loved and left their trace; and this still, glowing posture is the song of my species.

Sitting helps me overcome my deepest fears. I become freer to live from my heart and to face the consequences, but also to reap the rewards of this authenticity. Much of what I called pain was really loneliness and fear. It passes, dissolves, with that observation. The vibrations of my body are humming the song that can be heard only when dawn and dusk are simultaneous, instantaneous, continuous. I feel that a burst of stern effort is a small price to pay to hear this inner music—fertile music from the heart of life itself.

I sit to anchor and organise my life around my heart and mind, and to radiate out to others what I find. Though I shake in strong winds, I return to this basic way of living. The easy, soothing comfort and deep relaxation that accompany intense awareness in stillness, peel my life like an onion to deeper layers of truth, which in turn are scoured and soothed until the next layer opens. I sit to discipline my life by what is clear, simple, self-fulfilling and universal in my heart. There is no end to this job. I have failed to really live many days of my life, but I dive again and again into the plain guidance of self-containment and loving receipt. I sit to find and express simple human love and common decency.

(Dhamma Giri edition—July 1995)

Apply Dhamma in Life

The following has been adapted from Goenkaji's discourse on Day 30 of the 30-day course.

The most important thing is to apply Dhamma in life. If you merely take courses after courses—10-day courses or long courses—and do not apply it in life, Dhamma will become a lifeless rite or ritual. Different religions and sects have their own rites, rituals, and ceremonies. It would be very unfortunate if Vipassana courses also become a rite or ritual for a meditator.

Whenever you join a 10-day course or a longer course, you are eradicating your weaknesses and developing your strength. You have to use this strength in your day-to-day life. In a course, you work at the deeper level of your mind, eradicating layer after layer of complexes. After the course, if you again start accumulating the same complexes, the same impurities, the same defilements, then the purpose is not served. One has not understood what one is doing. The entire life pattern must change. Dhamma must manifest itself in day-to-day life.

One has to keep trying to apply Dhamma in life. "Whatever strength I have gained in a course like this, I will use it to ensure that my life becomes a Dhamma life. I will perfect my *sīla*, gain mastery over my mind and purify my mind. While facing different situations in life, I will practice Dhamma instead of generating unwholesome *saṅkhāras* (mental reactions)." In this way, you must keep watch over yourself. You have a human life and have come in contact with the wonderful Dhamma. You have developed confidence in Vipassana. Now you must make best use of it. Gaining a human life, coming in contact with Dhamma, and learning how to practise Dhamma—this is a rare opportunity indeed.

The goal is clear: to come out of all misery. This is possible only when one eradicates all the defilements. The aim: at least to reach the goal to become an ariya, a *sotāpanna*. Then Dhamma will take care because one is liberated from the four lower fields.

Before one becomes *sotāpanna*, one has to develop oneself to becomes a *cūḷa-sotāpanna*, a minor *sotāpanna*. A *sotāpanna* starts flowing in the stream of liberation, and is bound to reach the final goal of full liberation. A *cūḷa-sotāpanna* starts flowing in the stream of Dhamma and is bound to become a *sotāpanna*.

There are three important qualities in the life of a *sotāpanna*:

The first important quality: total liberation from all doubts and scepticism about Dhamma (*vicikicchā*). How can there be any doubt about Dhamma, about the path after one has directly experienced Dhamma, directly experienced the path, has walked on the path, and experienced the benefits. If one has doubts about Dhamma, about the path, about the technique, and feels that one has become a *sotāpanna*, it is a big delusion.

The second important quality: total liberation from attachment to all rites and rituals *(sīla-vata parāmasa)*. Every sect, every organized religion has some rites, rituals, and ceremonies. Some people develop tremendous attachment towards these rites, rituals and ceremonies, and feel that they will get liberated by practising them. A *sotāpanna* is liberated from this kind of delusion and understands that attachment to these rites and rituals cannot take one to the final goal. If one still has attachment towards them and feels that "I am a *sotāpanna*," it is a big illusion, a big delusion.

The third important quality: total liberation from the belief of some essence in this mind-matter phenomena *(sakkāyadiṭṭhi)*. For conventional purposes, to deal with people, one has to use these words—"I" and "mine". However in reality neither the physical structure nor the mental structure nor the combination of the two is "I" or "mine" or "my soul".

That becomes clear to a *sotāpanna* not by listening to discourses or by reading scriptures but by direct personal experience. Having divided, dissected, disintegrated, and dissolved the entire physical and mental structure, it becomes clear how the mind and matter interaction is going on constantly, how the illusion of "I" and "mine" is being created.

These three qualities become established in a *sotāpanna*. A *cūḷa-sotāpanna* develops these very qualities, because unless these qualities are developed, the goal of *sotāpanna* is far away.

A rare and wonderful opportunity has come in your life. Make full use of this opportunity for your own liberation.

Buddhuppādo dullabho lokasmiṃ.

One is fortunate to be born in an aeon in which 25 centuries back someone became fully enlightened. It is so rare for someone to become fully enlightened, a *sammāsambuddha*. One has to accumulate and perfect *pāramīs* for countless *kappas* (aeons); it takes a very long time. So many *kappas* are empty; there is no Buddha at all. We are fortunate that in this present *kappa*, Gotama became *sammāsambuddha* and even after 25 centuries, his *sāsana*, his teaching, the Dhamma, Vipassana, is still alive.

Manussa-bhāvo dullabho.

It is so rare to get a human life—such a valuable life. Nature has given such wonderful capability to human beings—to observe the truth within themselves. One observes the mind-matter interaction: how due to this reason, this happens; how if this is not there, this does not happen. The Dhamma becomes so clear to a human being because of the capability to objectively observe the reality within oneself.

People say that someone is fortunate if he or she dies as a human being and is born in the celestial world. But the Buddha says somebody in the celestial world who dies and is born as a human being is really fortunate.

A human life is a wonderful life. The faculty of a human being to be able to look within is so wonderful. This is the life when one can observe the reality as it is, go beyond the apparent truth and move towards the ultimate truth. We are fortunate, we have got this rare opportunity now; we are human beings.

Dullabhaṃ saddhammasavanaṃ.

However if a human being does not come across the truth, the law, the Dhamma; if he or she does not even get an opportunity to hear the Dhamma, one does not make any use of human life. One spends the whole life like any other being—an animal, a bird or a reptile. Just to listen to the truth about the Dhamma—this itself is so rare.

Dullabhā saddhā sampattiṃ.

Even if one has heard about Dhamma, listened to the words of Dhamma, it is so rare to develop confidence, devotion, faith in Dhamma.

Pabbajita bhāvo dullabho

Even if one develops faith in Dhamma, it is so difficult to leave all the multifarious responsibilities of the householder's life and live like a monk or a nun.

All these rare things have been attained. Now what remains is—establish yourself in Dhamma, strengthen yourself in Dhamma.

Handadāni, bhikkhave, āmantayāmi vo,

The Buddha invites his disciples, just before he passes away to heed his last words.

All his words are so wonderful. But his last words are like an invaluable heritage, an invaluable gift:

Vayadhammā saṅkhārā, appamādena sampādetha.

All *saṅkhārās* are *vaya-dhammā, anicca.* Whatever gets composed is bound to get decomposed, whatever arises is bound to pass away. This is the truth; this is the reality; this is the law; this is the nature; this is the Dhamma. Keep on realizing this reality diligently, *appamādena*—remaining alert, remaining attentive.

It is a wonderful opportunity to be a human being; to come in contact with the Buddha's teaching; to hear the beautiful truth of the Dhamma; to develop faith in the Dhamma; and to practise Vipassana, living the life of a monk or a nun.

Make use of all these in your day-to-day life. Dhamma is not just for 10 days; Dhamma is not just for 30 days; Dhamma is for the whole life. Every moment is so precious. Every moment for a human being who knows about Dhamma, who has realized the truth of Dhamma even a little, who knows how to practise Dhamma, becomes so precious. You can't afford to lose this opportunity.

Make use of it for your own good, for your own benefit, for your own liberation and for the good and benefit of so many others. There is so much suffering all around. There is no other way to come out of suffering.

May Dhamma spread for the good of many, for the happiness of many, for the liberation of many. **(Dhamma Giri edition—June 2007)**

SECTION FIVE

THE SPREAD OF DHAMMA

The Spread of Dhamma—Introduction

The opening article of this section ("The Swelling Stream of Dhamma") recalls S.N. Goenka's appointment as a Vipassana Teacher, the prophesy of the revival of this non-sectarian practice in India and the initial difficulties he faced.

The following article gives a detailed picture of the development of *Dhamma Giri*, the first Vipassana centre dedicated to this tradition in India and a catalyst for the spread of Dhamma worldwide.

Four articles follow which look at Dhamma service in different ways: as an opportunity to develop our *pāramī*; helping future generations learn Vipassana from an early age; working selflessly whilst planting seeds of Dhamma: developing equanimity and *mettā* towards fellow students and volunteer helpers.

In "Torchbearers of Dhamma" Goenkaji is addressing western meditators directly, reminding them of their responsibility to keep up their daily practice, maintain the purity of the technique and attract others to Vipassana through personal example.

"The Blade of Dhamma" is a talk given at an international Spread of Dhamma meeting focussing on the need for proper organisation as demand grows so that Vipassana continues to serve suffering humanity without serious obstacles.

The following three articles contain accounts describing the initial vision, construction and completion of the remarkable Global Vipassana Pagoda in Mumbai, India. This huge project was begun in 1997 to mark the approaching centenary of the birth of Sayagyi U Ba Khin (Goenkaji's Teacher) and as a symbol of India's gratitude to Burma for maintaining the gem of Dhamma across the centuries before returning it in its purity to the land of the Buddha. The Pagoda was finally inaugurated in February 2009 in the presence of thousands of meditators, dignataries and guests from around the world, including the President of India who herself had sat a 10-day Vipassana course. The Pagoda now hosts monthly one-day sittings for thousands of meditators and was the location chosen by Goenkaji in 2010 for a "Gratitude Gathering" with old students from the 1970s, to express his personal thanks to them for accepting the gift of Dhamma and helping him to develop his own *pāramīs*.

The final article of the section and the entire *Newsletter* collection was written by Goenkaji on the occasion of the enshrining of Buddha relics within the main dome of the Global Pagoda in 2006. It provides a fitting summary of Vipassana meditation now as in the past: a wholesome and harmonious art of living, a practical path to liberation.

The Swelling Stream of Dhamma

The following article by S.N. Goenka appeared in the Hindi Vipashyanā Patrikā in 1994 to mark the 25th anniversary of Goenkaji's teaching. This translation has been adapted from the original.

Words of Dhamma

Caratha bhikkhave, cārikaṃ bahujanahitāya bahujanasukhāya lokānukampāya atthāya hitāya sukhāya devamanussānaṃ.	Go your ways, oh monks, for the benefit and happiness of many, out of compassion for the world, for the good, benefit and happiness of gods and men.
Mā ekena dve āgamittha. Desetha bhikkhave, dhammaṃ ādikalyāṇaṃ majjhekalyāṇaṃ pariyosānakalyāṇaṃ sātthaṃ sabyañjanaṃ kevalaparipuṇṇaṃ.	Let no two go in the same direction. Teach, oh monks, the Dhamma which is beneficial at the beginning, in the middle, and at the end, both the spirit and the letter of it.
Parisuddhaṃ brahmacariyaṃ pakāsetha.	Make known the Noble Life which is fully complete and pure.

—Saṃyutta Nikāya, IV (I), 5.

June 20, 1969, was an extremely important day in my life. On that day my revered Teacher Sayagyi U Ba Khin appointed me a Vipassana teacher, entrusting me with a great responsibility. In the preceding years he had trained me as his assistant so that I might undertake this responsibility; now the time had come to fulfil it. The next day I was to leave Myanmar (Burma), my birthplace, and set out for India, the land of my ancestors. Vipassana had come to Myanmar from India about 2,500 years before. In its adopted land it had been preserved by an unbroken chain of teachers, down to Sayagyi. In India, however, the technique had been completely lost and people had even forgotten the name.

Now Sayagyi wished Vipassana to return to India, its country of origin. This would benefit the people of India and also enable Myanmar to repay its debt to India for this liberating technique. It was his strong Dhamma wish that this priceless spiritual teaching should not only return to India but, after becoming established there, spread throughout the world for the welfare of many. I had assured him that I would do my best to fulfil his noble wish.

Sayagyi firmly believed that India would readily accept its lost treasure. He often used to say that many people had been born in India at this time endowed with abundant *pāramitā* (merits), and that their previous meritorious deeds would naturally draw them to Vipassana.

In my ears again and again would ring my Teacher's voice, filled with *mettā:* "The clock of Vipassana has struck. Its revival is bound to come in India and it will happen now." This was the prophecy not only of my Teacher but also that of saints thousands of years ago. For me, his blessings and this unequivocal prophecy were like nourishing provisions sustaining me on my journey.

In the first days after coming to India, however, I found myself surrounded by difficulties and began to doubt whether I would succeed. Where should a course be held? How would it be organized? Who would organize it? Who would be prepared to leave family and household to spend 10 days with me? How few knew me in this country with such a vast population!

Closest to me were the members of my own family living in India. I had come with high hopes of help from them, but just before my arrival several of them had become followers of another path, Ananda Marg. I had learned of this even while I was in Myanmar. What I hadn't known was that those family members had become so extreme in their support for Ananda Marg that they would not even listen to explanations about Vipassana. The possibility seemed remote that they would join a Vipassana course and give the technique a try; and I could not see any possibility of their help in organizing a course.

At the same time, family members who had come from Myanmar and were Vipassana meditators were feeling dispirited because they had lost everything due to economic changes. I felt sure that none of them could help organize a course. Even more dire was the situation of some other Vipassana meditators who had recently come from Myanmar.

My mother faced her own dilemma. A Vipassana course was to be organized for her benefit, to enable her to free herself from mental distress. It was specifically for this purpose that I had come to India and for which the Burmese government had taken the then-unprecedented step of granting me a passport. After my arrival in India, my mother would frequently sit with me and meditate, and the experience made her eager to join a course if it could be organized. She did not want to disappoint her son who had come all the way from Myanmar, but she also did not wish to anger her other sons in India who followed the Ananda Marg path. In a very sad voice she would say, "You will have to see how I can sit the course."

The atmosphere was filled with disappointment and frustration. I thought that I would have to return to Myanmar without success. Despite my Teacher's confident prediction, a cloud of despair had cast its shadow; and although I thought that the clock of Vipassana had struck, the work of its revival would have to be done by other, fitter hands.

Sometimes, even in this unhappy atmosphere, there would be a ray of hope. Sayagyi had said that on my arrival in India nature would give a sign of my future success. I traveled by air from Yangon (Rangoon) and, as it happened, when I descended from the plane in Calcutta there was an earth tremor. The next day I read in the newspapers that it had affected a large area of northern India. To me it was as if the country was thrilled to regain the long-lost jewel of the Dhamma.

Signs of this kind had occurred in the time of the Buddha. Was this nature's way of expressing joy at the rebirth of his teaching through the return of Vipassana? However, when I recalled the present difficulties, I felt that perhaps the earthquake had just been a coincidence and that it was senseless to give it importance. I needed to understand and accept the existing situation, which was bleak.

Such storms of hope and despair raged in my mind. As the days passed a sense of despondency became heavier and deeply affected me. One evening I sat to meditate in this frame of mind. The meditation was very strong. Just a short while before its end, I found that dense clouds had gathered inside and in all directions there was total darkness. The atmosphere around was filled with doubts and tension but, when I examined the state of my mind, I found that it was not affected at all. Instead, it was firmly established in equanimity. Suddenly my mind was filled with a strong resolve: "What is to be will be. I am dedicated to Dhamma. Let Dhamma do as Dhamma wishes. If I am a worthy vessel of Dhamma and if I have a sufficient store of previous *pāramitā,* the darkness will dissipate. If it does not, I shall accept my unworthiness and return to Myanmar after meeting my family and friends."

As soon as I made this resolve, I felt strong *mettā* toward my brothers who were deeply involved in Anand Marg: "May they be happy. May they be successful." My mind was suffused with these emotions. Suddenly the darkness started to dissolve and within a few seconds was gone. In its place a stream of joy arose and enthusiasm started to overflow. No trace of despair remained anywhere.

After my meditation, I saw that a young man was waiting to see me: Vijay Adukia, the son of Dayanand Adukia and grandson of Mangalchand Adukia. Mangalchandji was the father-in-law of my younger brother and my associate in social service in Myanmar. He had also done a Vipassana course there. Vijay said, "If you wish to conduct a 10-day course, I shall arrange for a place. A portion of the Pancayatiwadi Dharamsala can be made available. I have already spoken to the management. If you wish, you can come and inspect it."

I cheerfully went to the course site but found it totally unsuitable for meditation. Aside from the noise and din of the city, there was filth everywhere. However, to find a vacant place for 10 days in a large, densely populated city like Bombay was an impossibility. Therefore, expressing gratitude toward the management of the facility, I immediately gave my acceptance.

Now the question was who would join the course. But I was confident that, just as a site had been found, a few people would also be prepared to participate.

Vijay himself said with great enthusiasm, "I shall be one of the students. I had wished to take charge of arranging the course but my father can do it. I'll sit the course instead."

My old friend and associate from Myanmar, Kantibhai G. Shah, had come to my home to see me. When he heard about the course he also said with great enthusiasm, "I'll be a student and our friend B. C. Shah will be another. I'll bring him along."

"Now the course will certainly be held," I said, "even if only two or three people participate."

My mother was sitting nearby. Her face, which always used to be so cheerful, looked forlorn. The waves of her sorrow tugged at my mind. When I lay down to sleep at night, her image came before my eyes again and again. I could understand her frame of mind only too well. She was torn between conflicting emotions. On the one hand, for her sake her son had come from far away to conduct a Vipassana course in which she wished to participate. On the other hand, her younger son would feel hurt if she did so.

I too was sad. One reason was that the prophecies made long ago appeared to be coming true: after perhaps 2,000 years a Vipassana course was about to be held in India. I had hoped that, by taking part in this historic Dhamma mission and helping to organize it, my entire family in India would share the merits. Now there did not seem to be the slightest possibility that this would happen.

Another reason for my sadness was that I wished to repay my debt of gratitude to my parents. In their old age I wished to make the effort to put them on the path of Dhamma. But I could not see any possibility of their joining the course. What could I do? I had only the strength of *mettā* to rely on. During that night I sent strong *mettā* to my parents and brothers. The next day I felt that the entire atmosphere was vibrating with enthusiasm. Early in the morning another old friend from Myanmar, Motilal Chaudhary, and Bharat, the son of Balchand Poddar, came to see me. Both were old students. When they heard about the course they said that they were ready to join it and assured me that they would also ask others to take part. I phoned Madras. Family members who had settled there were delighted when they heard the news about the upcoming course, and three of them decided to come to Bombay to participate.

My mother and father were observing all this. I could understand my mother's difficulties very well, but in the present situation I could not find the courage to say anything to her. And I knew only too well my father's stubbornness. He had joined Ananda Marg even though he was not greatly influenced by it. While living in Myanmar he had completed a Vipassana course with Sayagyi U Ba Khin, in which his Ānāpāna had been very powerful. Sayagyi had been very satisfied with him. There was only one difficulty barring him from taking part in the course: he did not wish to give up the performance of his daily religious rituals. I suggested to him that, just as someone else had been found to perform the rituals for him during the course he did in Myanmar, the same arrangement could be made here also. To my pleasant surprise, he accepted my suggestion at once. At this my mother summoned up her courage and said, "If you are going to meditate, I shall also, if not for 10 days then at least for five."

My happiness was limitless. Here was the chance for me to repay my debt to my parents. "Who knows," I thought, "the remaining family members who are Ananda Marg followers may experience the benefits of Vipassana at some time in the future, but these two have reached old age; they should sit now." And so it happened. Both parents participated in the first course from July 3 to 13, 1969, along with 12 other students. My mother remained for the full 10 days of the course and benefited greatly.

I was surprised to see that, although my Ananda Marg brothers did not offer to help on this first course, they did not put any obstacles in the way of this meritorious endeavor, nor did they express any opposition or feel the slightest annoyance. All our apprehensions proved to have been unfounded. My mind was suffused with feelings of gratitude toward them. At the conclusion of the course, I mentally shared the merits of this great Dhamma undertaking and made the Dhamma wish that sooner or later their merits would also bear fruit, that they might also taste the nectar of Vipassana and be happy.

These difficulties were only for the first course. Immediately afterward students who had taken part and experienced the benefits began to organize and to serve courses, one after another. Thus, after 2,000 years, the pure stream of Dhamma again began to flow in India. Since 1969 it has swelled into a mighty river, bringing happiness to people in India and around the world. The doors of liberation were opened for many, allowing them to realize true happiness.

May the Dhamma-Ganges of Vipassana gain more and more strength, and continue to benefit people throughout the world.

Editor's note: In 1996 approximately 400 courses were held in India, and another 300 were held in 35 other countries around the world. Over 38,000 students attended these courses.

Let Dhamma Spread

My dear Dhamma sons and Dhamma daughters: It is good that in the last 26 years Dhamma has started spreading, but it is also true that this is only a few drops in a big ocean. Yet, they are so valuable. The path is very long, but even the longest path of thousands of miles must start with the first step; during these 26 years we have taken that first step.

Now, just as Sayagyi said, the clock of Dhamma has struck. People have at least started understanding that there is a meditation technique like Vipassana, which is result-oriented, which gives results here and now. "People are getting benefited; let me also try." This in itself is a big achievement, a very big achievement; but it must spread.

A proper foundation has been prepared, and now is the time for Dhamma to spread everywhere. If a center is still not well established, not yet self-sufficient, and is not giving service to the number of people that it could, then to start another center nearby is not a good idea. But, if a center has become strong enough, then more and more centers should arise.

But how will this happen? More and more noncenter courses must be given in those parts of the country, those parts of the world, where Vipassana has not yet gone. We must take it there; let people taste Vipassana. This is the way it started in India, with these noncenter courses.

So now let there be more and more such courses around the world. Dhamma centers must be established, well maintained and self-sufficient. And then, let Dhamma spread, let it spread......

(Excerpted and adapted from S.N. Goenka's closing address at the 1995 Annual Conference at *Dhamma Giri.*)

Vyāpe visva Vipasyanā	May Vipassana spread throughout the world
Bhau jana hita sukha hoya.	For the good and happiness of many.
Jana jana kā kalyaṇa ho.	May everyone enjoy well-being.
Jana jana maṅgala hoya.	May everyone be happy.
Dāna sukhoṅ kā mūla hai,	Generosity is the root of happiness,
kare parigraha dūra.	removing acquisitiveness.
Halkā phulkā cita rahe,	The mind remains light and at ease,
maṅgala se bharapūra.	filled with well-being.

—Hindi doha by S.N.Goenka

(International edition—January 1998)

Dhamma Giri: Tenth Year Commemorative

This autumn marks the tenth year anniversary of the first official course at *Dhamma Giri*. It was in October 1976 that the Vipassana International Academy opened its doors to the general public for its first 10-day course. The opening of *Dhamma Giri* marked an important step in the spread of Dhamma in India. Since 1969, S.N. Goenka had conducted courses in that country using temporary facilities: temples, churches, mosques, pilgrims' rest houses, monasteries, schools, hotels. These "gypsy camps" were invaluable in scattering wide the seeds of Dhamma, but obviously it would be still more valuable to have a place specifically for the practice of Vipassana meditation. The importance of establishing a center was stressed by Sayagyi U Ba Khin when, in the early seventies, he was visited by the first of Goenkaji's students to come to Burma.

There were, however, formidable obstacles, not all of them financial. One was that while the Buddha is held in high respect in India, Buddhism is widely regarded with suspicion. If a center was founded to spread the teaching of the Buddha, it might be regarded as a sectarian institution, in which case its appeal would be limited only to the small minority of Buddhists in India. Aware of this danger, Goenkaji emphasized strongly the non-sectarian, universal nature of Vipassana meditation. He made clear that *Dhamma Giri* was not to be the property of any group, but was for the benefit of all who sought a way out of suffering.

Another problem was that the system of pure *dāna* [donation] was unfamiliar in India. At the gypsy camps, students paid for their own room and board. Given the circumstances, there was nothing wrong in such a system, but a Dhamma center, Goenkaji felt, could not operate on this basis. He recalled his Teacher's own policy Sayagyi had written, "There is no admission or subscription fee or fixed donation payable by my disciples... We accept aid only from disciples who have purified themselves with Vipassana meditation.. .. If one can help the people to enjoy the fruits of meditation and if they know that the results obtained are for their well-being, tangible, here-and-now, and concrete, you cannot prevent them from doing their might to give better facilities for the promotion of the Dhamma." The starting of a center was thus not just a matter of finding the right piece of land and the money to pay for it. There must be the proper foundation: the wish to experience and share with all others the benefits of Vipassana meditation. For the center to flourish, all who supported it and came there must understand this. Goenkaji was confident, however, that the Dhamma would overcome these obstacles. He worked tirelessly to realize his Teacher's goal of establishing a center from which the Dhamma could spread not only in India but around the world.

As this great project has developed many Vipassana meditators have become involved in it and in time thousands of them have come to *Dhamma Giri* to meditate and give their help in establishing the center. Their own words and those of Goenkaji help to tell the story of the early years of *Dhamma Giri*.

How *Dhamma Giri* was Purchased

In December 1973 I attended my first Vipassana course at Deolali, nearby to my home at Igatpuri. I found the course hard but rewarding. On the last day I learned by chance that Goenkaji had been looking for a site for a meditation center in the area of Bombay. At once the thought came to me that there could be no more suitable location for such a center than Igatpuri. I was eager for the inexhaustible spring of Dhamma to well forth from the town where I lived. I went to Goenkaji and invited him to stop for tea at my house on his way back to Bombay after the course. I assured him that he would not be delayed more than five minutes, since my home stood by the side of the road that he must travel from Deolali to Bombay. My plan was, once he was in my home, to broach the subject of a site for a center.

Goenkaji's reply was not at first encouraging "If I stop at every house where I am invited along the way, how will I ever reach my home?" he asked. But in response to my urgent requests he kindly accepted my invitation, only warning me, "See that the five minutes do not turn into five hours!"

I was filled with joy that my plan had worked so far, but also with trepidation that it might yet miscarry. In my anxiety I wanted to set out at once for my home, lest Goenkaji pass me on the way. He would be traveling by car, while I would have to take the bus or train, which naturally were much slower. It was now lunchtime. I went to the dining room to say goodbye to Shri Rangil Mehta, a fellow meditator who had given me a lift to the course. Hearing of my plan, he offered his assistance. "Let us have our lunch," he said. "Then we shall all go together in my car, and reach Igatpuri in no time."

All went as I had hoped. We were in plenty of time to welcome Goenkaji when his car

Dhamma Giri, the Plateau of Peace. Channels in the rocky face of the mountain behind are cut by the many waterfalls that veil the mountain during the monsoon (1983)

arrived at Igatpuri. As we were drinking tea in my home, I requested that if he could spare the time now, I might show him a few possible sites for a meditation center in the area of my town. He gave his consent, and with Mr. Mehta we set off to look at properties. The first one or two that I showed Goenkaji obviously did not meet with his approval. I asked for clearer guidelines about the kind of place that he had in mind. He told me, "I would like a site that is not in the midst of the town but not too remote either, where connections could easily be arranged for water, electricity, and telephone, and where access would not be too difficult." I immediately thought of showing him the land where *Dhamma Giri* now stands. At that time there was no proper road into the property, but Mr. Mehta did not hesitate to risk his car on the rough, uneven track. We went as far as the car could take us, and then got out. Goenkaji looked closely all about him, and within just a few minutes he decided that this was what he had been looking for. At that moment someone pointed out a cremation taking place at the foot of the hill on which we stood. I was worried that the proximity of a cremation ground would make Goenkaji change his mind about the site. But he said with a smile, "Good! This will continually implant the awareness of *anicca* [impermanence] in the minds of meditators."

View of the original buildings, taken from the area where the pagoda now stands (1975)

There and then Mr. Mehta offered to purchase the property and donate it to the Trust. Before we left he had noted all the details so as to conclude the transaction speedily. All of this took five hours—a long time for a cup of tea! Goenkaji was well justified in his suspicion that stopping at my house would take much more than five minutes.

That day—December 16, 1973—was the happiest of my life. Since then I have practiced Vipassana faithfully and given whatever free time I have to serve the Dhamma so that many may experience the happiness of liberation.

—Bhojraj Sancheti, Igatpuri, India

The First Meditators at the New Center

I first came to *Dhamma Giri* in early 1974. After a course near Bombay, I had asked Goenkaji for permission to visit the newly-purchased land. He told me to go ahead, and to contact Mr. Bhojraj in Igatpuri. I went there along with a friend, and Mr. Bhojraj took us up the hill. At that time the site consisted of three or four old bungalows and the surrounding land. There was a family of farmers still living in the little bungalow nearest the mountain. Mr. Bhojraj opened up the easternmost building for us, which is where the farmers used to keep their goats. The floor was covered with dung and the walls were black from years of cooking fires. I stayed about a week and then left. When I came back a few weeks later, Graham Gambie had arrived. Together we set up housekeeping and started meditating on the site. We wrote to Goenkaji and asked him what work we should do to start improving the place—cleaning, planting gardens, or whatever. He wrote back, "Dear Graham and Geo: Be happy! Meditate, meditate, meditate. Clean yourselves and clean the meditation center. Don't do anything else, just meditate." And that is what we did.

First there was some basic cleaning that was necessary for us to use the place. We carried buckets of water up from the well, threw them on the floor, and scrubbed away on our hands and knees. And then we started meditating, perhaps six to eight hours a day. It was hard enough with the farmers in the next building, arguing and yelling and screaming. But after a while the farmers moved out.

Then Sonu, the deaf laborer, was hired to work at the site. He started whitewashing the walls of the bungalow where we were living, which went from black to dark gray to light gray to white after about eight coats of whitewash. We would meditate in one room and Sonu would whitewash in another. When he had finished the room where he was working, he would move to the next and start whitewashing there. One day I must have been getting a little bored with meditating, so I motioned to Sonu that I would help him whitewash. In gestures he told me emphatically, "You meditate, I'll whitewash!"

During the monsoon season we would put our foam cushions above the stone floor on little 2-inch high wooden platforms, because it was so damp the cushions would soak up the water. One time while I was meditating, I felt a really strong pain in my big toe. I thought it was just a strange *saṅkhāra* [reaction], so I just sat and observed. And then I felt another one, and another one. So I looked down and there was this little mouse—he'd take a bite of my toe and slip underneath the platform after each bite. And the ants! I used to wrap myself up in this elaborate way so that it would take at least 45 minutes for the ants to find my neck or my eyelids or my face.

From time to time Goenkaji would come to lay out the building plans and inspect progress. I remember when he decided where the Pagoda would be. At that time the Plateau of Peace [where the Pagoda stands] was just a field without any trees, but we had a group sitting there: Goenkaji, Graham, Narayan Dasarwar [now manager of *Dhamma Giri*], and myself. I was there when the four Bodhi trees were planted on the Plateau of Peace. Graham had brought the trees from Sarnath, Bodhgaya, Sravasti, and Burma.

Building started in 1975. The Trust hired a contractor to construct facilities for about 80 people. At the same time Goenkaji gave the westerners living at *Dhamma Giri* permission to build thatched mud huts for meditators, in traditional Indian village style. Once construction started, there was a whole encampment of laborers and their families and animals living on the site.

—Assistant Teacher Geo Poland, Canada

In the early days before there was any building going on, everyone who was there would meditate six to eight hours a day. There was more to do in terms of keeping yourself alive then; there was no water, electricity, or plumbing, just an empty building to stay in.

Dhamma Giri wasn't a retreat environment. It was like living in a hut out in the desert. We were living on an isolated hilltop with four or five mango trees and the wind howling around, and the rain. There were snakes and jackals and vultures, and many kinds of insects. The insects really owned and ran the building, the people were the intruders. Working with the Indians was great. Sonu was there from the beginning. He has a great personality. Because he's deaf and mute, his instructions are always in sign language. He had a novel way of identifying each of the foreigners, according to some physical characteristic. Geo Poland, because he is a doctor, was signed as the needle pusher with no hair. And Graham, who wore round glasses, was signed like binoculars held in front of the eyes. One day Sonu was replacing some tiles on a roof and another worker came and took the ladder away. Since he couldn't talk, he was just left there gesturing wildly. And if he wanted to get your attention without going up to you, he would throw rocks at you. So you would see these rocks and know Sonu wanted you.

We were always so busy, everyday. I don't think we sat around and thought about what it was going to be like in 10 years. It was more, what have we got to do tomorrow? Goenkaji did encourage us with news about what was going on, and how this would be a center for future generations, and so on. But the day-to-day jobs have a way of shouldering their way to the front. When we planted all the trees we knew one day it would be a wonderful forest, but as you're considering the forest, you know that you have to water this one and that one and prune those...

—Luke Matthews, Canada

Sonu is still working at Dhamma Giri today as one of the head laborers, and has been shown the first steps of meditation by Goenkaji.—Editor

---

A course for old students was held at the new center in May, 1975. The following is from the Vipassana Newsletter, July–August 1975:

Academy's First Course

A total of 76 students attended the historic first course of four days at the Vipassana International Academy to make every particle of the land vibrate in Dhamma.

In a very short time the Igatpuri Academy was extensively repaired and all necessary facilities such as lighting, temporary meditation hall, dining tent and bathroom were installed.

Naturally there were numerous initial difficulties which were quickly overcome. A tube well was drilled, but at the last moment it was found to be dry. Water for the course was brought by tanker.

The course, in severe heat, proved a grueling but wonderful experience. Goenkaji meditated almost the whole time in the meditation hall with the meditators.

One of the original thatched mud huts

Goenkaji sent special *mettā* to all the creatures living on the land the night the first group *mettā* session was held. He announced that no creature from now on need fear for its life in the Dhamma atmosphere. No one would kill them or give orders for them to be killed....

During the course Goenkaji carefully checked all sections of the land and selected the site for the first new buildings, which will be a kitchen and a large hall...

To make clear...that the Dhamma is a priceless gift, Goenkaji also has announced a new arrangement for covering the cost of food and accommodation at the Academy. In future students will not pay for their food and other expenses, but will donate according to their means and the feeling of their hearts for the benefit of students who will follow them at the Academy. In this way their happiness at receiving the Dhamma will be shared with others, and the wheel of Dhamma will keep rolling for the benefit of all. The intention of this move is to eliminate any trace of commercialism from the Dhamma institute.

Dhamma Giri in the First Year After its Opening

I arrived at *Dhamma Giri* in October 1976, a few days after its official opening. The first 10-day course was in progress, attended by 130 people, about the limit that the Academy could then accommodate. I was asked to help out until the next course began. My first jobs were scraping whitewash off the tiles in the new bathroom and clearing a walking path around the Plateau of Peace. I was surprised by the place. I had thought I was coming to a center that was fully, if newly, built. Instead it seemed to me a raw, unfinished building site. Some structures were incomplete; all were surrounded by rubble and debris. Only a few trees and gardens had yet been planted.

Still, the center had a stark beauty. In the evening, while Goenkaji was giving the Hindi discourse in the meditation hall (then located beside the dining room), I would sit outside and watch the shadows deepen on the surrounding hills. This was the first course at *Dhamma Giri*, and many people from the town wanted to come at least to hear the discourses. There was no room for them in the hall, so a loudspeaker was set up outside and carpets were put down near the mango tree in front of the gate. Each evening 50 to a 100 people would come and sit there. They were simple people of all ages, in traditional Indian dress. They listened intently to Goenkaji's words as their ancestors had listened to the Buddha speak. Then they gathered up their sleeping children and in the darkness they hurried home.

From November I started to sit, and continued in consecutive courses into early 1977. My plan was to keep going until March, when I would head on my way to carry on with my life elsewhere. It didn't work out that way. By January I very much needed a break and was contemplating going away for a vacation. I am always grateful to Graham Gambie who encouraged me instead to stay and serve at *Dhamma Giri*, an experience that taught me at least as much as sitting had.

Serving at V.I.A. was a little different then from today. There were no Indians and no hired workers involved in the day-to-day management. There were also very few organized office procedures. At one time I was responsible for manning the office, answering the telephone, dealing with students, supervising workers and watchmen, handling the petty cash, replying to letters, keeping accounts—all simultaneously. To do all that, and do it smilingly with equanimity was quite a test, and my failures taught me as much as my rare successes. I quickly realized that I had much to learn about Dhamma, and decided to extend my stay at V.I.A. indefinitely.

As the hot season came on, *Dhamma Giri's* perennial water problem became severe. The line connecting us to the municipal system seemed to be obstructed, and there were endless delays in having it cleaned out. Goenkaji asked me to write a letter on the subject to the Igatpuri Municipality. I wrote that if the problem was not solved soon, we might be forced to close the meditation center. Before sending the letter I showed it to Goenkaji for his approval. He told me to change it. "Our job is to open meditation centers," he said. "It is the job of Māra [the forces opposed to Dhamma] to close them." June brought the onset of monsoon.

Courses stopped and only a handful of people remained at *Dhamma Giri*. Within a few days the land was carpeted in fresh green, and on every side the Hill of Dhamma was surrounded by flowing streams. At that time it seemed to me a true island of peace, wrapped in mist and cut off from the world. Those of us who stayed took turns serving and doing self-courses. With Goenkaji's encouragement, Shanti Shah began teaching us Pāli. It was inspiring at last to understand the meaning of the chants that we had heard so often during courses. Every weekend Goenkaji would come to visit *Dhamma Giri* and attend our class. He seemed as delighted with our progress as we were. For hours he would explain Dhamma to us or tell us stories of his experiences in Burma.

Those early days at *Dhamma Giri* remain unforgettable to me. In them so many seeds were planted that were to come to fruition in later years.

When I return each year to V.I.A., it is the trees that convey most vividly the change in the place. I remember one morning during the monsoon of 1977, when a 100 silver oak seedlings lay in a little pile under the mango tree outside the office. Today those seedlings are each 20 feet tall and form the border of the Plateau of Peace. I remember when the trees along the drive from the gate to the old bungalows barely reached my shoulder. I remember when I first came that the Burmese Bodhi tree in the central garden between the men's dormitories was so weak that it drooped from a stake. Now its trunk is thick and straight, its roots deep, its branches thick, giving pleasant shade—a visible symbol of the growth of *Dhamma Giri*.

—Bill Hart, Canada

Once the newly opened Academy was functioning smoothly, it was possible to think of further expansion. The first priority was to improve the meditation facilities by providing cells where students could work in seclusion. Accordingly, construction of a meditation pagoda began on the Plateau of Peace in 1978. Dozens of meditators from the west came to *Dhamma Giri* specially to participate in this project. Alongside Indians they worked as carpenters, masons, electricians, and general laborers, often under conditions of great difficulty. With their help it was possible to inaugurate the first stage of the Pagoda in March 1979.

Original bungalows with mango trees that were standing on the site when it was purchased (1980)

New accommodation (1985)

Dhamma Giri in 1978–1979

The train rumbled to a halt. Maureen and I scrambled for our backpacks and wearily

Students completing installation of metal umbrella, in preparation for the inauguration of the Pagoda (March 15, 1979). In the center of the upper storey of the Pagoda is an octagonal meditation room for the Teacher. Surrounding this are eight cells for students, connected to the central room by communicating doors. The lower storey is built on the same plan, with additional concentric rings of cells surrounding the central core. The roof is in the shape of a Burmese pagoda but differs from a traditional pagoda in that it is hollow inside, thus forming a dome over the central meditation room. Similar smaller domes top the adjoining cells. The design follows that used at the center of Sayagyi U Ba Khin in Burma.

pushed and shoved our way onto the platform of Igatpuri Station. We were greeted by a bunch of small kids, mouths crammed with sugarcane, yelling "What is your name?" and "Give me a stamp!" Above, flocks of black crows squawked noisily. The air was thick with smoke from charcoal burners, which had been brought out into the street in preparation for the midday meal. Screeching train whistles competed with the high-pitched horns of brightly-decorated trucks. Added to the traffic din was the incessant wailing of popular Indian vocal music piped through antiquated loud-speaker systems. The sweet aroma of freshly ground spices permeated the air.

It was a walk of about 20 minutes to *Dhamma Giri*, through the sprawling back streets and alleys, crowded with people, children, cows and ox-carts. A dry, dusty track linked the town with the Academy.

Physically, *Dhamma Giri* was no luxury hotel, but its facilities were basic and practical. The buildings were primarily of stone and concrete. About 25 mud and stick huts helped accommodate the ever-increasing numbers of people who came to practice there. The grounds were landscaped, with young trees and a lush garden obviously well-tended. It was particularly pretty at sunrise and sunset, when soft light highlighted the surrounding dry mountains.

Maureen and I eagerly joined the first 10-day course of the winter season (1978–1979). The large hall was jammed with an interesting mixture of westerners and Indians of all classes. During the course I began to piece together a deepening understanding of the practice and its implications in my daily life. I began to understand more clearly how it all fit together, and could directly correlate theory to my own experience. There seemed a cleanliness in what I was learning. The powerful atmosphere at *Dhamma Giri* was most conducive to making strong efforts. The presence of a number of eager students who had been practicing for years gave further inspiration.

At the end of the first 10 days, Maureen and I decided we would continue another 10 days in a self-course. After 20 days we felt sure that our long journey to the East had been well worth it. We decided we would stay on at *Dhamma Giri*.

Staying means work whether you sit and work at the practice or help around the center. Maureen found a niche in the office. I was fortunate to work on the construction of the Pagoda. This is a large, circular, concrete construction with a roof in the shape of a traditional Burmese pagoda and rows of cave-like cells for individual meditation in seclusion.

Living at *Dhamma Giri* provided us with the ideal environment to do intensive meditation and become more established in the technique, and also to give service. It was an excellent balance, alternating periods of meditation and periods of work.

Six months passed before we made our final descent down the dusty track, through the bustling town of Igatpuri to the train station. We both felt a quiet and deep respect for Goenkaji, who stood as such a fine example of both theory and practice.

—Bruce Stewart, New Zealand/U.S.A.

Initially meditators often had to share cells, since in its first stage the Pagoda contained only 32. Sometimes as many as six or seven people sat together in one cell.

Meditators helping in construction of Pagoda (1978)

Masons working on Pagoda roof (early 1979)

Seen from the mountain behind, the lush sight of *Dhamma Giri* in its wider surroundings (1985)

Each year more cells have been added, and the number now exceeds 200. In 1980 a large meditation hall was added next to the Pagoda. At the same time the residential facilities have been expanded and improved. Recently a second meditation hall was added. Extensive tree-planting has also been undertaken to create a green zone around the perimeter of *Dhamma Giri*. A large water-tower was completed this year, and as an experiment a dam has been built to create a reservoir. A printing press has been established, and under the auspices of the Vipassana Research Institute, a one-year Pāli studies program is being offered annually.

But the most important development has not been in bricks and mortar. Year by year the meditation atmosphere has strengthened at *Dhamma Giri*. As soon as it was possible to provide students with the facilities to live and meditate in seclusion, Goenkaji began to conduct 30-day courses at the Academy. A still longer course is planned for early 1987. Those who come to V.I.A. have the opportunity to practice seriously and intensively in a highly supportive environment, and so to take further steps along the path to liberation.

Today this unique center is a wonderful example of what can be done with hard work and with Dhamma. To meditators around the world it gives support and inspiration for the practice of Vipassana meditation.

The following extract is from an article written by Goenkaji in 1979 to mark his completion of 10 years as a Teacher of Vipassana meditation.

I do not devalue what has been done for the spread of Vipassana in the last 10 years, since to do so would be to de-value the selfless service given by so many people. But the fact remains that up to now only a first step has been taken in the work, and a small step. From a firm base in India, the light of Vipassana must spread everywhere around the world.

It is a lifetime job. It is a steep ascent of the mountain. Upon the way are many obstacles and hindrances, those within and those without.... To overcome these difficulties requires great strength of Dhamma, perseverance, forbearance, zeal, and egolessness.

At times when faced with great difficulties, I find that I have stooped beneath their weight. Very soon, however, I have stood up, brushed the dust from my knees, and started walking with increased Dhamma strength. Whatever portion of the journey has been completed gives the inspiration and strength to walk on. And the greatest help upon the path is gratitude. This is the support for the journey ahead.

Therefore gratitude keeps overflowing in my mind, firstly to the Enlightened One who rediscovered this lost technique and used it for his benefit, and who with free hand and compassionate heart distributed it for the benefit of one and all I am grateful to the entire chain of teachers from the Buddha to Sayagyi U Ba Khin who maintained this wonderful technique in its original form, thereby permitting me to learn it in its purity. I am grateful to all the members of my family whose co-operation has been so helpful in the Dhamma work. I am grateful to all my comrades and friends in the Dhamma, all who have given me their co-operation and assistance, whose companionship has given me sustenance on the path.

If during the last 10 years by my deeds of

body, speech, or mind I have committed any wrong action knowingly or unknowingly, intentionally or unintentionally toward anyone, I ask pardon.

May all beings be happy!
May all beings be peaceful!
May all beings be liberated!

—Traveler on the Dhamma Path, S.N. Goenka

Dharmagiri se Dharama ki
Ganga pravahita hoya,
jana-jana ka hove bhala,
jana-jana mangala hoya

May the Ganges of the Dhamma
flow from *Dhamma Giri*,
bringing happiness to everyone,
bringing blessings to all.

—Hindi doha of S.N. Goenka

(International edition—December 1986)

Dhamma Giri: Silver Jubilee Commemoration

Words of Dhamma

...leṇatthañca sukhatthañca, jhāyituñca vipassituṃ. Vihāradānaṃ saṅghassa, aggaṃ buddhena vaṇṇitaṃ; tasmā hi paṇḍito poso, sampassaṃ atthamattano. Vihāre kāraye ramme, vāsayettha bahussute...

Sheltering and conducive to concentration and insight, a place of meditation is praised by the Buddha as the greatest gift to the Saṅgha. Therefore, a wise man, considering his own welfare, should have pleasant dwellings built, in which those who have heard much about the Dhamma, may stay (and practise it).

—Cūḷavagga (Vinayapiṭake)

This autumn marks the 25th anniversary of the first 10-day course at *Dhamma Giri*. The gates of the Vipassana International Academy were opened to the public in 1976. Goenkaji conducted the first 10-day course at *Dhamma Giri* from 27 October to 7 November 1976. Eighty-nine students, 38 old and 51 new students, participated in that course. The opening of *Dhamma Giri* marked an important step in the spread of Dhamma. Since 1969, Goenkaji had conducted courses in temples, churches, mosques, pilgrims' resthouses, monasteries, schools, and hotels. These "gypsy camps" (non-centre camps) were invaluable in the spread of Dhamma, but obviously it would be still more valuable to have a place specifically for the practice of Vipassana meditation. The importance of establishing a centre was stressed by Sayagyi U Ba Khin when, in the early seventies, he was visited by the first of Goenkaji's students in Myanmar.

The Growth of *Dhamma Giri*

Once the newly opened Academy was functioning smoothly, it was possible to think of further expansion. The first priority was to improve the meditation facilities by providing cells where students could work in seclusion. Accordingly, construction of a meditation pagoda began on the Plateau of Peace in 1978. Dozens of meditators from the west came to *Dhamma Giri* specifically to participate in this project. They worked alongside Indians as carpenters, masons, electricians, and general labourers, often under difficult conditions. With their help, the first stage of the pagoda was inaugurated in March 1979.

Initially meditators often had to share cells, since in its first stage the pagoda contained only 32. Sometimes as many as six or seven people sat together in one cell.

Each year more cells were added. In 1980, a large meditation hall was built next to the pagoda. At the same time the residential facilities were expanded and improved. After a few years, a second meditation hall was added and extensive tree planting was undertaken to create a green zone around the perimeter of *Dhamma Giri*. The original hall has been expanded and six more rings of cells have been added to the cell complex. In the early 1990's, an outer ring of 32 cells was built on the upper level. This served as a base for a larger hollow pagoda, within which the original pagoda remains intact. This magnificent Myanmar-style structure rises 60 feet above the second level of cells. At present, there are more than 350 cells in the pagoda, comfortable accommodation for more than 700 students, living quarters for Dhamma servers and kitchen staff in addition to a bookstore, carpentry and maintenancee offices etc. There are separate meditation halls for males and females on a 10-day course or for two different types of courses held simultaneously. A large kitchen complex, which was originally run by a couple of cooks with a few pots and pans, now uses modern appliances and caters to over 900 people daily.

Continuous gardening, landscaping and tree planting have transformed the site. Thousands of trees and shrubs have been planted, and more are being planted all the time. What began as a dry, barren, scrubby hill has now become a lush garden of trees and flowering shrubs, which gives food and shelter to numerous birds as well as shade, delight and protection to the meditators.

Adjoining the meditation centre is the Vipassana Research Institute, which was established in 1986 to conduct research into the *pariyatti* (theory) and *paṭipatti* (practice) of the Buddha's teaching.

On the adjacent land to the east of *Dhamma Giri*, Sayagyi U Ba Khin village is quickly taking shape, where meditators will be able to live in a conducive Dhammic atmosphere.

Dhamma Tapovana, to the west of *Dhamma Giri*, is the first centre built exclusively for long courses. The second phase of construction has now been completed with 100 single accommodation units ready for use. Work on cells was recently completed, and expansion of the dining hall and toilet blocks has been completed. The new units were recently used in a 20-day course; the first combined male and female long course at *Dhamma Tapovana*. A 45-day course, the first outside *Dhamma Giri*, was held there in July and August 2001. The first ever 60-day course conducted by Goenkaji will be held in *Dhamma Tapovana* from 2 January 2002. The course is open to teachers and senior assistant teachers who have sat two 45-day courses.

But, the most important development has not been in bricks and mortar. Year by year, the meditation atmosphere has strengthened at *Dhamma Giri*. As soon as it was possible to provide students with the facilities to live and meditate in seclusion, Goenkaji began to conduct 30-day courses at *Dhamma Giri*. Those who come here have the opportunity to practise seriously and intensively in a highly supportive environment, and so, to take further steps along the path to liberation.

Today, this centre is a wonderful example of what can be done with hard work and with Dhamma. To meditators around the world, it gives support and inspiration for the practice of Vipassana meditation.

(Dhamma Giri edition—November 2001)

No Force Can Stop the Dhamma

S. N. Goenka

The following is adapted from Goenkaji's opening address at the Annual Meeting at Dhamma Giri on January 16, 1994.

Words of Dhamma

Na paresaṃ vilomāni,
na paresaṃ katākataṃ;
attanova avekkheyya,
katāni akatāni ca.

—Dhammapada, 50

Let not one seek the faults of others, Nor
the things left done and undone by others.
Instead, let one reflect on one's own deeds
Done and undone.

All of us are sons and daughters of the Buddha. We have inherited from him compassion for others, to help them to come out of their misery. The one and only aim of a Dhamma server, a Dhamma manager or a Dhamma teacher is to help more and more suffering people to come out of their misery. We are paid back for all our efforts when we see others coming out of their misery, and we feel joyful.

We are not spreading Dhamma to make a sect out of it—such madness should never come in the mind. Buddha gave Dhamma for the individual to come out of misery, not to establish a sect. A person may call oneself by any name or belong to any community, colour or gender, this is not our concern. We should think, "He or she is a miserable person. How can I help them come out of misery?" This is all, nothing else.

I would like to emphasize two things. The first is to sow the seed of Dhamma in the coming generation. Here is a generation whose minds are very fertile. If we sow the seed of Vipassana Dhamma at a young age, we are preparing these children to live a happy, peaceful life, a good human life. Children are not bound by attachment to rites, rituals or philosophical beliefs. They should be given pure Dhamma at this age. We have to give more and more children's courses. Secondly, anyone who is giving any kind of service, whether a Dhamma teacher or server, is a representative of Dhamma.

You are sons and daughters of the Buddha, and so, you have a great responsibility. If someone points the way, before taking that path, people will look at the finger pointing. If it is dirty, stained with blood, people will hesitate. You are serving so that people can take Dhamma's way. Your way of life and your behaviour with people should be very clean. This alone will inspire others to walk on this path. Again and again a Dhamma server, a Dhamma trustee, a Dhamma teacher, has to keep examining oneself: "Have I done anything wrong? If so, I must rectify it. I must amend myself.

Even as a normal human being, it is in my interest to rectify myself. But now that I represent Dhamma it is all the more important that I rectify myself." All of you must examine yourselves: "In performing my duty, what mistakes have I made?" "I made this mistake—I spoke rudely to somebody. My words were very harsh." Or, "I was angry. I had no love or compassion while serving." Or any other mistake. First accept it, and then make a strong decision that in future it should not happen again. It is true that you are not yet fully liberated from all impurities; they keep arising.

But be very careful not to allow them to overpower you, especially when you are serving people in Dhamma. When you accept a mistake, it is like taking the lid off—you stop suppressing the wrong you have done. Another great advantage is that the more you accept your mistake open-heartedly, your ego will start deflating. If you keep your mistakes secret, you are helping your ego to inflate; you are harming yourself and harming Dhamma. This is not good for you. So, accept your mistake and take a strong decision that in future this will not happen again. This will help you to come out of ego and to learn how to serve in a humble way. This is *anattā*—egolessness. By this, we are not instituting a rite or ritual; rather, it is a healthy process of cleansing.

Dhamma work means cleaning oneself and helping others to learn how to clean themselves. I am sure all of you here are giving your time, energy and service to help others, not to inflate your egos. Dhamma will spread. No force in the world can stop it from spreading. As Sayagyi used to say, "The clock of Vipassana has now struck." We are fortunate to be tools of Dhamma with a wonderful opportunity to develop *pāramī* for our own liberation.

We must be very grateful to all those people who come to take Dhamma because they are giving us an opportunity to develop our *dāna pāramī*. The *dāna* of *Dhamma* is the best *dāna*. Make proper use of this opportunity.

May all of you grow in Dhamma. May all of you glow in Dhamma. You are Dhamma's representatives; let people be attracted by your service. May this year bring more and more people to the path of Dhamma. May this year help more and more people to come out of their misery. May many more people come out of their misery. May Dhamma spread. May all be happy, be peaceful, be liberated.

(Dhamma Giri edition—July 2004)

Benefits of Dhamma Service

S.N. Goenka

The following is based on a talk given by Goenkaji for 10-day students at Dharmaṣriṅga, Kathmandu on 15 April 2000.

You have completed a 10-day Vipassana course. But this is not enough. Now you have to learn how to apply it in your day-to-day life. When you go out, you will have to face the world. And whatever equanimity you have learned here, see that you apply it in your life in spite of all the difficult situations. You know, and I also know, that the world is such that it is so difficult to maintain equanimity in life. But this is what you have to learn.

For that, one important way is that you learn to apply equanimity in an atmosphere of a Dhamma centre where a course is going on. You can come for some time whenever you are free and give service, 10 days of Dhamma service. The atmosphere here is definitely better than the atmosphere outside. Outside, the entire atmosphere is full of negativities. Here, the students who come will also generate negativity time and again. But the atmosphere will not be so strong. You can face it. So first, you learn in a Dhamma centre how to remain equanimous dealing with people who are generating negativity. This is a training ground for you.

And moreover, you will not be serving the entire day. Whenever you are free, you have an opportunity to meditate. This is how you will strengthen yourself.

Besides this, there are many other benefits of giving Dhamma service. One important benefit is that you will develop your *pāramīs*. It is only your *pāramīs* that will take you to the final goal. And you get a good opportunity here while you are serving people to develop your *pāramī*.

One *pāramī* you will develop is *mettā*. Whenever you serve people, naturally you generate *mettā* for them, love and compassion for them. And that helps you to develop your own *pāramī* of *mettā*.

Another important *pāramī*, especially for a householder, is the *pāramī* of *dāna*. It is a very important *pāramī*. When you give *dāna* of money and of other things required by people in the world, this is good. But here the *dāna* is the *dāna* of Dhamma, the greatest *dāna* in the world.

Why is it the greatest? Because the law of nature is such that whatever the seeds you plant the fruit will be exactly according to that and multiplied. When you give food to somebody, then in return when the time ripens, you will get food in bigger quantities.

You are now joining a course to give Dhamma. Of course, the teacher gives Dhamma. And it takes time for someone to reach the stage of becoming a full-fledged teacher or even an assistant teacher. But still you can be a partner in this Dhamma service, in this *dhammadāna*.

Understand, a teacher cannot give

dhammadāna unless there are proper facilities. So those people who are helping to construct proper facilities are also partners in giving Dhamma. Similarly, Dhamma cannot be given if the management is not proper. So those who are managing a Dhamma course are also partners in *dhammadāna*. And so also, Dhamma cannot be given unless there are good Dhamma workers to help. So, you are also becoming a partner. And you get the benefit of this.

And I know, from my own experience, how much benefit one gets. From the time I finished my first course until I was appointed a full-fledged teacher after 14 years, I kept going to my teacher and to the centre to give Dhamma service. I benefited immensely.

Similarly, the students who give Dhamma service keep on reporting to me that, "By giving one 10-day Dhamma service, I received so much benefit."

When you plant the seed of Dhamma and giving the *dāna* of Dhamma is planting the seed of Dhamma you receive a large quantity of Dhamma in return for yourself. Your Dhamma becomes stronger and stronger. This is a very good benefit you are going to get by giving Dhamma service.

Another big benefit is that you get so much satisfaction. When you received Dhamma, so many Dhamma workers served you. Now you feel that you are paying your debt of gratitude by serving other people in the same way. "Others have served me. Now I better serve others." This is a great satisfaction.

Another great satisfaction is that at the end of serving a course, you will feel so much joy. And this is not ordinary joy. This is a very sublime joy, *muditā*, sympathetic joy. You notice when people join the course, their faces are full of melancholy, sadness, having this kind of misery or that kind of misery. But on the tenth day, when they leave the course, there is a glow on their faces, so much happiness and so much joy. And when you generate sympathetic joy, you also become so happy. This is a great advantage of Dhamma service.

Dhamma is not only for your own liberation. Of course, the teaching of the Buddha is that you liberate yourself, but at the same time, you help others to get liberated. And you are doing the same thing by giving Dhamma service. You are trying to liberate yourself from misery and you are helping others to get liberated from misery.

Therefore, I keep on advising my students that they must find time to give Dhamma service for at least one 10-day course. As you find time to take your own 10-day course, similarly it is very important to give service for one 10-day course.

At times, you cannot find 10 days. All right, then serve as many days as possible. Maybe during the weekend you can come for two days. You may discuss this with the management, and if they agree, you can come for two or three days or even one day and give service. Service is always good for you.

May you all develop in Dhamma, get established in Dhamma, for your good, and for the good of so many others. May you all keep on growing in Dhamma, may you all keep on glowing in Dhamma.

(Dhamma Giri edition—April 2001)

The Value of Dhamma Service

The following is an excerpt from a talk given by S.N. Goenka at the Vipassana Meditation Centre, Blackheath, New South Wales, Australia.

Words of Dhamma

Sabbe saṅkhārā aniccā 'ti;
yadā paññāya passati,
atha nibbindati dukkhe —
esa maggo visuddhiyā.

'Impermanent are all compounded things.'
When one perceives this with true insight,
then one becomes detached from suffering;
this is the path of purification.

—Dhammapada, 277

What is the purpose of Dhamma service? Certainly not to receive board and lodging, nor to pass the time in a comfortable environment, nor to escape from the responsibilities of daily life. Dhamma workers know this well.

These people have practiced Vipassana and realized by direct experience the benefits it offers. They have seen the selfless service of the teachers, management and Dhamma workers—service that enabled them to taste the incomparable flavor of Dhamma. They have begun to take steps on the Noble Path, and naturally have started to develop the rare quality of gratitude, the wish to repay their debt for all that they have received.

Of course the teacher, management and Dhamma workers gave their service without expecting anything in return, nor will they accept any material remuneration. The only way to pay back the debt to them is by helping to keep the Wheel of Dhamma rotating, to give to others the same selfless service. This is the noble volition with which to give Dhamma service.

And as Vipassana meditators progress on the path, they emerge from the old habit pattern of self-centeredness and start to concern themselves with others. They notice how everywhere people are suffering: young or old, men or women, black or white, haves or have-nots; all are suffering. The meditators realize that they themselves were miserable until they encountered the Dhamma. They know that, like them, others have started to enjoy real happiness and peace by following the Path. Seeing this change stimulates a feeling of sympathetic joy, and strengthens the wish to help suffering people come out of their misery with Vipassana. Compassion overflows, and with it the volition to help others find relief from their suffering.

Of course it takes time to develop the maturity and receive the training necessary to teach Dhamma. But there are many other ways to serve people who have come to join a course, and all of them are invaluable. Truly it is a noble aspiration to be a Dhamma worker—a simple, humble Dhamma worker.

And those who practice Vipassana start realizing the law of nature: actions of body or speech that harm others will also harm those who commit them; while actions that help others, bring peace and happiness to those who perform them. Thus helping others is also helping oneself. It is therefore in one's own interest to serve. Doing so develops one's *pāramī* (wholesome qualities) and makes it possible to advance more quickly and surely on the Path. Serving others is, in fact, also serving oneself. Understanding this truth stimulates the wish to join in the noble mission of helping others to come out of their misery.

But what is the proper way to serve? Without knowing this, workers cannot help others or themselves; instead, they might even do harm. However noble the Dhamma mission may be, there can be no true benefit in serving if the volition of the worker is not sound. The service will not be beneficial if it is given to inflate the worker's ego, or to obtain something in return—even if only words of praise or appreciation.

Understand that you are learning how to apply Dhamma in day-to-day life. After all, Dhamma is not an escape from daily responsibilities. By learning to act according to the Dhamma in dealing with the students and situations here in the little world of a meditation course or center, you train yourself to act in the same way in the world outside. Despite the unwanted behavior of another person, you practice trying to keep the balance of your mind, and to generate love and compassion in response. This is the lesson you are trying to master here. You are a student as much as those who are sitting in the course. Keep on learning while serving others humbly. Keep thinking, "I am here in training, to practice serving without expecting anything in return. I am working so that others may benefit from the Dhamma. Let me help them by setting a good example, and in doing so help myself as well."

May all of you who give Dhamma service become strengthened in Dhamma. May you learn to develop your good will, love and compassion for others. May all of you progress in Dhamma, to enjoy real peace, real harmony, real happiness.

(International edition—September 1991)

Questions On Dhamma Service

Question*: What is the most important quality needed while serving the Dhamma?*

Goenkaji: If you don't have *mettā*, it is better that you don't give Dhamma service. Sometimes a Dhamma server shouts like a policeman or a policewoman at students who do not observe the rules, and this is totally wrong. Every Dhamma server is actually a representative of the Dhamma; students watch their behaviour and if they are just as arrogant as others, the students will lose confidence in the Dhamma.

Therefore Dhamma service is a great responsibility. If someone cannot work with *mettā* in a humble way, it is better to refrain from taking this responsibility.

Question: *Why is abstaining from sexual misconduct and intoxicants so important for a Dhamma server?*

Goenkaji: They are important in order to progress in Dhamma. All the *sīlas* are important for a Dhamma server, but these two are the most important. If you keep taking any intoxicant you will remain a slave to intoxication, and you cannot progress in Dhamma; the mind cannot be balanced when it is enslaved. You must become your own master, and intoxication cannot make you your own master.

Similarly for sexual misconduct: by practising Dhamma, both husband and wife will ultimately reach the stage where they naturally live a life of celibacy. But if there is a relationship with more than one person, sexual desire will continue to increase. It is like adding petrol to a fire that you want to put out.

So the first discipline is that a sexual relationship should only exist between spouses. If both are good Vipassana meditators, when passion arises they observe the sensations arising and accept the fact, "There is passion in my mind." As they observe the sensations they will probably come out of passion. But if they don't and have bodily relations, there is nothing wrong because they have not broken their *sīla*. I have seen many cases where, if they keep working like this, people easily come out of passion and still feel so contented, so happy. The need does not arise. A sexual relationship is actually designed by nature for reproduction, but it is human beings' weakness to go against nature and use it only for passion.

Slowly, if you keep working with Vipassana, you will come out of passion and reach a stage where there is a natural celibacy—a celibacy achieved through suppression doesn't help—and this natural celibacy will help you to develop so much in Dhamma. You progress by leaps and bounds once you reach that stage.

Question: *What are the benefits of bowing down to pay respect?*

Goenkaji: In the eyes of most people when you bow down to somebody you pay respect to that person, and that is all there is to it. For a Vipassana meditator it is really worthwhile keeping the attention at the top of the head and bowing down to somebody who is giving *mettā*.

I remember my Teacher instructed us how to bow down: The first time should be with awareness of sensations at the top of the head and the understanding of *anicca* (impermanence), the second time should be with the understanding of *dukkha* (suffering), and the third time should be with the understanding of *anattā* (lack of self). At times when we bowed down, he would ask, "Did you bow down properly?"

When you are observing *anicca* in this area you understand, "Look, everything is changing." When you observe *dukkha* you understand, "Whatever is changing is a source of *dukkha*; it can't be a source of happiness." With *anattā* you understand, "There is no 'I' in this, no 'mine', it is just a mind-matter phenomenon." So the way to bow down is with understanding and awareness of sensations at the top of the head.

Question: ***I know that an experienced Dhamma server should treat new students and visitors with more mettā than old students. How can one do this?***

Goenkaji: By practising Dhamma more and more. When your mind becomes purer, naturally you will have more *mettā*. In an earlier question you asked why it is important to practise daily. Understand, if you don't practise daily you will not have any *mettā*, and if you have no *mettā* you cannot serve. So practise daily, make yourself strong in Dhamma, and naturally your *mettā* will become strong and have a great impact on the students who visit.

As I said, those who come to a course always look at the Dhamma servers, the teacher and all those who manage the centre. If they find these people are not practising what is being taught here, they will think that this is a sham. They will say to themselves, "Look, the technique has not helped those who practise here, why should I waste my time?"

Be very careful: Make yourself strong in Dhamma so that you can give more *mettā*. Keep the atmosphere full of *mettā*, full of *mettā*. If you do that you will be successful and the centre will be successful; more and more people will be benefited.

Question: ***If our senior in Dhamma takes an independent decision which goes against the guidelines you have formulated, what should we as Dhamma servers do?***

Goenkaji: Very humbly and politely place your view before this person, saying, "Well, according to my understanding of the guidelines, this is an incorrect decision. I believe the guidelines suggest another course of action." Then your senior can explain the reasons for his or her decision. If you still find there is a difference of opinion you can say, "Since we do not agree on this matter I will write to a senior teacher or to Goenkaji. Let us explain the situation to a senior and let him or her decide." But never write to a senior without first discussing your difference of opinion with this person, otherwise it would be backbiting, a breakage of *sīla*. Be careful not to break your vocal *sīla*.

Often people write letters to me saying, "So-and-so is behaving like this. So-and-so is doing this." Then I ask whether they have discussed the matter with the person they are complaining about and they reply that they have not. In such a situation why write to me?

It is very important that you talk over the problem with the person concerned first. Most of your difficulties will be settled when you discuss the matter directly—not with a negative attitude but a positive attitude, making an effort to understand the other person's view. Maybe your view is wrong or maybe the elder's view is wrong, and when you discuss with them things will become clearer. If you find that the situation is not becoming clearer, then there is nothing wrong in informing other elders.

Question: ***How does one find the balance between selfless service and taking care of oneself?***

Goenkaji: If one cannot take care of oneself, what service will one give? First take care of yourself, and then start giving selfless service.

In daily life, there are many ups and downs. To maintain equanimity and to generate love and compassion despite these vicissitudes is the training of Vipassana. When Vipassana meditators give Dhamma service, they learn in a healthy atmosphere how to apply Dhamma in life.

While giving service you come across different types of meditators. Some may be lazy, or talkative, or rude. Sometimes an immature Dhamma server reacts in kind and replies rudely or behaves like a gaoler. But you are trained that, in spite of any mistakes made by the students, you must not become angry. Instead you must maintain a balanced mind filled with love and compassion. You may make mistakes and learn to correct yourself, and in this way, you learn how to face unwanted situations equanimously. In the atmosphere of a Dhamma centre or course, it is easier to learn how to face various situations, and then you can start to apply this wisdom in your daily life. This is the training ground for each server to learn how to live a good life.

The Buddha said that a good Dhamma person has two qualities: the quality of selflessly serving others and the quality of gratitude for help received. These two qualities are rare.

A Dhamma server has the opportunity to develop both qualities. You practise serving others without expecting anything in return, and you start to develop a feeling of gratitude towards the Buddha, who discovered this wonderful technique and gave it to the world, and towards the chain of teachers, right from the Buddha up to today, who maintained this technique in its pristine purity. One feels like repaying the debt of gratitude by serving others in order to fulfil the mission of the Teacher.

One feels so happy and contented serving others and helping them to come out of their misery. Therefore Dhamma service works both ways: It helps others, and it helps the Dhamma server too.

May you all gain strength in Dhamma for your own benefit, and may you continue to serve others for the good and benefit of so many.

(Dhamma Giri edition—March 2008)

Torchbearers of Dhamma

This talk, given by S.N. Goenka to old students at V.M.C., Dhamma Dharā, Massachusetts, in September 2000, has been edited and adapted for the Newsletter.

Words of Dhamma

Sabba pāpassa akaraṇaṃ; *kusalassa upasampadā;* *sacitta pariyodapanaṃ.* *Etaṃ buddhāna sāsanaṃ.*	Abstain from evil actions; perform pious actions; purify your mind. This is the teaching of all the Buddhas.

—Dhammapada, 183

Tumhehi kiccaṃ ātappaṃ, *akkhātāro tathāgatā;* *paṭipannā pamokkhanti,* *jhāyino mārabandhanā.*	You yourself must make the effort; the Enlightened Ones only show the way. Those who practice meditation will free themselves from the chains of death.

—Dhammapada, 276

My dear Dhamma sons and daughters:

Many of you have been serving me in Dhamma for two to three decades. I received an invaluable jewel from my Dhamma father, and now you have it as well. See that you preserve it. See that Dhamma is maintained in its pristine purity.

An old student, whether of a few courses or many years' practice, is a torchbearer of Dhamma. You are an example. People watch how you deal with situations, how you behave; they look to see whether significant change has come in your life. They will hear many good things about Vipassana but will become convinced of its value only when they see good results.

All old students have a dual responsibility. One responsibility is to establish yourself in Dhamma very strongly. This is in your own interest and also in the interest of so many others who need Dhamma. The other responsibility is to see that Dhamma spreads around the world, especially to your near and dear ones, your friends, your relatives, those who know you.

Never try to push Dhamma on them. If someone wants to know about Dhamma, very politely and humbly explain what Dhamma is and how it has helped you, and how it helps so many others around the world. And explain how the Buddha taught a good way of life that is happy, healthy, harmonious and wholesome.

He was not a founder of any religion.

A great misconception about the Buddha, which we must try to remove, is that he taught a religion. When one talks of religion today, one thinks of rites, rituals, ceremonies, dogmas, beliefs. These things have nothing to do with the teaching of the Buddha. He taught Dhamma; and when he sent out the 60 *arahant* messengers of Dhamma, giving them the highest teaching, he exhorted them, *Caratha bhikkhave cārikam*—"Oh bhikkhus, go forth. Go to serve suffering humanity. More and more people should know about Dhamma."

As the Buddha said, Dhamma is beneficial in the beginning, the middle and the end. It is beneficial to practice the beginning of Dhamma, *sīla* (morality), which helps in this and future lives. Proceeding further, one practices *sammā samādhi*, or concentration of mind with an object that is not imaginary—with the reality, the truth that one experiences. This too gives great benefit. The mind comes under control and is directed toward exploring the truth within, free from all imagination, blind beliefs, dogmas or cults. This is the truth pertaining to oneself, the truth pertaining to mind and matter and the interaction of the two. One understands the universal law of nature at the experiential level.

The highest step, *paññā*, is purification of mind, and not just at the surface level. The Buddha said, *Sa citta pariyodapanaṃ*—"You have to purify the totality of the mind." Unless the roots of impurity are eradicated, unless the mind is pure to the depth, in totality, one is not liberated from misery, one is not freed from the cycle of endless birth and death. It is *pannã* that leads to full liberation. *Sīla, samādhi, pannã*—that's all; there is nothing to be added or subtracted. The Dhamma is complete, *paripuṇṇaṃ,* and it is ultra-pure, *parisuddhaṃ.*

Never condemn a person who is practicing something else. That would be harmful. Never find fault with others. If a friend asks, you may explain, "This is enough—*sīla, samādhi, paññā.*" Of course one also naturally develops love, compassion and goodwill, but nothing else is to be added. If we start finding fault with others, it will be an unwholesome action on our part. Every religion, every tradition has something or other in it that is good. Every religion of the world accepts a moral life, a disciplined mind, a pure mind full of love and compassion. Give importance to these good qualities in other religions and ignore the differences. People would come to the Buddha to argue with him, but he would never argue. "When you start arguing and debating," he said, "it is harmful, it is dangerous. Let us see not where we differ but rather where we agree, and let us give importance to those points. Let us leave aside our differences; there is no use in discussing them."

Everyone agrees on the value of living a life of *sīla*, cultivating *samādhi* and purifying the mind by *paññā*; on these points there can be no disagreement. Buddha put his emphasis on these three only. The same thing applies to any old student: whenever you are discussing with others, don't indulge in any arguments. Don't try to find fault with others. Rather, encourage them: "You agree to *sīla*; we also practice *sīla*. You agree to concentration of mind; we also practice concentration of mind. You agree to purification of mind; we also practice purification of mind. If you want to know how we practice, come give this technique a try." Don't say, "Yours is bad and ours is good." Instead simply say, "Come and see—*Ehi passiko*. If you find it really is good for you, for others, for everyone, then accept it and live this life."

Buddha's teaching takes you to the depths where you start realizing why you must live a life of *sīla*. Every tradition urges us to practice *sīla*; but then says that it is for the good of the society, for the good of others. But the Buddha said, "It is for *your* good, and *also* for the good of others. This is what a good Vipassana meditator starts realizing. Experiencing your sensations, you start understanding, "Whenever I break *sīla*, I have to generate some impurity or the other and I start suffering. If I don't generate impurity, I don't perform any unwholesome action. If my *sīla* is perfect, I save myself from all kinds of misery, and I help others because they don't suffer on account of me." This one can understand only by experience. It is not a subject of argument. When you start experiencing the truth of sensations and how you continue to suffer at the deeper levels of the mind, then you realize why you should live a life of *sīla*.

And why did Buddha teach us to develop *samādhi* by observing respiration? Partly because it is nonsectarian, anybody can practice it. But another reason is that this practice leads us to *paññā* at a deeper level. Observing breath not only concentrates the mind; it enables us to investigate the truth about the interaction of mind and matter according to our own experience, not merely to develop *paññā* intellectually. Many traditions agree that the entire universe is *anicca* (changing), that the cycle of birth and death is *dukkha* (suffering), and that the ego is a big obstacle that must be left behind. It is not something difficult for people to understand. But the Buddha taught the same thing experientially.

If you invite people to come and learn to meditate, they need not abandon their own beliefs. Rather, by practicing, they start going deeper, understanding the pure Dhamma of *sīla, samādhi* and *paññā* at a more profound level, and they derive so much benefit. The real substance of Dhamma lies in *sīla, samādhi, paññā*. Let more and more people come and meditate and understand how it really works.

The volition should be to help people, not to try to prove that what we do is superior. It won't help to say, "You don't know the proper meaning of *sīla*, you don't know what is real *samādhi*, you don't know what is real *paññā*." Give a good example to people. Whenever you talk with somebody who is not on the path, speak with compassion, not ego. Never think you are superior and others are ignorant. Our job is to help people as we were helped by this technique—to share our happiness with others.

The best way of encouraging people to come to this path is to give them a good example. Let them see that here is somebody on the path of Vipassana, living so peacefully, with love, compassion and goodwill for others. Your example will be beneficial to you because you are progressing on the path by living such a life; at the same time, so many others will be attracted to the Dhamma. Have compassion, and remember your dual responsibility: "I must progress on the path and also encourage others to come to the path and progress on it."

You progress only when you maintain your practice morning and evening. If you take courses, whether of 10, 20 or even 30 days, and you miss your daily meditation, you will not really benefit. A course ought to strengthen your practice, your understanding of Dhamma at the experiential and intellectual level. But only applied Dhamma will give real benefits.

If you do not practice morning and evening every day, you will notice that real progress is missing. Morning and evening sittings are very important.

Also, throughout the day, from time to time examine how you deal with situations you encounter. Are you able to handle them better than before? The more you find you are progressing on the path, the more you will be encouraged to practice. If you find that there is no improvement, either you have stopped practicing or you are not practicing properly.

I repeatedly warn students that Vipassana is not intended for the enjoyment of pleasant sensations, but despite my advice some of them make that their aim. They think, "I must get a free-flow of very pleasant vibrations. If I'm not getting it, I'm not progressing." They are completely wrong. The equanimity you have developed is the measure of your progress. The Buddha explained: To dig out the stock of your *saṅkhārās* of craving, make use of the pleasant sensations; to dig out the *saṅkhārās* of aversion, make use of your unpleasant sensations. Both types of sensation are equally important as tools to help us eradicate the deep-rooted *saṅkhārās* that we have accumulated. If you ignore this advice and instead feel depressed with gross sensations and elated with pleasant ones, you are simply repeating what you have been doing your whole life and for so many lives. In the name of Vipassana, you have started playing the same game. How can you progress?

Keep in mind that equanimity is most important for you. The type of sensation you feel does not matter. Whenever a deep-rooted *saṅkhāra* comes to the surface, it will produce a particular type of sensation, but don't assume that every sensation you feel is because of a *saṅkhāra*. When you are meditating, it is true that most of the sensations are because of *saṅkhārās*, but there are many other causes for sensations to arise. Whatever the cause, if a sensation occurs and you don't generate a new *saṅkhāra*, the purpose is served: naturally the old accumulated stock will start to come up to the surface of the mind and be eradicated.

Understand this and work intelligently, diligently. Keep progressing in Dhamma. See that the Dhamma continues from generation to generation. Dhamma should continue to serve people for centuries, and that is possible only if you, the torchbearers, are strong in Dhamma, established in Dhamma, good examples of Dhamma.

Maintain Vipassana's pristine purity. It doesn't matter if somebody else has started defiling it, polluting it. But those who are on the path and those who have understood the importance of this purity, should maintain this pristine purity for their own good and also for the good of future generations. If you start polluting the technique, then there is no chance of it being maintained for a very long time. Others may do whatever they wish, but at least one stream, one flow of pure Dhamma, will continue. People will understand the difference between the two and this will help for generation after generation.

A big responsibility rests on you. Keep the purity of Dhamma. Keep the torch of Dhamma shining. Remain strong in Dhamma yourself. Be a good example to others. May all of you live a very happy, pure, Dhamma life. May all of you encourage so many others to come on the path and live a pure Dhamma life.

May all be happy, be peaceful, be liberated.

(International edition—September 2001)

The Blade of Dhamma

S.N. Goenka

The following is the opening address given by Goenkaji at the Meeting on the Spread of Dhamma, held at Dhamma Giri from March 1–4, 1988.

Words of Dhamma

Anupubbena medhāvī	Gradually, little by little,
thokathokaṃ khaṇe khaṇe	moment by moment, a wise person
kammāro rajatass 'eva	should remove one's impurities
niddhame malam attano.	as a smith removes [the dross of] silver.

—Dhammapada, 239

Companions on the path of Dhamma. We have assembled here again this year to discuss how best the Dhamma can be disseminated, so that more and more suffering people can benefit from it.

The work is growing speedily and satisfactorily. Many assistant teachers have been appointed; many Dhamma workers are giving their service for the spread of Dhamma; many meditation centers have been established. There will be still more in the future. As the work increases, it becomes essential now to organize it properly, so that divisive tendencies may not weaken the Dhamma in the future. But organization brings problems with it. In fact we stand now at a crossroads. One wrong step and the movement will proceed toward its downfall, harming humankind. One right step and the movement will develop for the good and benefit of many. Organization is needed for the Dhamma to spread widely, but the danger is that this will turn Dhamma into an organized religion, a sect. If so, the essence of Dhamma will disappear, and instead of helping, it will start causing harm.

The situation, therefore, is very delicate. On the one hand, order and organization are necessary for the proper spread of Dhamma. But creating a hierarchy, from Teacher to assistant and on down, all working in a regimented way with rigid rules—this is how sects are established. Once there is a hierarchy, ego rears its head: "I am placed in this position. All who are junior must obey and pay respects to me. My word is final. I am so important! Certainly Dhamma must spread to help suffering people. But where do I stand in the organization? What is my position, my status? Is my service appreciated? Look, I have left the comforts of home. I have left my work, my family, and have given my whole life. I don't want money; I don't want people to bow before me, but there must be some appreciation of all I've done!"

From this madness starts the cult of personality; from here sectarianism starts. We must remember that Dhamma is important, nothing else. The attitude of each of us should be: "Whatever part I play in the spread of Dhamma, I do so because I am asked to, and perhaps because of some special skill I have. Tomorrow if I am asked to do something else instead, I'll be happy with that. What does this 'I' matter? Dhamma is important. Service is important. Giving benefit to others—that is important. The happiness of more and more people—that is important. Nothing else. Nothing else." This is the proper volition with which to serve.

Only you can know whether truly you have this volition, and so you must examine repeatedly whether you are really working without ego, without expecting anything in return.You must judge for yourself. One way to do so is by checking to what extent you have developed sympathetic joy and compassion, *muditā* and *karuṇā*. The stronger these two pure mental qualities develop in you, the weaker your egotism has become. Keep applying this yardstick to yourself.

Suppose a comrade is given a particular position in the organization. Suppose a fellow worker receives praise for his service. What happens in my mind then? Do I rejoice in their success? Do I feel happy that my comrades are doing wonderful work which people appreciate? Or have I started developing jealousy and envy, thinking, "How about me? If he surpasses me, what will happen?" Such a mad attitude shows that one has not understood Dhamma. If somebody is progressing on the path, there will be joy to see another person also progress; there will be joy at seeing another person serve Dhamma well, helping others. If there is a trace of jealousy, then understand: "In spite of all my attempts to delude myself and others, I am far from the path of Dhamma. Look, there is no sympathetic joy in me at all." Or suppose somebody has made a mistake. Maybe it is a real error on that person's part, or maybe my colored glasses, my own prejudices make me see it as such. In either case, what happens in my mind? Do I generate hatred and aversion toward this person? If so, I am far away from Dhamma. I ought instead to feel compassion: "Look, my companion has slipped, has become weak. What should I do to support him, to give him strength so that he may come out of this weakness?" Here a big delusion can arise. One may say: "I have no hatred towards this person who blundered." But inside there will be a pleasant feeling; one rejoices to see a comrade falling down. One thinks, "Now people will know what a mad, ego-centered fellow this person is. Now all his reputation will go away. Now the Teacher will know that this fellow is useless, and he will be toppled!" Is this kind of feeling in your mind? Examine yourself; no one else can do it. If you find any such thought within you, understand that you are far away from the path. First establish yourself in Dhamma. Only then can you serve others. A blind person cannot show the way to another blind person. A lame person cannot support another who is lame. And to establish yourself in Dhamma, you must dissolve your ego. If at every opportunity you put yourself forward so others may know that "Here is an important person," then you are far away from Dhamma. Are you projecting your ego in the name of serving selflessly? If so, whether you are a teacher, organizer or Dhamma worker, your service will spoil the Dhamma. You will not really be serving anybody because you are not serving yourself. Serve yourself in Dhamma, and keep examining that your ego is dissolving little by little. Only then will you be fit to serve in the organization.

Five centuries ago in India there was a saint named Kabir whose words are very appropriate on this occasion. He said,

Kabirā khadhā bajāra meṇ,
liyā gaṇḍhāsā hātha,
"Sīsa utāre bhuin dhare
cale hamāre sātha!"

In the marketplace Kabir
offered an axe and cried,
"Chop off and cast away your head
if you'd walk by my side!"

Today the same clarion call is made again. The axe offered is the fine blade of Dhamma. Use it to cut off your head—your ego—and throw it in the dustbin. Then you are fit to accompany me.

I know many of you will accept this call. Many of you have accompanied me in the past for long years. Many of you, I know, will accompany me for all of this life, and perhaps in future lives as well. But do so having cut off your heads; dissolve your egos. Then the Dhamma will remain Dhamma; it will not become a sect. The Buddha started teaching the Dhamma in its pure form, and for generations it spread without losing that purity. Now the time has come for it to arise and spread again. See that it starts flowing in its original, pure form, so that for at least a few centuries it may continue. And in order that this may happen, those who really want to serve must serve themselves first. Those who want to spread the teaching of purification must first purify themselves. Come out of ego. Come out of ego. It has no place on the path of Dhamma.

In the next days you are going to have important discussions as you prepare codes of discipline for assistant teachers, for organizers, for the Dhamma workers, for centers. This is an historic gathering taking historic steps. One wrong step, and future generations will not receive the Dhamma in its purity. For this reason, in all that you do, that you decide, that you codify, Dhamma should remain most important, not any particular person. If now you start giving importance to an individual, you give an opportunity for ego to enter. This is running in the opposite direction from the Dhamma. Remember, one's position in the organization does not matter at all. Do not be concerned with projecting your own image; otherwise Dhamma will become lost in the background, and that means that everything good in the practice is also lost in the background. Instead, project the Dhamma. All importance should be given to Dhamma; the focus should be on Dhamma, the applied Dhamma. People may come and go, but the Dhamma must remain so that many can benefit from it.

Whatever decisions you make, therefore, whatever discipline you codify, see that those who make the code follow it. The one and only aim must be *bahujana hitāya, bahujana sukhāya*—that is, the good and happiness of many. The one and only volition must be *lokānukampāya*—compassion for all beings. More and more people must benefit from Dhamma, must come out of their misery, must start enjoying real peace, real harmony.

May your efforts meet with overflowing success. I see the future very bright ahead. May all of you shine with Dhamma in this brightness so that people become attracted toward you—that is, toward the Dhamma in you. Attract them as examples of the Dhamma, as representatives of the Dhamma, as servants of the Dhamma.

Work in Dhamma to help suffering people everywhere. May all of you be successful.

(International edition—December 1988)

The Global Vipassana Pagoda: Lighting a Beacon to the World

William Hart

Words of Dhamma

Tapo ca brahmacariyañca, ariyasaccāna dassanaṃ; nibbānasacchikiriyā ca, etaṃ maṅgalamuttamaṃ.

Ardent practice, a life of purity,
Witnessing the Noble Truths,
Experiencing *nibbāna* —This is the highest blessing.

—Khuddaka pāṭha, 5–11 Maṅgala Sutta

To mark the centenary of the birth of Sayagyi U Ba Khin, an extraordinary project is taking shape in Mumbai. There, in the suburbs of India's most modern city, a crossroads of East and West, the foundations have been laid for a unique monument: the Global Vipassana Pagoda.

For ages, graceful pagodas have dotted the landscape of Myanmar. Their soaring spires have represented humanity's aspirations to the highest spiritual goals. By their very form they have served as visible reminders of the path of liberation, the teaching of the Buddha. The most famous and revered of Myanmar's pagodas is the world-renowned Shwedagon in the capital city of Yangon. It dominates the city skyline, beckoning to people from afar; and it has been the model for countless other pagodas, including those built atop the meditation cell complexes at Vipassana meditation centers.

Each pagoda honors the past: the matchless Teacher who showed the world the way to enlightenment. At the same time a pagoda is a beacon guiding us toward the future of freedom from misery through the practice of Vipassana meditation.

The world needs such a beacon today.

Although tens of thousands of people have learned Vipassana in the last three decades, many more remain unaware of the message of the Buddha. And in India, that message is still misunderstood: there people are taught to honor the Buddha as a god but to reject his teaching as a heresy.

The Global Vipassana Pagoda is designed to break through this shell of ignorance. Towering over 100 meters into the sky, it will attract visitors from India and abroad; and in a gallery with compelling displays, it will present the truth about India's greatest son—and the world's greatest benefactor. Indians in large numbers will have the opportunity to learn about the life and universal teaching of the Buddha; they will rediscover the most precious part of their national heritage. As for the millions of people from other countries who pass through Mumbai each year, many will be drawn to the Global Pagoda; and when they return to their homelands they will carry an interest in Vipassana and perhaps the wish to join a course. The Pagoda thus will inform and inspire multitudes.

But a Vipassana Pagoda must do more than that; it must provide an opportunity to take steps on the path to Enlightenment. And so the structure will contain a hall in which up to 8,000 people can sit together and practice Vipassana meditation. This is in fact its main purpose. Old students will gather in the hall on Sundays and holidays for group sittings or one-day courses; and by their meditation together, they will create a powerful Dhamma atmosphere.

2500 years ago, Myanmar received the Teaching of the Buddha from India, and through the centuries it preserved Vipassana, the gem of Dhamma, in its pristine purity. But according to an ancient prophecy, after 2,500 years the Dhamma would return from Myanmar to India and would spread from there around the world.

Earlier, this century, Sayagyi saw that the time had come for the prophecy to be fulfilled, for Myanmar to repay its debt of gratitude to India. Although he himself could not go to India during his lifetime to teach Dhamma, he trained our Teacher, Goenkaji, to do this as his representative. Because of him, the land of India again has the jewel of Vipassana; and we, Goenkaji's students, have learned the technique of liberation.

As Goenkaji often says, "Without Myanmar there would have been no U Ba Khin, without U Ba Khin there would have been no Goenka, and there would have been no gift of Dhamma to students around the world." In the very first words of every course he declares his gratitude to his Teacher; and before teaching Ānāpanā and Vipassana, he chants:

Guruvara terī aurase,
devūṅ dharama ka dāna;
Guruvara tera pratinidhi,
devūṅ dharama ka dāna.

Revered Teacher, on your behalf,
May I give the gift of Dhamma;
Revered Teacher, as your representative,
May I give the gift of Dhamma.

Goenkaji attributes all the enormous successes of the last 35 years to U Ba Khin. Each student of Vipassana will naturally feel gratitude to Sayagyi U Ba Khin and Myanmar for the gift of Dhamma, and gratitude for the opportunity to develop our *pāramīs* by helping in U Ba Khin's great mission.

Now, we have an opportunity to show our gratitude to U Ba Khin. We do so first of all by practicing what he taught, establishing ourselves in Vipassana. And having done so, we can work to fulfill his mission by helping the teaching to spread still more widely, to millions of suffering people around the world.

In every part of the globe, dedicated meditators are patiently working to help others learn Vipassana. However humble the efforts of these Dhamma servers, the fruit yielded will be wonderful because of the purity of volition behind the efforts. And crowning all of these Dhamma efforts will be the Global Pagoda. It will be visible proof of the re-awakening of the Buddha's teachings in India, and the acceptance of the teachings around the world. The Global Pagoda will be an expression of gratitude to Myanmar, the country that preserved Vipassana, the practical essence of the Buddha's Teaching. It will embody as well our gratitude to U Ba Khin, who enabled each of us today to find the path to liberation.

All Vipassana meditators are welcome to contribute to the Global Pagoda Project, even in a small way; and by thus expressing their gratitude to Sayagyi U Ba Khin, to Myanmar and to the Teaching, they will share in the great merits of the project.

The Global Pagoda will be a beacon to the world, drawing large numbers of people everywhere to the incomparable teaching of Vipassana. This is the message carved in the stones of the Global Pagoda, a message that speaks to people of any nationality, of any religion or no religion. It is a message of hope, of liberation, of peace.

The Global Pagoda brings this message to the people of the world. For all of us, it is a summons in stone. Start climbing!

(Dhamma Giri edition—August 2005)

Realizing the Dream of Dhamma

S. N. Goenka

The following is a translation of Goenkaji's remarks to about 5,000 Vipassana meditators attending the first one-day course under the main dome of the Global Pagoda in Gorai, Mumbai, on March 19, 2006. It has been adapted for the Newsletter.

My mind is filled with joy at seeing this large gathering of the Vipassana family. In future, within this great dome, thousands of people will sit together and meditate. A small glimpse of that scene is before my eyes. The Buddha said, *Samaggānaṃ tapo sukho*—"To gather together and meditate brings joy." A very fruitful joy.

This is a land for meditation. Whenever I come here, my mind feels delight. At the time when a Dhamma son donated this priceless land, I did not fully understand. But afterwards, each time I came here, strong faith developed in my mind that this land is very pure, it is a land for meditation. Many saints have meditated in this vicinity. Therefore this land has drawn all of us to come here. Tremendous is the attraction of this land!

In the time of the Buddha, an ascetic named Dāruciriya was meditating in this area when he heard that someone in the world had become a *sammāsambuddha*. He resolved to meet the Enlightened One in order to learn the path of liberation. Dāruciriya walked from here to Sāvatthī, encountered the Buddha, reached liberation, and became an *arahant.*

Another incident that happened here comes before my eyes: A man from this region named Puṇṇa went to Sāvatthī for his business, and there he met the Buddha. He was fortunate, he learned Vipassana. He was even more fortunate; he progressed rapidly on the path of Vipassana. His business remained important to him. However, he could not help thinking, "This is such a wonderful teaching, but the region where I live knows nothing of it. Nobody even knows that there is such a technique that offers liberation from the cycle of life and death. If people there learn and practice it, they will get the same benefit."

With deep enthusiasm he went to the Enlightened One and said, "Sir, I request your permission to go back to my home and proclaim there the doctrine taught by the Buddha. Allow me to make Vipassana known to the people."

The Buddha smiled and asked, "Are you aware that in your region, people will strongly oppose you. They will heap abuse on you. What will you do then?"

"Lord, with folded hands I shall humbly say, 'You are so kind, so good! You have only heaped abuse on me, you have only used a few harsh words. Someone else might have pelted me with stones. You did not throw stones at me. You are so kind!'"

"And if they start throwing stones at you, what will you say then?"

"With folded hands I shall say, 'You are so kind! Someone else who had become angry might have beaten me with sticks. You only threw stones at me. You are truly kind.'"

"And if they started beating you with sticks, what will you say then?"

"With folded hands I shall say, 'You are so kind! You have only beaten me with sticks. Someone else would have attacked me with a sword. You did not attack me with a sword. You are indeed kind.'"

"And if some of them attack you with swords, what will you say then?"

"With folded hands I shall say, 'You are so kind, so good! So many people in this world are miserable. In their great misery, they commit suicide. You are saving me from that evil act. You are truly merciful!"

The Buddha said, "Good! You have ripened in Dhamma. Now, you are fit to preach the doctrine."

This is the region in which the ascetic Puṇṇa spread the Buddha's teachings. And the archeological remains in this region, the nearby caves and statues, show that people gladly accepted the Buddha's teachings.

In our own time, when the foundation stone of this pagoda was being laid, someone asked me, "Sir, why did you choose this place?"

I replied, "I did not choose the place. The place chose me."

The entire picture is revealing itself. The greatness of this land! The purity of this land! Somewhere nearby there used to be a large port known as Suppārakapattana. It was a huge centre of business activity in ancient India, as Mumbai is today. And near this place many ascetics used to perform penances. When Vipassana started spreading, people started practicing it in large numbers.

The same is happening today. Not only in India but around the world, people are accepting Vipassana, they are accepting the words of the Buddha. In doing so, they have not joined a sect. What matters is not to call oneself a Buddhist but to practice Vipassana, to practice the Noble Eightfold Path taught by the Enlightened One, to practice *sīla, samādhi, paññā*, and to really benefit from the teaching of the Buddha.

The teaching of the Enlightened One does not belong to any particular caste, creed, race or sect; it is universal. And everyone accepts it. Today, there is not a single religious group whose followers do not come to join Vipassana courses. And not only that, their leaders and their teachers come to learn Vipassana.

I am dreaming of a day when as many as 10,000 people will gather here in this dome to meditate. Some will call themselves Hindus, some Buddhists, some Jains, some Muslims, but all will practice Vipassana.
All will practise *sīla, samādhi, paññā*. This is the greatness of the Buddha's teaching. It is universal, for one and all.

This magnificent pagoda is a symbol of the deep gratitude we feel, a symbol stretching toward the sky. My mind feels infinite devotion, infinite gratitude toward those who preserved the words of the Buddha in their pure form, as well as the practice in its pristine purity.

This pagoda is not intended for prayers or rites and rituals; it is meant for meditation. This is a land for meditation. Even in the past, how many saints have meditated on this land! Again people will meditate, for centuries they will meditate. And all humanity will benefit.

Meditators of this generation carry a great responsibility. Practice Dhamma not just for your own benefit, your own liberation, but for the benefit of suffering people around the world—for their liberation. Ripen yourselves to help others ripen. When Dhamma arises, it brings great benefit to one and all.

The Enlightened One explained that when one helps others with proper volition, no other wish arises but the urge to help, to serve. One thinks, "How can others be helped? How can others get this teaching? How can others receive benefit? How can they become liberated from misery?"

Every meditator must realize, "The way to serve is without expecting anything in return. How can I help for the benefit of many? How can I serve? What can I do so that more and more people benefit?" That is the proper volition for serving.

And along with the wish to help others is a feeling of gratitude. Gratitude to Gotama the Buddha, who rediscovered the teaching and used it not simply for his own benefit but for the liberation of so many other people. Gratitude to Emperor Asoka, who preserved the teaching by sending it to neighboring lands, so that it stayed alive after it was lost in India.

Gratitude toward those neighboring countries, which carefully kept the teaching in its pristine purity.

Gratitude to the saints of those countries, the chain of teachers, who kept the living practice of the Buddha's teaching down to the present day.

Gratitude to Ledi Sayadaw, one of these saints from Myanmar, who had great foresight. He thought to himself,"The time has almost come, this teaching must go back to India. But how? Preparation is needed."

So he trained a lay person to teach Dhamma. Deep gratitude to Saya Thetgyi who became a model of the ideal Dhamma teacher and trained my Dhamma father, Sayagyi U Ba Khin.

Sayagyi too realized that the prophesied time was almost at hand. He said, "The clock of Vipassana has struck! Now it will spread around the world."

Because of them, the Dhamma has returned to India and has started spreading around the world for the benefit of many.

To those who came before, let us feel gratitude. And to those still waiting for the Dhamma, let us develop *mettā*, the wish to serve without expecting anything in return.

(International edition—May 2006)

Inauguration of the Global Vipassana Pagoda

Words of Dhamma

Āraddhaviriye pahitatte,	Resolute, intent,
Niccaṃ daḷha parakkame;	constantly striving ardently—
samagge sāvake passa,	behold these meditators assembled!
etaṃ Buddhānavandanaṃ.	They truly honor the Buddha.

—Mahāpajāpatigotamītherīapadānaṃ—2/7–171

Note: This is one of the verses engraved in stone on the exterior of the Global Vipassana Pagoda.

A long-cherished dream of Goenkaji was fulfilled on February 8, 2009, with the inauguration of the Global Vipassana Pagoda on the outskirts of Mumbai. Attending the event were thousands of meditators, dignitaries and guests from around the world, including the President of India, Mrs. Pratibha Patil.

President Patil hailed the Global Vipassana Pagoda as a monument of peace and harmony that would help to dispel hatred and violence. She noted that she herself had taken a 10-day Vipassana course, and described Vipassana as a way to gain control over the mind, develop purity of heart and live a more balanced life.

In his speech, Goenkaji stressed that the Buddha was not the founder of a religion but instead the teacher of a simple, scientific way to develop peace and harmony for oneself and others—a way that can be applied by people of any religion or background. Goenkaji also emphasized that the Global Vipassana Pagoda was not a site for religious ceremonies but instead a place for the practice of Vipassana meditation.

A day earlier, on February 7, Goenkaji, Mataji and thousands of Vipassana meditators and guests watched the traditional raising of the *Dhammadhaja* (flag of Dhamma) and crystal to their position at the very top of the Pagoda, completing the structure. This was followed by *Saṅgha-dāna* (offering of a meal and gifts) for bhikkhus from Myanmar, Thailand, Śri Laṅka and India.

Towering 325 feet, the Global Vipassana Pagoda is a symbol of gratitude to the Buddha and the chain of teachers who preserved the Dhamma for 2,600 years. Modelled on the Shwedagon Pagoda in Yangon, it also gives visible expression to India's debt to Myanmar, from where the teaching of Vipassana returned to the land of its origin in modern times.

Unlike the Shwedagon, the Global Vipassana Pagoda is a hollow structure containing a domed hall. At the apex of the dome, a golden Dhamma wheel marks the point where relics of the Buddha have been enshrined, donated by the government of Śri Laṅka and the Mahabodhi Society of India.

The hall has a capacity of about 10,000 and has already been used for one-day Vipassana

The completed structure of the Global Vipassana Pagoda. The brass umbrella at the top stands approximately 20 feet high

The President of India, Mrs. Pratibha Patil, greets Goenkaji at the inauguration ceremony

A close-up of the very top of the Global Vipassana Pagoda. The natural rock crystal is over two feet long and has been carved in the shape of a lotus bud

courses.

The Global Vipassana Pagoda is Asia's tallest stone monument and took 11 years to build. For the structure, a system was devised of interlocking stones grooved to stay in place. Each stone had to be cut individually and adjusted by hand to match the intricate design. Some stones weigh as much as 700 kilograms. The use of stone and lime mortar provides far greater strength and longevity than concrete and steel; the Global Vipassana Pagoda is expected to stand for hundreds of years. This is the largest dome in the world without interior support. It is 280 feet in diameter and 90 feet high.

Two 60-foot pagodas flank the main structure. One of these will contain meditation cells. The Pagoda complex will also house libraries and information galleries presenting the life and teaching of the Buddha.

Next to the Global Vipassana Pagoda stands a Vipassana meditation centre, *Dhamma Pattana*, where 10-day and old-student courses have been held regularly since October 2007.

The Pagoda was opened to the public after the official inauguration. It is expected to attract thousands of pilgrims and seekers of peace, and to help large numbers of people from India and around the world become aware of the teaching of the Buddha.

For more information, visit the Global Vipassana Pagoda website: *www.globalpagoda.org*
(International edition—April 2009)

Vipassana: The Practical Path to Unity in Diversity

S. N. Goenka

The sacred Buddha relics were enshrined within the main dome of the Global Pagoda on 29 October 2006 in the presence of venerable bhikkhus from many countries, Goenkaji and Mataji, honourable dignitaries, and thousands of Vipassana meditators. The following is an article by Goenkaji on this historic occasion. It has been adapted for the Newsletter.

The Path to Peace and Happiness

In multi-religious and multi-cultural societies such as in India, Vipassana is a wonderful, practical path to unity in diversity. Vipassana, an ancient, timeless heritage of India, is the quintessence of all religions: how to live a moral life, to be a master of one's own mind, to purify the mind. No religion objects to these ideals. No right-thinking person objects to these ideals. Vipassana is the effective, universal method to achieve these ideals.

In past millennia, and in the present day, we are seeing how Vipassana enables one to live a happy, harmonious life. When more individuals achieve inner peace, peace is achieved in homes, in the neighbourhood, in villages, towns, cities and countries.

Universal Non-sectarian Path

This unifying process of peace and harmony is visible in Vipassana courses worldwide. During a Vipassana course, people from all religions, castes, nationalities, races and social strata sit together to practice this ancient path. Thousands of Hindus, Muslims, Christians, Sikhs, Jains, Buddhists and Jews have taken Vipassana courses. They follow the same code of discipline and gain benefit from the Vipassana course.

Vipassana courses have been taken not only by the followers of all religions but also by their leaders. Many religious leaders have later told me, "Goenkaji, in the name of Vipassana, you are teaching our religion!" Vipassana courses have been held in temples, mosques, churches, and monasteries.

True Dhamma

In the ancient Pāli language, Vipassana means to see things as they are, not as they seem to be. Gotama the Buddha re-discovered this ancient scientific path to real happiness. This is the true *Saddhamma*, the truth of the laws of nature applicable to all beings in the universe.

The Buddha did not claim any monopoly on this path; neither did he intend to start any sect, cult or ritualistic religion. He told people who came to debate and sometimes to quarrel with him: "Let us keep aside our differences. Let us talk about what we agree upon. I am teaching *sīla* (morality) *samādhi* (mastery of the mind) and *paññā* (purification of the mind)."

The Science of Mind and Matter

The Buddha was a super-scientist who rediscovered certain universal truths using his own body and mind as the laboratory instruments. He discovered that, at the actual level, there is no solidity in the entire universe, that all material phenomena are made up of tiny *kalāpas* (sub-atomic particles) that arise and pass away with such great rapidity that they give the appearance of solidity. These *kalāpas*, the basic building blocks of the material universe are nothing but mere vibrations. The Buddha said:

Sabbo ādīpito loko,
sabbo loko padīpito;
sabbo pajjalito loko,
sabbo loko pakampito.

The entire world is in flames,
The entire world is going up in smoke;
The entire world is burning,
The entire world is vibrating.

—Therīgāthā 200

The Role of Bodily Sensations

The Buddha discovered that the key to liberation lies in experiencing the different physical sensations in the body and their nature of arising and passing away (*anicca*). He also realized that misery arises because of the blind reaction of craving and aversion to these sensations.

One comes out of the habit pattern of misery when one learns to remain equanimous with every sensation, pleasant or unpleasant, with the experiential realization that they are all impermanent, changing every moment. This ability to remain equanimous eradicates old impurities and helps one to change the behaviour pattern of the mind.

The Importance of Morality (*Sīla*)

At the start of the Vipassana course, the student undertakes to observe a moral code of conduct. The student experiences how morality is the essential foundation to inner peace and happiness, not merely an empty, unrealistic ideal. One cannot do any harm to others without first harming oneself:

Pubbe hanati attānaṃ;
pacchā hanati so pare.

Ānāpāna

The student in a Vipassana course starts meditation practice with Ānāpāna – observation of the natural incoming and outgoing breath, as it is, without regulating the natural reality of the breath. The student is instructed not to add any shape, colour, form, philosophy or image to the breath. As the natural breath is linked directly to the mind, one observes the mind by observing the breath. For instance, when one is angry, the breath becomes hard and irregular; when one is calm and peaceful, the breath becomes soft and subtle.

The truth of the natural breath can be experienced by anyone; this is not the monopoly of any religion or country. Then the student observes the touch of the breath at the point below the nostrils, above the upper lip where the breath touches.

When the student starts observing the point of contact of the breath with the body, he or she begins to experience the truth of sensations on the body: any physical feeling like heat, cold, vibration, tingling, itching, pain, etc.

Vipassana

During the practice of Vipassana, the student is instructed to observe the truth of sensations throughout the body. It is a choiceless observation. The student is instructed not to give any importance to any particular sensation or to have any bias or preference for any sensation.

The student proceeds from the gross truths to the subtler truths to ultimately reach the subtlest truth. He observes the mind-matter phenomenon, the truth of the so-called 'I', the truth about the causes and effect of suffering and the way out of suffering. He makes this observation within the framework of the body, without any illusion, delusion, imagination or visualization.

The Vipassana student observes the truth of the moment, as it is. So he experiences the truth of the changing reality, from moment to moment, within the framework of the body. Nature is playing its role, one just observes. One realizes how difficult this is! One also realizes how necessary and beneficial this is!

From Reaction to Equanimity

Soon, the Vipassana practitioner experiences how the mind is blindly reacting to these bodily sensations with craving or aversion, with attachment or hatred. He experiences how this habit pattern to the pleasant or unpleasant reality of sensations—which is not in his control—causes a vicious cycle of suffering and misery. Apparently, one seems to be reacting to objects, situations and people in the outside world. In reality, one is constantly reacting to the sensations caused by the outside objects coming in contact with the sense doors of eyes, ears, nose, body, tongue and mind. This deep-rooted habit pattern of blind reaction is the cause of suffering of oneself and others.

By training the mind to objectively observe the sensations, instead of blindly reacting to them, the Vipassana student progresses on the path leading to real happiness. Every time a negative thought or emotion arises, instead of suppressing or blindly expressing these negativities, the student enjoys the benefits of the middle path of mere observation. One realizes that nothing can arise in the mind without a sensation arising on the body. One experiences how the negative habit pattern starts weakening at the root level by dispassionate observation of the sensations. When no new fuel is added to the fire, the fire gradually dies out. One starts experiencing real happiness in life, the happiness of a pure, peaceful mind.

Mettābhāvanā (Loving Kindness)

Towards the end of the Vipassana course, the student learns how to share this peace and harmony with all others. When one truly benefits, then one cannot resist sharing the benefits with others. The practice of mettābhāvanā, an essential part of Vipassana, enables one to share one's peace, happiness and harmony with all beings. One wishes for the well being of others from the depth of a purified mind. By the practice of *mettā*, one becomes peaceful and happy and the entire atmosphere around is suffused with peace and harmony.

The Universal Law of Nature

This practical path to real happiness can be called by any name. For conventional, linguistic purposes, it is called Vipassana. Just as the law of gravity works in the same way irrespective of whatever name we give it, the practice of coming out of suffering by objective observation of sensations is beneficial to all, irrespective of whatever it is called.

People from all religions and backgrounds understand this universal truth: one has to have a balanced, pure mind to be happy amidst the vicissitudes of life. They also understand that the saints of the past must have been practising this technique of developing equanimity to sensations. How else could they generate infinite compassion for the very people who were torturing them to death, as many noble saints of the past from all religions did?

Core of Purity

Every religion has a wholesome essence of love, compassion and goodwill. The outer shells of each religion are different: the various rites, rituals, ceremonies or beliefs. However, all religions give importance to purity of mind. Vipassana helps us to experience this wonderful, happy unity in diversity.

Emperor Asoka: Respect for All Religions

One of the truest followers of the Buddha's teaching was Emperor Asoka. In one of his rock edicts, he gave us this benevolent message:

"One should not honour only one's own religion and condemn other religions. Instead one should honour other religions for various reasons. By so doing, one helps one's own religion to grow and also renders service to the religions of others. In acting otherwise, one digs the grave of one's own religion, and harms other religions as well. Someone who honours his own religion and condemns other religions, may do so out of devotion to his religion thinking 'I will glorify my religion,' but his actions injure his own religion more gravely."

Let all listen: Concord is good, not quarrelling. Let all be willing to listen to the doctrine professed by others.

When this important quality of respecting other religions arises, there will be no sectarian conflicts. One who respects the noble qualities of other religions, instead of finding fault, becomes a true and inspiring representative of his religion.

By practising tolerance for all religions, Emperor Asoka did not become a weak ruler. There is no record of any communal conflict or foreign invasion during his reign after he renounced violence. On the contrary, his reign was the golden age of Indian history.

Sayagyi U Ba Khin: A Life of Integrity

My Vipassana teacher and Dhamma father, Sayagyi U Ba Khin, is an inspiring example of how Vipassana enables one to live an active, honest, beneficial, and efficient life and to serve others tirelessly and selflessly. He was the first Accountant General of independent Myanmar and a trusted confidant of the Prime Minister of Myanmar. Yet Sayagyi U Ba Khin did not hesitate to point out any impropriety in the government that conflicted with established laws and norms. He took immediate action against any action to bribe him. He often took a strong position against the government. Yet the government kept extending his period of service and postponing his retirement and even changed governmental regulations to allow him to serve longer!

People from all religions came to take Vipassana courses from Sayagyi U Ba Khin, even though he called himself a staunch follower of the Buddha's teaching. I was a leader of the Hindu community in Myanmar when I approached him to take my first Vipassana course. He told me, "I will not convert you to a Buddhist. I will teach you a technique that will make you a better human being."

(Dhamma Giri edition—November 2006)

From Bondage to Liberation

I took the Vipassana course and all my doubts and fears were removed. I found that Vipassana is Bhagavad Gītā in practice. This is the only conversion that Vipassana does: the conversion from misery to happiness, from ignorance to enlightenment, from bondage to liberation.

As more and more individuals in the world experience this path of converting themselves from misery to happiness, all violence will be eradicated and there will be peace and prosperity all around. This happened during the reign of Emperor Asoka and I have no doubt that it will again happen in the future.

May all beings be happy,
be peaceful,
be liberated!

Vipassana Meditation Centers

Courses of Vipassana meditation in the tradition of Sayagyi U Ba Khin as taught by S. N. Goenka are held regularly in many countries around the world.

Information, worldwide schedules and application forms are available from the Vipassana website.

www.dhamma.org

ABOUT PARIYATTI

Pariyatti is dedicated to providing affordable access to authentic teachings of the Buddha about the Dhamma theory (*pariyatti*) and practice (*paṭipatti*) of Vipassana meditation. A 501(c)(3) nonprofit charitable organization since 2002, Pariyatti is sustained by contributions from individuals who appreciate and want to share the incalculable value of the Dhamma teachings. We invite you to visit *www.pariyatti.org* to learn about our programs, services, and ways to support publishing and other undertakings.

Pariyatti Publishing Imprints

Vipassana Research Publications (focus on Vipassana as taught by S.N. Goenka in the tradition of Sayagyi U Ba Khin)

BPS Pariyatti Editions (selected titles from the Buddhist Publication Society, copublished by Pariyatti in the Americas)

Pariyatti Digital Editions (audio and video titles, including discourses)

Pariyatti Press (classic titles returned to print and inspirational writing by contemporary authors)

Pariyatti enriches the world by

- disseminating the words of the Buddha,
- providing sustenance for the seeker's journey,
- illuminating the meditator's path.

www.ingramcontent.com/pod-product-compliance
Lightning Source LLC
Chambersburg PA
CBHW081227090426
42738CB00016B/3212
9781681723549